D1738884

Order ID: 111-9926043-6566612

Thank you for buying from meremc_books on Amazon Marketplace.

Shipping Address:
Susanne Lohmann
10403 Colina Way
Los Angeles, CA
90077-2000

Order Date: Sat, Feb 6, 2021
Shipping Service: Free Economy
Buyer Name: Susanne
Seller Name: meremc_books

Quantity	Product Details
1	**On Critique: A Sociology of Emancipation [Paperback] [2011] Boltanski, Luc** **SKU:** 03062017 **ASIN:** 0745649645 **Condition:** Used – Like New **Listing ID:** 0306X23ST9P **Order Item ID:** 53103218299242 **Condition note:** In excellent condition, Like New! Pages are clean and unmarked.

Returning your item:

Go to "Your Account" on Amazon.com, click "Your Orders" and then click the "seller profile" link for this order to get information about the return and refund policies that apply.

Visit https://www.amazon.com/returns to print a return shipping label. Please have your order ID ready.

ON CRITIQUE

ON CRITIQUE

A SOCIOLOGY OF EMANCIPATION

LUC BOLTANSKI

Translated by Gregory Elliott

polity

First published in French as *De la critique* © Editions GALLIMARD, Paris, 2009

Ouvrage publié avec le soutien du Centre national du livre – ministère français chargé de la culture

Published with the support of the National Centre for the Book – French Ministry of Culture

This English edition © Polity Press, 2011

Reprinted 2013

Polity Press
65 Bridge Street
Cambridge CB2 1UR, UK

Polity Press
350 Main Street
Malden, MA 02148, USA

ISBN-13: 978-0-7456-4963-4 (hardback)
ISBN-13: 978-0-7456-4964-1 (paperback)

A catalogue record for this book is available from the British Library.

Typeset in 10.5 on 12 pt Sabon
by Servis Filmsetting Ltd, Stockport, Cheshire
Printed and bound by MPG Books Group, UK

The publisher has used its best endeavours to ensure that the URLs for external websites referred to in this book are correct and active at the time of going to press. However, the publisher has no responsibility for the websites and can make no guarantee that a site will remain live or that the content is or will remain appropriate.

Every effort has been made to trace all copyright holders, but if any have been inadvertently overlooked the publisher will be pleased to include any necessary credits in any subsequent reprint or edition.

For further information on Polity, visit our website: www.politybooks.com

For Jean-Elie Boltanski

I've got to tell you: me, all my life, I've thought for myself; free, I was born different. I am who I am. I'm different from everyone. . . I don't know much. But I'm suspicious of lots of things. I can say, pass it to me: when it comes to thinking ahead, I'm a dog handler – release a little idea in front of me and I'm going to track it for you into the deepest of all forests, amen! Listen: how things should be would be to get all sages, politicians, important elected representatives together and settle the issue for good – proclaim once and for all, by means of meetings, that there's no devil, he doesn't exist, cannot. Legally binding! That's the only way everyone would get some peace and quiet. Why doesn't the government deal with it? Oh, I know very well, it's not possible. Don't take me for an ignoramus. Putting ideas in order is one thing, dealing with a country of real people, thousands and thousands of woes, is quite another. . . So many people – it's terrifying to think about it – and not one of them at peace: all of them are born, grow up, marry, want food, health, wealth, fame, a secure job, want it to rain, want things to work. . .

João Guimarães Rosa, Diadorim

CONTENTS

PREFACE

This book originated in three talks given at the Institute for Social Research in Frankfurt in November 2008. Professor Axel Honneth, with whom I have kept up a very rewarding dialogue for several years now, took the initiative of entrusting me with the task, at once stimulating and intimidating, of making this contribution to the series of Adorno Lectures. I hope he will accept my warm thanks for having provided me with the opportunity to present, in synthetic form, some observations that have accompanied my thinking over the last three years.

In returning to these lectures with a view to publication, I have been unable to resist reintroducing a number of arguments that I had to eliminate so as not to exceed the time allotted me. In addition, I have integrated into the body of the text some more up-to-date considerations on contemporary forms of domination, which I had the opportunity to present in October 2008 at Humboldt University in Berlin, in the context of a lecture which the Centre Marc Bloch organizes annually to mark the start of the academic year. The three Adorno Lectures have thus, as it were, been opened up, giving rise to the six segments that make up this work. Nevertheless, conscious of the difficulty presented by the transition from lecture form to book form – a task virtually impossible in as much as the two formats involve different methods of argument and stylistic practices[1] – in writing them up I have sought to preserve, at least to some extent, their initial oral character. They must therefore be read as if they were a series of six talks. Consequently, readers should not expect to find a finished work, whose composition would have taken me many more years of labour and whose size would be (will be?) much greater, but only a series of remarks, whose articulation has certainly not yet reached the desired level of integration and coherence, as if they had been set down on paper in preparation for composing a book. Or, if you like, at best a sort of *précis* of critique.

The six segments can be assembled in twos to form three different parts. The first two concern the issue of the relationship between sociology and social critique. This is a question that has never stopped haunting sociology since the origins of the discipline. Should sociology, constituted on the model of the sciences, with an essentially descriptive orientation, be placed in the service of a critique of society – which assumes considering the latter in a normative optic? If so, how should it go about making description and critique compatible? Does an orientation towards critique necessarily have the effect of corrupting the integrity of sociology and diverting it from its scientific project? Or, on the contrary, should it be acknowledged that it in a sense constitutes the purpose (or one of the purposes) of sociology, which, without it, would be a futile activity, remote from the concerns of the people who make up society? Questions of this kind have periodically arisen in the course of the history of sociology, hitching up with other pairs of oppositions en route – for example, between facts and values, ideology and science, determinism and autonomy, structure and action, macrosocial and micro-social approaches, explanation and interpretation and so forth.

Having, in the first segment (which may be read as an introduction), rapidly presented some concepts that can be used to describe the structure of critical theories in social science, in the second I dwell on a comparison between two programmes to which, in the course of my professional career, I have sought to make a contribution. The first is the *critical sociology* of the 1970s, particularly in the form given it in France by Pierre Bourdieu. The second is the *pragmatic sociology of critique*, developed by some of us in the Political and Moral Sociology Group of the Ecole des Hautes Etudes en Sciences Sociales (EHESS) in the 1980s and 1990s, which was fashioned *both* in opposition to the first *and* with a view to pursuing its basic intention. In particular, in this chapter readers will find a reciprocal critique of each of these programmes, from the perspective of their contribution to social critique.

Segments 3 and 4 can be read as a second part, wherein is expounded in its main lines an analytical framework intended to formulate afresh the question of critique, such as it is given free rein not in the theoretical space of sociology, but in everyday reality. But this framework also has the aim of providing tools that make it possible to reduce the tension between critical sociology and sociology of critique. It therewith pursues an objective of pacification. This framework is developed from the postulate (of the order of a thought experiment) that the organization of social life must confront a radical uncertainty as regards the question of *how things stand with what is*. It dwells on institutions, considered in the first instance in their semantic functions, as instruments geared towards the construction of reality through the intermediary, in particular, of operations for qualifying entities – persons and objects – and defining test formats. The possibility of critique is derived from a contradiction, lodged at the heart of institutions, which can be described as *hermeneutic contradiction*. Critique is therefore considered in its dialogical relationship with the institutions it is arrayed against. It can be expressed either by showing that the tests as conducted (i.e. as instances or, as analytical philosophy puts it, as tokens) do not conform to their format (or type); or by drawing from the world examples and cases that do not accord with reality as it is established, making it possible to challenge *the reality of reality* and, thereby, change its contours. The distinction between *reality* and *world* supplies the conceptual framework of these analyses.

Segments 5 and 6 form a third part, more sharply focused on current political problems. Segment 5 presents some summary applications of the analytical framework outlined in the two preceding segments, devoted to describing different regimes of domination. The term 'domination' – in the sense in which it is used in this little *précis* – refers to historical situations where the work of critique finds itself particularly impeded in various ways depending on the political context, and also in more or less apparent or covert fashion. In this segment I pay particular attention to a mode of domination – which can be characterized as managerial – that is in the process of being established in Western democratic-capitalist societies. Finally, Segment 6 (which may be read as a provisional conclusion) aims to sketch some of the paths critique might take today in order to proceed in the direction of emancipation.

To conclude, I shall add that the issue of critique and the problems posed by the relationship between sociology and critique, to which I have devoted much of my work for many years, have not only captivated me by their theoretical attraction. For me, and no doubt more generally for sociologists of my generation, who came into the discipline in the years immediately preceding or following May 1968, they have a quasi-biographical character. We have gone through periods when society was populated by powerful critical movements and then through periods marked by their retreat. But today we are perhaps entering a phase that will witness their return.[2] This History with a capital 'h' is bound to have an impact on the little history of sociology.

ACKNOWLEDGEMENTS

To thank all those who made a contribution to the development of this work is a task impossible to acquit without omitting or neglecting someone. My thanks go in particular to the members of the Political and Moral Sociology Group (GSPM), to my students at EHESS, and to the numerous researchers who have stimulated my thinking by intervening either in my doctoral seminar or in that of the GSPM. I am especially indebted to Damien de Blic, Eve Chiapello, Elisabeth Claverie, Bernard Conein, Nicolas Dodier, Arnaud Esquerre, Bruno Karsenti and Cyril Lemieux, who, with great generosity, have read, criticized and commented on earlier stages of this work. Tomaso Vitale of Milan University has also been an exacting reader and an impassioned (and stirring) interlocutor. I have also benefited from discussions with students or colleagues from history (Ariane Boltanski, Robert Descimon, Simona Cerutti, Nicolas Offenstadt), anthropology (Catherine Alès, François Berthomé, Matthew Carey, Philippe Descola), literature (Philippe Roussin, Loïc Nicolas), and law (Olivier Cayla, who was generous enough to trust me with the as yet unpublished manuscript of his thesis, Paolo Napoli, and espe- cially my dear late friend, Ian Thomas). In addition to the attention of Axel Honneth, at Frankfurt my work benefited greatly from the help given by Mauro Basaure, who was an intermediary of inexhaustible intelligence and good will between the Institute for Social Research and the GSPM, but also from the observations of other researchers at the Institute – in particular, Robin Celikates and Nora Sieverding. I am grateful to Sidonia Blätter, Eva Buddeberg and to the two dis- tinguished translators who rendered these lectures – written and delivered in French – into the language of Adorno: Bernd Schwibs and Achim Russer. I am also grateful to Gregory Elliott who, having worked on eight hundred pages of *The New Spirit of Capitalism*, has, once again, brought his elegant style to this English translation. I must finally add that this text could not have been finished without the vigilant skill of my brother, the linguist Jean-Elie Boltanski, who has followed every step of its preparation. But in order for it to become a book, friendly attention was once again required from my editor Eric Vigne, who perseveres against the current in publishing writings which, without his stubborn efforts, would simply be condemned to disappear in the incessant flow of messages saturating our computers.

Drafts of this work have been presented and discussed in various seminars or conferences and, in particular, in the conference in Frankfurt that assembled researchers from the GSPM and the Institute for Social Research in November 2006; in the conference on common sense organized by Sandra Laugier at Amiens University in December 2006; in the seminar organized in May 2007 at the Ecole normale supérieure (Lyon, literature and social science) by the directors of the journal *Tracés*, Arnaud Fossier and Eric Monnet, and, in the same month, during the important day school on 'Anthropology and Pragmatics' organized by Carlo Severi at the Musée de Quai de Branly in Paris; in the Hannah Arendt symposium at the New School for Social Research in New York in December 2007, on the initiative of Nancy Fraser; and then, at the same institution, during a workshop organized by Janet Roitman and Anne Stoler in May 2008; in Antonio Negri's seminar in January 2008; and in the conference on individualism organized by Philippe Corcuff, whose comments were very useful to me, at Cerisy in June 2008.

— 1 —

THE STRUCTURE OF CRITICAL THEORIES

Power or Domination. Society or Social Order

I shall approach critical sociologies starting from the concept of *social domination*, a polemical notion if ever there was one, because it has been a major axis of critical theories while having often been rejected by other currents in sociology, at least when the term domination is used not only to refer to different ways of placing power in the service of politics, whatever it might be – as is more or less the case with 'modes of domination' in Max Weber – but also serves to identify and condemn manifestations of power deemed extreme and abusive. As we shall see in the next talk, critical sociology has made abundant use of it in this sense and the pragmatic sociology of critique has simply ignored it. However, do not expect me to outline a conceptual history of this notion, which would take me far beyond not only the time in which I shall address you but also, alas, my competence. I shall instead base myself on this problematic notion in order to seek to clarify the relationship between sociology and critique, and examine the ways in which they might converge in compromise formations that are never free of tensions.

An initial characteristic of sociologies of domination is that they fashion a synthetic object, in the sense that it cannot give rise to direct observation, so that revealing it is necessarily the result of a reconstruction on the part of the analyst. All sociology can observe is power relations. For standard sociology, reference to power goes hand-in-hand with the identification of asymmetries, but they are diverse, partial, local or transitory. The existence of different sources and sites of power creates a web in which these powers can become entangled, contradict and even neutralize one another. The fact of

1

exercising power or of being subjected to power does not escape the consciousness of actors and power relations are invariably visible to the eyes of an observer. Power can therefore easily form the object of an empirical sociology, on the one hand because social relations are shot through with forms of power that are fairly readily observable, at least in certain situations; and on the other hand because power relations are, in many cases, inscribed in pre-established formats that are themselves stabilized in the form of customs or registered in texts – for example, juridical texts and other forms of regulations. As Max Weber showed, power thus tends to be rationalized, whatever its modalities, in the sense that its structures and exercise are subject, at least formally, to *requirements of justification* that impart a certain robustness to them. It is by invoking these requirements that those who hold power can claim it to be 'legitimate', thereby compelling those who challenge it to *rise in generality* in such a way as to subject the very principles they invoke to critique.[1] By contrast, to characterize a form of power as 'arbitrary' signifies that it is impossible to take its measure by referring it to a pre-established format ensuring its exercise a certain consistency and thereby to stress the difficulties facing those who endure it in forming predictable expectations of it. Because it must be both asserted and justified, power speaks of power.

The same is not true of domination. Critical theories of domination posit the existence of profound, enduring asymmetries which, while assuming different forms in different contexts, are constantly duplicated to the point of colonizing reality as a whole. They adopt the point of view of the totality.[2] The dominated and the dominant are everywhere, whether the latter are identified as dominant class, dominant sex or, for example, dominant ethnicity. What is involved is not only not directly observable, but also invariably eludes the consciousness of actors. Domination must be unmasked. It does not speak of itself and is concealed in *systems* whose patent forms of power are merely their most superficial dimension. Thus, for example, contrasting with the demand *to get done*, rendered manifest by an order given in a hierarchical relationship, are manoeuvres or even, in still more tacit fashion, social conditions deposited in an environment, which combine to determine an actor to do something for the benefit of another as if she were doing it of her own accord and for herself. It is therefore as if actors suffered the domination exercised over them not only unwittingly, but sometimes even by aiding its exercise.

As a result, theories of domination must select an object slightly different from that of sociologies which, for convenience sake, we shall call standard. This discrepancy is the result of different forms

2

of totalization. As an empirical activity, sociology can describe different dimensions of social life (and different forms of power) without necessarily aiming to integrate them into a coherent totality – on the contrary, even seeking to bring out the specificity of each of them. By contrast, theories of domination unmask the relations between these different dimensions so as to highlight the way they form a system. Where sociology takes as its object *societies*, however it identifies them (and it could be shown that it invariably involves nation-states, as is obviously the case, for example, in Durkheim),[3] theories of domination, relying on sociological descriptions, construct a different kind of object that can be referred to as *social orders*. In fact, it is only once this object has been constructed that an approach to society as a totality considered critically can be posited;[4] and that a mode of domination can be described in its generality (and also, in numerous cases, that *contradictions* immanent in this order can be identified, whose exposure furnishes a basis for its critique. In fact, contradictions are distinguished from the disparate only within a unified framework).[5] The substitution of social order – an object that is manifestly constructed – for social relations – an object supposed to follow from empirical observation – represents the strength and weakness of critical theories of domination. They are always liable to be denounced as illusory – that is to say, as not offering pictures which provide a good likeness of reality, but merely being the expression of a rejection of reality based on nothing but particular (and contestable) points of view or the desire (and resentment) of those who condemn it.[6]

Morality, Critique and Reflexivity

Compared with the so-called natural sciences, the specificity of the social sciences is that they take as their object human beings grasped not in their biological dimensions, but in so far as they are capable of reflexivity (that is why it is appropriate to distinguish between the social and the human sciences). Considered in this respect, human beings are not content to act or react to the actions of others. They review their own actions or those of others in order to make judgements on them, often hinging on the issue of good and evil – that is, *moral judgements*. This reflexive capacity means that they also react to the representations given of their properties or actions, including when the latter derive from sociology or critical theories.[7]

The moral judgements formulated by actors in the course of their everyday activities often take the form of *critiques*. Moral activity is a predominantly critical activity. The sociological *doxa* taught to first-year students (often invoking a popularized form of Weberian epistemology) consists in making a sharp (if not always clear) distinction between, on the one hand, critical judgements delivered by so-called 'ordinary' people and sustained by 'moralities' or 'cultures', which form part of the legitimate objects of description, and, on the other hand, critical judgements made by sociologists themselves (renamed 'value judgements'), which are to be banished (axiological neutrality). This distinction is based on the Weberian separation of *facts* from *values*.[8] Critical theories of domination necessarily rely on descriptive social science to paint a picture of the reality subject to critique. But compared with sociological descriptions that seek to conform to the vulgate of neutrality, the specificity of critical theories is that they contain critical judgements on the social order which the analyst assumes responsibility for in her own name, thus abandoning any pretention to neutrality.

Ordinary Critiques and Metacritical Positions

The fact that they are backed up by the discourse of truth of the social sciences endows critical theories of domination with a certain robustness in describing the reality called into question, but complicates the critical operation itself, which is essential to them. This confronts them with a dilemma.

On the one hand, it prevents them making judgements that rely directly on the resources, invariably exploited by ordinary critique, represented by spiritual and/or moral resources of a local character. Metacritical theories cannot judge the city as it is by comparing it with the City of God, or even by introducing a secularized but specific moral ideal that the metacritical theoretician naively adopts on her own account in order to judge (and condemn) society as it is, as if it involved not one moral conception among others, but the moral ideal in itself (which would contradict the comparativist requirement to place the moral ideals present in all known societies on an equal footing). That is why critical theories of domination are clearly distinguished from the very many intellectual movements which, basing themselves on moral and/or religious exigencies, have developed radical critiques and demanded from their followers an absolute change in lifestyle (e.g. primitive Christianity, Manichaeanism, millenarian sects, etc.).

On the other hand, however, critical theories of domination are not abstract organums suspended in the heaven of metaphysics. The existence of a concrete relationship with a set of people (defined as public, class, group, sex or whatever) forms part of their self-definition. Unlike 'traditional theory', 'critical theory'[9] possesses the objective of *reflexivity*. It can or even *must* (according to Raymond Geuss) grasp the discontents of actors, explicitly consider them in the very labour of theorization, in such a way as to alter their relationship to social reality and, thereby, that social reality itself, in the direction of *emancipation*.[10] As a consequence, the kind of critique they make possible must enable the disclosure of aspects of reality in an immediate relationship with the preoccupations of actors – that is, also with ordinary critiques. Critical theories feed off these ordinary critiques, even if they develop them differently, reformulate them, and are destined to return to them, since their aim is to *render reality unacceptable*,[11] and thereby engage the people to whom they are addressed in action whose result should be to change its contours. The idea of a critical theory that is not backed by the experience of a collective, and which in some sense exists for its own sake – that is, for no one – is incoherent.

This dual requirement places a very strong constraint on the structure of critical theories. On the one hand, they must provide themselves with normative supports that are sufficiently autonomous of the particular moral corpuses formed from already identified religious or political approaches, and identified with as such by specific groups whose critical stances they arm. In fact, were this not the case, the opponents of these theories (even those who might initially have been favourable to them) are bound to reduce them to these positions and, consequently, to denounce their local character, bound up with particular interests. They will then dissolve into the sea of ordinary critiques that accompany relations between groups and form the fabric of everyday political life, in the broad sense. But, on the other hand, they must try to meet these ordinary critiques as if they derived from them and were merely unveiling them to themselves, by inducing actors to acknowledge what they already knew but, in a sense, without knowing it; to *realize* what this reality consists in and, through this revelation, to take their distance from this reality, as if it was possible to exit from it – to remove themselves from it – in such a way as to conceive the possibility of actions intended to change it. When this second condition is not fulfilled, critical theories can be rejected by consigning them to the sphere of 'utopias';[12] or, as Michael Walzer more or less does (in connection with the work of Marcuse in *The Company of Critics*) by regarding them as nothing more than the lamentations of rootless intellectuals, cut off from the sense of reality that comes from belonging to a community and, as a result, having abandoned even the desire of acting to transform it.[13]

The kind of critical judgement built into theories of domination therefore has complex relations with the critiques formulated by people in the course of everyday life. It never coincides with them and subjects them to more or less sustained attention depending on the case, ranging from rejection (critiques formulated by actors derive from illusions, particularly moral illusions) to partial acknowledgement (there is something in these ordinary critiques that can pave the way for Critique with a capital 'c'). But in any event, a distinction is maintained between the partial critiques developed by the actors on the basis of their experiences and the systematic critique of a particular social order.

For this reason we shall say that critical theories of domination are *metacritical* in order. The position adopted, geared to the critique of a social order in its generality, distinguishes metacritical positions from occasional critical interventions which, from a position of scholarly expertise, call into question, with a view to reparation or improvement, some particular dimension of social relations without challenging the framework in which they are inscribed. But metacritical constructions must also be distinguished from the multiple critical stances adopted by ordinary people who, in the course of political action and/or the disputes of daily life, denounce people, systems or events that are characterized as unjust by reference to particular situations or contexts. In the rest of these talks, when we speak of *critique*, it is to these socially rooted, contextual forms of criticism that we shall be referring, while reserving the term *metacritique* to refer to theoretical constructions that aim to unmask, in their most general dimensions, oppression, exploitation or domination, whatever the forms in which they occur.

Simple Exteriority and Complex Exteriority

The two operations whose ideal type I have tried to trace – the sociological operation of describing society and the critical operation addressed to a social order – share the common feature that they need to situate themselves in a position of *exteriority*. But the kind of exteriority to be adopted is not the same in both cases. We shall speak of *simple exteriority* in the case of description and *complex exteriority* in the case of value judgements that are based on metacritical theories.

6

The project of taking society as an object and describing the components of social life or, if you like, its framework, appeals to a *thought experiment* that consists in positioning oneself outside this framework in order to consider it as a whole. In fact, a framework cannot be grasped from within. From an internal perspective, the framework coincides with reality in its imperious necessity. This engineering perspective is the one often adopted by sociologists when they are attuned to the officials in charge of large organizations (be it firms or organizations dependent on the state) and prove open and attentive to the problems facing these officials and the issues they pose. This position is one of *expertise*. The expert is asked to examine the problematic relationship between elements (e.g. between women's access to wage-labour and the birth rate), which have already been subject to formatting in a language of administrative or economic description used by those in charge to govern.

Sociological work answering to this kind of demand, which developed in the United States in the 1930s and 1940s, today makes up the bulk of the output identified with sociology the world over. It has two key objectives, which are complementary. The first is to increase the rationality of organizations and enhance their productivity, which subordinates sociology to *management*. The second is also to limit the costs, but this time the so-called 'human' costs, entailed by managerial policies geared to profit. In the second case, sociology is called on to help put in place 'palliative care', as one says in medicine – that is, either to sketch the shape of 'social policies' or to provide justifications to those who implement them on the ground (i.e. 'social workers') and sustain their morale. However, in both cases this work by experts identifying with sociology can be realized (it would be better to say *must be*) without problematizing the general framework upon which the 'variables' considered depend.

The social sciences free themselves from expertise, and hence define themselves as such, by positing the possibility of a project of description which is that of a general social anthropology (in a number of cases appealing to comparativism) from a position of exteriority. In the case of ethnology or history, adoption of a position of exteriority is favoured by the distance – geographical in one instance, temporal in the other – that separates the observer from her object. Because it derives in a sense from constraints that are independent of the observer's will, the move towards exteriority has been able to remain more or less implicit in the case of these disciplines.

In the case of sociology, which at this level of generality can be regarded as a history of the present, with the result that the observer

7

is part of what she intends to describe, adopting a position of exteriority is far from self-evident. The fact that its possibility even poses a problem in a sense leads the move to externalization to become self-conscious. This imaginary exit from the viscosity of the real initially assumes stripping reality of its character of implicit necessity and proceeding as if it were *arbitrary* (as if it could be other than it is or even not be); and then, in a second phase, restoring to it the necessity it had initially been divested of, but on which this operation of displacement has conferred a reflexive, general character, in the sense that the forms of necessity identified locally are related to a universe of possibilities. In sociology the possibility of this externalization rests on the existence of a laboratory – that is to say, the employment of protocols and instructions respect for which must constrain the sociologist to control her desires (conscious or unconscious). It is thus that descriptive social sciences can claim that they sustain a discourse of truth. It must be added that this truth claim, which is bound up with a description carried out by occupying a more or less extra-territorial post vis-à-vis the society being described, generally gives the social sciences, whatever they are, a critical edge (and this even, albeit in highly limited fashion, in the case of expertise). For, if the very substance of their object was constantly in full view of everyone, the social sciences would simply have no reason to exist. In this sense, we can therefore say that sociology is already, in its very conception, at least potentially critical.

In the case of theories of domination, the exteriority on which critique is based can be called *complex*, in the sense that it is established at two different levels. It must first of all be based on an exteriority of the first kind to equip itself with the requisite data to create the picture of the social order that will be submitted to critique. A meta-critical theory is in fact necessarily reliant on a descriptive sociology or anthropology. But to be critical, such a theory also needs to furnish itself, in ways that can be explicit to very different degrees, with the means of passing a judgement on the value of the social order being described.

The Semantic Dimension of Critique of Domination. Domination vs. Exploitation

Metacritical theories of domination are often combined with theories of exploitation. The term exploitation has an economic orientation. Exploitation refers to the way that a small number of people make use of differentials (which can be very diverse in kind) in order to extract a profit at the expense of the great majority. In theories of domination, reference to exploitation serves to indicate the *purpose* of domination (as if domination in the pure state, which would have no rationale but itself, was difficult to conceive). On the other hand – that is, considered from the perspective of a critique of exploitation – domination also possesses a character of necessity. It is difficult to conceive exploitation that is not dependent on some form or other of domination (if they were not dominated, why would human beings let themselves be exploited?).

However, it must be stressed that the concept of domination does not have a strictly economic orientation, but rather (if I can put it like this) a *semantic* one. It is directed at the field of the *determination of what is* – that is to say, the field in which the relationship between what (borrowing terms from Wittgenstein) can be called *symbolic forms* and *states of affairs* is established. We can also say, in a different language inspired by law, that the critique of domination concerns the establishment of *qualifications* – that is (as we shall see in more detail later), the operations which indivisibly fix the *properties* of beings and determine their *worth*. This work of qualification generally relies on *formats* or *types*, invariably combined with *descriptions* and/ or *definitions*, which are themselves stored in various forms (such as regulations, codes, customs, rituals, narratives, emblematic examples, etc.). These formats incorporate classifications (and, in particular, classifications making it possible to distribute people between groups or categories) and combine them with rules that exercise a constraint on access to goods and their use. They thereby play a major role in the formation and stabilization of asymmetries.

Metacritical theories of domination tackle these asymmetries from a particular angle – that of the *miscognition* by the actors themselves of the exploitation to which they are subject and, above all, of the social conditions that make this exploitation possible and also, as a result, of the means by which they could stop it. That is why they present themselves indivisibly as theories of power, theories of exploitation and *theories of knowledge*. By this token, they encounter in an especially vexed fashion the issue of the relationship between the knowledge of social reality which is that of ordinary actors, reflexively engaged in practice, and the knowledge of social reality conceived from a reflexivity reliant on forms and instruments of totalization[14] – an issue which is itself at the heart of the tensions out of which the possibility of a social science must be created.

9

Some Examples of Compromise between Sociology and Social Critique

A re-reading of the sociological traditions which, to various degrees, incorporate a critical dimension, undertaken with the two constraints that have just been mentioned in mind, would doubtless make it possible to identify the main compromises that have been forged to combine the requirement of descriptive neutrality (simple exteriority) and the search for bases paving the way for critique (complex exteriority). As is the case every time we find ourselves in the presence of theoretical corpuses, subject as such to internal consistency – at least relative – while being haunted by a structural tension, the possibilities are certainly not unlimited. Without any pretention to exhaustiveness, but simply with the aim of exhibiting the kind of arrangements sociology resorts to in order to link itself to critique, we can very schematically indicate some of the compromises that seem to have been most frequently forged, and which can combine several of the possibilities we shall now describe.[15]

A first set of possibilities consists in taking sociological and normative advantage of a philosophical anthropology (which can be made more or less explicit). The ability of human beings to live in society will be associated with the existence in all human beings of properties and characteristics that can be specified differently depending on the anthropology in question (rationality; the capacity to exchange goods; the capacity to communicate by conforming to requirements of relevance; sympathy for the suffering of others; recognition etc.). Critique will then consist in showing how the existing social order does not allow members, or some of them, fully to realize the potentialities constitutive of their humanity. These constructions owe much of their critical power to the fact that they bank on a *common humanity* and therewith contain exigencies of equality of treatment between members of the same society. A satisfactory society is one *without leftovers* and the existing social order can be criticized in as much as it excludes, oppresses, scorns and so on, a greater or lesser number of its members, or simply prevents them from realizing what they are capable of as human beings.

But this kind of construction must confront two tricky problems in particular. The first consists either in criticizing any difference – which might seem unrealistic and consequently unconvincing – or justifying the distinction between acceptable differences and unacceptable differences, from the standpoint of the philosophical anthropology adopted. The second stems from the fact that the philosophical

anthropology which serves as a basis for critique must be both sufficiently robust and sufficiently general to resist critiques that aim to
reduce it to a particular moral or religious tradition (as in the case of
the accusation of ethnocentrism); and, at the same time, sufficiently
precise to be declined in different forms in such a way as to enable
the condemnation of specific social orders. We can add that this kind
of normative support can either be treated in an a-temporal fashion
or historicized, paving the way for an evolutionism or progressiv-
ism, but increasing the constraints of justification required to achieve
recognition in the framework of the social sciences, by demanding
recourse to a philosophy of history compatible with the longitudinal
descriptions furnished by historians.

A different set of possibilities, less ambitious on a critical level than
the previous ones but better placed to take advantage of the specific
resources supplied by sociological description, consists in extracting
the normative position serving as a basis for the critique to which a
certain social order is subjected from the description of that order
itself and, as a result, giving less weight to a normative anthropology
placed in a quasi-transcendental situation. A first mode of this type
can consist in playing on the differential between the *official* and the
unofficial. It will then be shown that the ideal this order lays claim to
does not correspond to its actual outcomes and, consequently, to the
real condition of its members or some of them. Critique then takes
as its main target the fact that the order in question does not *in fact*
conform to the values it assigns itself *in principle*.

A second mode paves the way for a critique of law from an analysis
of the condition of customs. A certain condition of the social order
will then be open to being criticized as 'pathological' (as Durkheim
put it) when the rules posited in an established form (i.e. most often,
in modern societies, 'legal' form), whose transgression is accompanied by sanctions, do not – or no longer – have their guarantor in
constraining norms 'immanent in the social', which by this token
are recognized or even internalized by actors. This critical position
is rendered more robust when it can enter into a compromise with a
historical perspective, as is the case when analysis intends to emphasize that the law has remained unchanged whereas customs have
changed (or 'evolved'), so that the condition of the law *lags behind*
the condition of customs.

In these first two modes of internal critique, the normative basis
(which can remain implicit) is that of a transparent, authentic society.
A good society is one where all, and especially the political elites
in power, agree on the effective implementation of the officially

proclaimed ideals – especially those inscribed in law – and/or where legal norms, on which sanctions of state origin rely, are the reflection in the legal order of the 'collective consciousness' and, therewith, of the moral norms acknowledged by all members (or a majority of them) in the social order.

A third mode among the critical operations open to sociology, while remaining very close to the descriptive requirements it is intent on submitting to qua 'science', consists in taking hold, to make normative use of them, of the moral expectations which actors disclose in the course of their actions, in the belief that they attest to the existence of a *moral sense* in actors. Contrary to interpretations of action in essentially opportunistic terms, it is credited with sufficient permanence and robustness for sociology to undertake its modelling. In this case, the metacritical orientation will therefore be developed by collecting and synthesizing the *critiques* developed by 'people themselves' in the course of their everyday activities. It will particularly rely on moments of dispute, when actors express their moral claims, and also on collective interaction in the course of which they engage in *experiments* and when, employing the 'creativity of action', they 'perform' the social in an innovative way. From a position of this kind, one of the difficulties encountered is constructing a critique that can resist the accusation of expressing nothing but the particular viewpoint of the particular group or groups of actors on which observation has focused. That is why the metacritical position adopted will rely less on a substantive normativity than a procedural one. Its main objective will be to sketch the contours of a social order where different points of view can be expressed, opposed and realized through experiments. By contrast, a social order where the conduct of such experiments is impeded by the exercise of authoritarian power will come under fire from critique.

The metacritical positions we have just schematically described share the common feature that they incorporate moral judgements, whether these are formed from an anthropology or derived from the social order submitted to critique. However, there is another path leading to critique which, bracketing moral references (or claiming to), is based in the main on the unmasking of *immanent contradictions*, be these specific to a determinate social order or present in a larger set of social orders. In this case, critique is not taken on by the sociologist in a personal capacity, in the manner of an ordinary individual judging the state of reality on the basis of values. It derives from the observation (or prediction) that the order in question cannot (or will not be able to) survive, because it cannot find the requisite resources to resolve these contradictions in itself. To various degrees, this assumes the adoption of a historical perspective.

To exploit this possibility, it is necessary to pursue the sociological and historical description and analysis of the cases under consideration sufficiently far to identify these contradictions, construct a genealogy of them, clarify their future and, above all, associate them with conflicts that counter-pose groups or classes in which these contradictions are embodied. A common characteristic of constructions based on a metacritical position of this type is rejection of the idea of a common good, or even that of a space of debate where different points of view confront one another, and their replacement by notions of struggle, power, domination and power relations between antagonistic groups. Different critical orientations can be developed on this basis, depending in particular on whether these struggles are envisaged above all *negatively*, in so far as they entail the destruction not only of a particular order but of any social order, or *positively*, in as much as they enable the emergence of new possibilities and the dialectical supersession of the contradictions whose expression they are.

In the first case, these contradictions and antagonisms are associated with conflicts between values (and/or interests) which are regarded as being, in essence, without a generally justifiable solution, either in the sense that there exists no value of a superior logical level making it possible to rank them or because no historical dialectic is envisaged. The possibilities for a compromise between sociology and critique are then rather limited and essentially distributed between two options. The first can consist in stressing the dissociation between sociological analysis and political action, regarded as being inhabited by logics that are not merely different but largely incompatible. As a 'scholar', the sociologist strives to understand the meaning actors confer on what occurs and to deploy probable chains of causality; as a man of action, the 'politician' makes choices. The sociologist can do nothing but enlighten the politician on the likely consequences of different possible choices and/or criticize political decisions deemed 'irresponsible', but only in the sense that those who take them have refused to face the consequences of their choices and thus acted in bad faith.

Another, moral radical option associates sociology with the preservation of order. The sociologist will then assign herself the task of criticizing political actions or arrangements that undermine order, weaken authority, blur the values that give members of society moral 'reference-points' and so on. This can lead to placing sociology – including in respects that warrant being called 'critical', even if they are orientated towards the 'right' rather than the 'left' – in the service of strengthening the authority of the state – that is, at the service of an authoritarian state.

The numerous critical sociologies which identify, to varying degrees, with the Marxist tradition are no doubt those where the issues of truth, power and exploitation are most clearly articulated. This articulation takes shape around a central contradiction that derives from the separation between theoretical activity, intended to be purely 'intellectual', and practical and productive activity. This separation is placed in a causal relationship with the formation of *social classes* – that is to say, both with the development of exploitation and with the monopolizing of power by certain groups (the dominant classes), at the expense of other groups (the dominated classes). At the level of a sociology of knowledge, these critical positions make it possible to denounce the supremacy accorded speculations developed in *theoretical* fashion ('ideological', in the sense that they state reality from the standpoint of the dominant interests), over modes of access to knowledge that go to the root of things because they derive directly from *practice*, particularly in its productive dimensions.

By comparison with sociologies which (often in the tradition of Hobbes) foreground struggle and contradiction, a particularity of critical sociologies geared to emancipation is that they seek to render two kinds of sociological description compatible. The first unmasks the social forces and instances of exploitation and domination and, as a result, locates violence at the heart of social life. But this first kind of description is insufficient to establish a metacritical position. In fact, if it is of the essence of every society to generate violence and domination, this *fact*, highlighted by sociological science, provides virtually no purchase for the construction of a radically critical approach. The overthrow of a social order where one form of domination is exercised will necessarily be followed by the formation of another social order where the forces of domination will be different, but not less. For critique to be possible, this first (pessimistic) description must be combined with a second (optimistic) description which, basing itself on the historicist forms of the Enlightenment project of liberation, points the succession of social orders in the direction of emancipation – which assumes recourse not only to a philosophy of history, but also to a philosophical anthropology more or less necessary to impart content to the idea of liberation.

As is well known, the tension between these two different kinds of sociological description constitutes one of the specific problems that must be confronted by constructions claiming to represent the working-class movement. In effect, to be deployed, description in terms of forces and relations of power must appeal to the language of causal determination taken from science in its positivist orientations. It will therefore stress the power of mechanisms of oppression, the way that the oppressed always find them already there, even before their entry into the world, and the way in which they endure them passively, or even, to account for their *alienation*, the fact that they adopt the (self-styled) values through which they find themselves subjugated, internalized in the form of *ideologies*. By contrast, description in terms of a progressive development pointing towards emancipation and based, not on a linear, inevitable evolution, but on the actions of human beings who rebel but who are endowed with reason(s), must instead stress the autonomy of human beings capable, in certain historical conditions, of becoming conscious of their alienation and rising up against the forces that dominate them. This second demonstration, which is necessary to the construction of a metacritical position, is far from being incompatible with a sociological description, but it requires resources that are significantly different from those employed by description of the state of power relations and leads analysis to turn instead towards sociologies of action, which acknowledge the intentionality of actors, their capacities for *realizing* (in the dual sense of conceiving and achieving) their true interests and desires, for fashioning new interpretations of reality and placing them in the service of a critical activity. Hitching up these two kinds of sociological description is far from unproblematic, for reasons that we shall seek to clarify in the rest of these talks.

The Intrication of Sociology and Critique

As suggested by the preceding pages, the distinction between metacritical orientation and sociological orientation is analytical in character. In the practice of sociologists, the two projects never stop intersecting. But in my opinion it nevertheless has the virtue of bringing out one of the main *tensions* that haunt sociological activity and possibly social science as a whole. This tension can be more or less manifest. It is particularly visible in the case of sociologies that most radically adopt a critical aim: *critical sociologies*. However, even in the case of sociologies that do not foreground their critical dimension, it can be said that this tension is ever present, at least in a way, *by default*. No doubt it never reveals itself so clearly as in the attempt, at once worthy – because it conveys a genuine concern for scientificity

– and pathetic – because it is necessarily doomed to fail – to join the so-called positive sciences, in what is most contingent and open to challenge in them. I am thinking here, in particular, not so much of the requisite precision of observation as of the marks that accompany its discursive formulation: the accumulation of external marks of impersonality ('we' or 'one' instead of 'I'); of the proliferation of references to other unknown researchers, of whom one does not wish to know anything, and whose dispersed works are now only identified by a name, accompanied by a date and, for the purposes of precision, a page number, the whole enclosed in the gravestone of a parenthesis; sometimes also of the mania for quantification, expressed in an ostentatious accumulation of figures and tables; or again of 'sharp' controversies polarized over the latest argument thought to make the difference – something that avoids examining shared premises, which are often overshadowed; and so on. In short, of all the manoeuvres intended to install the discourse in the organic texture of a body (the 'scientific community'), or in the framework of a network with 'global' ramifications, as if the destruction of the oeuvre in favour of an automaton emerging from the aggregation of a multiplicity of partial interventions sufficed to remove the risk of partiality – that is, to dissolve the ghost of critique.

Now, it is enough to examine a tiny fraction of the history of our disciplines to see that metacritical theories develop at the same time as the descriptive social sciences which they put to work; and that these two kinds of project, which are in part incompatible, are nevertheless profoundly interdependent. But this is also to say that metacritical theories must concede the possibility of a simple exteriority. It is even doubtful if they could readily abandon any claim to impartiality – as intellectuals in too much of a hurry to engage in political struggles sometimes seem to believe. It remains the case that critique's dependence on sociology has as its corollary sociology's dependence on critique. In fact, in their very conception, sociological descriptions are orientated to the kind of uses that metacritical theories will make of them. These uses will largely constitute their main justification. Who would be interested in a sociology for sociology's sake (in the way people refer to 'art for art's sake') – that is to say, a sociology, which, exhausting itself in ever more sophisticated and meticulous descriptions, has no other objective than its own fulfilment as a discipline of knowledge? And furthermore, if it is accepted that this discipline can only have as its object the ways in which people, through their reflexive activity, make and break collectives, we can examine what the very content of this 'knowledge' might be. The processes through which the actors in social life constitute the wholes of which they form part, and cause them to last or subvert them, are themselves articulated, in large measure, with the possibility of critique, not only when they challenge existing orders, but also when they are led to justify them. Sociology would be a strange activity if, out of a sort of misplaced modesty or sheepishness, it forbade itself a practice that contributes so significantly to the determination of its object. By dint of wishing to place the social world at a distance, as if in order to dominate it from without, it would deprive itself of what gives it a social foundation.

— 2 —

CRITICAL SOCIOLOGY AND PRAGMATIC SOCIOLOGY OF CRITIQUE

I shall now try to employ the schema I have just sketched in order to examine the way in which the link has been made between sociological description and social critique in the framework of the two programmes I referred to at the outset – critical sociology and pragmatic sociology of critique.

Critical Sociology

The second half of the 1960s and the 1970s were marked in France by the development of various critical trends, often Marxist in inspiration and, in particular, of movements claiming the heritage of the Frankfurt School. In this context, the originality of the *critical sociology of domination* established by Pierre Bourdieu and his team was its disengagement from predominantly philosophical approaches and its anchorage in the practice of sociology conceived as a 'profession' combining concept creation and empirical field work as closely as possible.[1] Bourdieu's critical sociology is unquestionably the most audacious enterprise ever attempted to try to conjoin in the same theoretical construction highly constraining requirements supervising sociological practice and radically critical positions. That is also why we can find in this oeuvre most of the problems posed by the linking of sociology and critique to which I have just referred.

The original theoretical framework constructed by Bourdieu to integrate sociology and critique saw itself as a continuation of the 'classics'. It contains elements taken from Durkheimian sociology, G.H. Mead's pragmatism, Schutz's phenomenologically inspired sociology, or the cultural anthropology of the first half of the twentieth century, itself born from the confluence of ethnology and psycho-analysis. However, as regards the problematic of domination in the strict sense, it is above all the dual contribution of Max Weber and Marx that is called upon. It is therefore not surprising if we find in Bourdieu's oeuvre a tension between, on the one hand, an approach devoted to the factual description and analysis of the modalities of domination such as they can be observed in different societies (the 'modes of domination') and, on the other, a challenge to domination which, in the spirit of currents of Marxist inspiration, is geared towards an emancipatory aim. Nevertheless, unlike what is found in most of the currents identifying with Marxism (and perhaps under the influence of Durkheim), in Bourdieu's case the enterprise of emancipation is mainly based on the practice of sociology itself. In this instance, sociology is therefore both the instrument for describing domination and the instrument for emancipation from domination.

Adoption of this dual orientation renders the tension contained in the project of a critical sociology especially salient. It directly concerns the linkage between a *sociology* which, although it contains numerous contributions from phenomenology and inter-subjective approaches, is always self-defined more or less by reference to the requirements of objectivity and axiological neutrality, and a *social critique*. The problem is on what the latter can be based. Refusing to search for a basis, on the one hand, in reference to morality or values (a position condemned as moralism) and, on the other, in a quasi-evolutionism making of the development of self-proclaimed democratic capitalist nation-states a sort of ideal towards which the end of history is necessarily directed (as in certain currents identified with Talcott Parsons[2] or Seymour Martin Lipset, of whom Bourdieu is unsparing in his criticisms), but also in a philosophy of history of the Marxist variety (the succession of modes of production and the exacerbation of contradictions), Bourdieu's critical sociology must invoke various 'lateral possibilities' without, however, seeking to specify their import.

The Problems Posed by Use of the Notion of Domination in Critical Sociology

I shall not spell out in detail the way in which the notion of domination is employed in Pierre Bourdieu's critical sociology – something that would involve us in extended exposition – and shall take it as well known.[3] I shall restrict myself to recalling rapidly the objections which, some twenty years ago now, led me to distance myself from *critical sociology* and attempt to broach the issue of critique by a different route – that of a *pragmatic sociology of critique* – of which I shall shortly present the main outlines.

The problems posed by the way in which the notion of domination was employed in critical sociology derive from the fact that it is at once too powerful and too vague in character. Extensive use of the notion of domination leads to conceiving virtually all relations between actions in their vertical dimension, from explicit hierarchical relations to the most personal of links. By the same token, what the sociologist will establish, in critical fashion, as a relationship of domination is not necessarily presented or even lived by actors in this register; and the latter might even turn out to be offended by such a description. (If, for example, as a sociologist you explain to a man engrossed in the enchantment of love that the passion he experiences for his companion is *in fact* merely the result of the effect of social domination that she exercises over him, because she comes from a higher class than his, you risk meeting with some problems in getting your viewpoint accepted.) This extension of the notion of domination leads to extending the notion of *violence* in such a way as to stretch *physical violence*, which is experienced and described, at least in a number of cases, precisely as violence by the actors themselves, in the direction of a *symbolic violence* (a key notion in Bourdieu's sociology), which invariably is not experienced as such.

To explain how and why actors are dominated without knowing it, the theory must accord great importance to the *illusions* that blind them and appeal to the notion of the unconscious. An initial consequence is that actors are often treated as deceived beings or as if they were 'cultural dopes', to use Harold Garfinkel's phrase. Their critical capacities in particular are underestimated or ignored. Another consequence is that preponderant weight is given to the dispositional properties of actors, at the expense of the properties inscribed in the situations into which they are plunged, and an attempt is made to explain virtually all of their behaviour by the internalization of dominant norms, above all in the course of the education process. It takes the form of an *incorporation*, which inscribes these norms in the body, like habits – a process that accounts for the reproduction of structures. However, by the same token, *situations* are neglected, sometimes in favour of dispositions and sometimes of structures. While situations can be observed and described as clearly by the actors who are continually immersed in them in the course of their everyday life as by sociologists, knowledge of structures is accessible exclusively to the latter. Their unmasking in fact requires the use of instruments of a macro-social character and, in particular, statistical instruments, based on the construction of categories, nomenclatures and a metrology. But this is also to say that the instruments on which the exposure of structures is going to be based are largely dependent on the existence of powerful centres of calculation invariably placed under the supervision of states or inter-state organizations. It follows, as numerous works over the last thirty years have shown, that these macro-social instruments, as well as the categories and metrologies on which they are based, must themselves be regarded as products of social activity and, in particular, the activity of states, so that they occupy the dual position, embarrassing to say the least, of instruments of social knowledge and objects of that knowledge.[4]

Finally, a third consequence is to increase the asymmetry between deceived actors and a sociologist capable – and, it would appear from some formulations, the only one capable – of revealing the truth of their social condition to them. This leads to overestimating the power of sociology as science, the sole foundation on which the sociologist could base his claim to know much more about people than they themselves know. Sociology then tends to be invested with the over-weening power of being the main discourse of truth on the social world, which leads it to enter into competition with other disciplines laying claim to the same imperialism. Above all, however, the critical enterprise finds itself torn between, on the one hand, the temptation of extending to all forms of knowledge the unmasking of the 'ideologies' on which they are based and, on the other, the need to maintain a reserved domain – that of Science – capable of providing a fulcrum for this operation. Finally, let us add that the intensification of the difference between sociological science and ordinary knowledge leads to an under-estimation of the effects of the circulation of sociological discourses in society and their re-appropriation/re-interpretation by actors – which is rather problematic in the case of a sociology that claims reflexivity. These repercussive effects of sociology in the social world are especially important in contemporary societies on account of the fact, in particular, of the enhanced role of secondary and university education (not to mention the role of the media), which leads actors to seize on explanatory schemas and languages derived from social science and to enlist them in their daily interactions (particularly in the course of their disputes).[5]

On the other hand, we might reckon that this paradigm does not make it possible fully to account for action and hence the disputes actors engage in. In fact, the attempt to maintain an interface between cartographic descriptions and interactionist descriptions seems to lead to over-determining the latter, by too hastily interpreting the behaviour of actors in accordance with dispositions identified from descriptions of the structuralist variety – dispositions that would be manifested in pretty much the same fashion whatever the situation (something well conveyed by the term *agent*, preferred to that of *actor*). The stress put on the circular relations between underlying structures and incorporated dispositions thus combines to reduce the uncertainty confronting actors in the situations in which they must act.[6] But the notion of action is only really meaningful against a backdrop of uncertainty, or at least with reference to a plurality of possible options.[7] In contexts where everything seems decided in advance, the very concept of action tends to become void of meaning. This applies in the first instance to disputes, of which not only the outcome, but also the facts invoked by the different partners and their interpretations, are uncertain. For the same reasons social change itself, and also the role played by critique in processes of change, are difficult to accommodate in this framework.

Other problems are posed to the articulation between the two uses of sociology: as an instrument of description and as a weapon of critique. On the one hand, domination is described – in a Weberian optic – as a factual condition that can be identified, in various forms, in most known societies. On the other, domination, unmasked in a *social order*, is submitted to critique as it would be in work inspired by Marx or, at least, geared to a project of emancipation – which assumes a normative basis. In this paradigm, the stress laid on social Science as the main access road to truth (a position common to most of the critical French authors of the 1960s and 1970s, concerned to free themselves from an idealist philosophy still preponderant in the academy), has the effect of making most of the normative resources – of which we have given a brief description above – that could support a project of a metacritical kind unavailable. In particular, what is bracketed is reference to a philosophical anthropology, which, however, is one of the supports to which metacritical endeavours most often resort. But the critical project is not thereby abandoned. It follows that critical postures, which it is difficult to adopt as such out of a fear of falling short of the requirements of Science, are in a sense embedded in the fabric of the description, and this largely via rhetorical means capable of generating indignation in the reader. By the same token, we might ask to what extent the descriptions themselves are not over-determined by these rhetorics, which would not have been the case – or at least not to the same extent – if the problems posed by the articulation between descriptive orientations and normative aims had been explicitly acknowledged.

The Programme of a Pragmatic Sociology of Critique

The programme of a *pragmatic sociology of critique*, established in the 1980s by sociologists some of whom had initially worked in the framework of the Bourdieusian paradigm, aimed to reformulate the question of critique by seeking to get round the difficulties just mentioned.[8] What was rejected in particular was the asymmetry between the sociologist enlightened by the light of his science and ordinary people sunk in illusion, which seemed to us not to be confirmed by field work and, in addition, to contain the risks – signalled in polemical terms by Jacques Rancière in *The Philosopher and his Poor* – of being recuperated in favour of a new kind of Platonist idealism (the omniscient sociologist replacing the philosopher-king in the ambition of guiding society).[9]

This querying of the paradigm of critical sociology concentrated on its *descriptive* – that is, specifically sociological – dimension and not on its critical aspects (as would have been the case if the rationale of the move had been a political shift to conservatism or, as with numerous French intellectuals at the turn of the 1980s, a lurch from Marxism to liberalism). We wanted to pursue, and even increase, anchorage in a rigorous empirical sociology, which seemed to us to represent a fundamental contribution of the work developed in the framework of this paradigm, by offering better descriptions of the activity of actors in particular situations. To this end, it seemed to us to be necessary to bracket an unduly powerful explanatory system, whose mechanical utilization risked crushing the data (as if the sociologists already knew in advance what they were going to discover),[10] so as to observe, naively as it were, what actors do, the way they interpret the intentions of others, the way they argue their case, and so on. To be brief, our move therefore consisted in re-tilting from a critical orientation to the search for a better description, which once again attests to the unstable character of sociological constructions that foreground the issue of critique, and perhaps of sociology in general, haunted as it is by the tension between its descriptive exigencies and its normative orientation.

However, we did not abandon the project of a critical sociology. Our attention to close-up description of the deeds and gestures of actors had the character (if I may be permitted this economic metaphor) of a *detour of production*. Via this detour, we thought we would ultimately be better placed to revive critique, while affixing it to social reality. In fact, it seemed to us necessary to firm up our powers of persuasion in an intellectual and political context – that of the 1980s – marked by a relative abandonment of paradigms stressing the vertical dimension and the opacity of the alienated consciousness of agents, in favour of paradigms directed instead towards horizontal relations (in particular, analyses in terms of networks) and modalities of action interpreted in terms of strategic motivations and rational choices.

The strategy implemented consisted in *returning to things themselves*, as phenomenology puts it. Now, to return to things themselves in the case of critique is to make one's first objective observing, describing and interpreting situations where people engage in critique – that is, *disputes*. The shift we made therefore took the form of a series of pieces of field research, borrowing the methods of ethnological observation, focused on disputes in situations pertaining to domains of objectivity that were as diverse as possible. But this change of perspective in respect of field work would have lacked coherence if it had not been accompanied by a readjustment of the theoretical framework.

This programme exploited the resources supplied by currents inspired to various degrees by *pragmatism*. Often taking very different paths, these currents shared the common feature that they refocused the sociologist's attention on actors *en situation*, as the main agencies of performance of the social, at the expense of a cartographic description of the world already there. This could involve currents directly inspired by American pragmatism, as in the case of interactionism and, less directly, ethnomethodology. But we must also mention currents which, rooted in the French intellectual context, adopted part of the pragmatist legacy, often via a complicated route running through the work of Gilles Deleuze (as in Bruno Latour). It could also involve currents which, without being directly linked to pragmatism, directed the sociologist's attention to language and the interpretative work *en situation* performed by actors, whether it be the analytical philosophy of the second Wittgenstein or Paul Ricoeur's attempt to bring about a convergence between analytical philosophy and phenomenology.

From this disparate range, particular use was made of currents connected with linguistics – on the one hand, linguistic pragmatics, which directed attention to *indexicality* and the formation of meaning *en situation*; on the other, generative linguistics, from which, in particular, the notion of *competence* was taken (in, it must be admitted,

24

unorthodox fashion). We used it to refer to generative schemas whose presence must be assumed to account for the capacity of actors to produce acceptable critiques and/or justifications *en situation* – that is to say, their sense of justice or their moral sense. We can therefore more or less link to the spirit of pragmatism the way in which the sociology of critique undertook to describe the social world *as the scene of a trial*,[11] in the course of which actors in a situation of *uncertainty* proceed to *investigations*, record their *interpretations* of what happens in *reports*, establish *qualifications* and submit to *tests*.

As is suggested by the reference to generative linguistics, this programme retained an objectivist character and even, in some respects, a structuralist orientation, directed not towards a social morphology that was cartographic in style, but a modelling of the cognitive and deontic equipment – that is, the competences – whose existence must be assumed in order to understand how actors succeed – notwithstanding the disputes that oppose them or even, to be more precise, through the very intermediary of these disputes – in coordinating their actions or getting their interpretations to converge. We were even rather hostile to those currents (like interpretative anthropology) which, in the same period, foregrounded the impossibility of the observer putting the interpretative categories she owed to her own rootedness in an era and culture at a distance, or even to the currents that practically took no account of the resources of which actors disposed locally (as in some hard versions of ethnomethodology).

According to this project, sociology's principal task was to explain, clarify and, where possible, model the methods employed in the social world to make and break bonds. In this sense, sociology is treated as a second-rank discipline which, rather like linguistics, presents in a certain format subject to requirements of ordering and clarity a competence which is that of the actors themselves, but of which they are not fully conscious when they exercise it. Sociology achieves its objective when it provides a satisfactory picture of the social competences of actors. The form of truth it seeks to attain thus approximates to *acceptability* in the sense of linguistics.

At the level of metacritical orientation, which we shall examine in more detail shortly, the intention was to make a form of normativity emerge from the description. Work was initially directed towards clarifying the normative positions on which actors can base themselves, in order either to criticize or to justify themselves in the face of critique. But this in such a way as to open up the possibility of a metacritical project that would be based on the collection and clarification of the critiques developed by actors themselves in the circumstances of everyday life. To put it in the terms of one of those who contributed to the development of this programme: having recognized that the exteriorities to which critical sociologies lay claim are always *incompletely external*, it was a question of exploring the possibility of a *complex interiority*, comprising, in addition to egress from the context and its critique, a third movement aiming to integrate what external critique still owes to the context it critiques.[12]

Research on the ground that deals with disputes in highly diverse areas has been conducted in connection with this programme: disputes in the workplace and firms;[13] in health contexts[14] (in connection, in particular, with the Aids epidemic);[15] in the world of the media;[16] in banks;[17] in committees responsible for valuing and selecting cultural goods,[18] recruiting salaried workers,[19] or distributing private or public goods in educational establishments[20] or municipalities.[21] Or, again, in bodies charged with product-labelling,[22] or in connection with protecting the environment.[23] And even within an institution as seemingly monolithic as the Roman Catholic Church, on the question of whether the Virgin Mary really did appear to some Bosnian shepherds.[24]

Another side of the programme took as its object various 'affairs' (often related in France to the model constituted by the Dreyfus Affair) – that is to say, more or less major and more or less protracted disputes, depending on the case, during which a conflict is carried into the public sphere.[25] In the course of these affairs, a problem, originally local, is extended and takes on a general character. Unlike a scandal,[26] which can elicit unanimous indignation, an affair entails the formation of opposing clans, because it always contains a reversal of the accusation. The defence of an individual, whom certain authorities have accused of a crime, is taken up by a collective that aims to show that he or she is in fact a victim and turns the accusation around against the accusers. The various conflicting parties then seek to mobilize as many actors as possible in favour of their cause. When it succeeds (if we can put it like this), the affair tends to colonize different sectors of society and to cross the boundaries separating different worlds: political, intellectual, economic and so on. Several incompatible narratives publicly come into conflict, keeping up an uncertainty about 'what really occurred' until the dénouement.

The *actors* whom these works have made visible were very different from the *agents* who feature in the critical sociology of domination. They were always active, not passive. They were frankly critical, even critical rather in the manner of critical sociologists, forever unmasking the hidden intentions and biases of their opponents – often related to their social position – mobilizing to this end various schemas taken from critical sociology, diffused by education or the media. They made their demands, denounced injustices, produced evidence in support of their complaints, or constructed arguments to justify themselves in the face of the critiques to which they were themselves subjected. Envisaged thus, the social world does not appear to be the site of domination endured passively and unconsciously, but instead as a space shot through by a multiplicity of disputes, critiques, disagreements and attempts to re-establish locally agreements that are always fragile.

In synergy with field research, theoretical work was undertaken to model the activity of actors and the competences employed during disputes. In particular, stress was laid on the sense of justice. In *On Justification*, Laurent Thévenot and I attempted to construct a model of the competences that enable actors to make critiques or to justify themselves in the face of critique. Without describing this model of the meaning of injustice in detail – which would take too long – I shall indicate some elements useful for the remainder of this talk.

To invoke justice in disputation of this type, tools must be activated (which we called *principles of equivalence*) that make it possible to assess, *in a certain respect* to be specified, the relative value of the beings engaged in the dispute, or (to use our vocabulary) their *worth*. Basing ourselves on field work, we identified six principles of worth operative in the different situations of everyday life. These principles were formalized starting from classical political philosophies. On the basis of each of these principles, a form of common good can be exhibited that we called a *polity* [*cité*].[27] These different principles of worth possess a common underlying structure or, if you like, *grammar*. The latter is based on a construction that makes it possible to reduce the tension between two constraints: a *constraint of equality* (what we called a requirement of *common humanity*) and a *constraint of order*. In a certain situation, beings who in principle are equal by virtue of their membership of a common humanity are placed in hierarchical or asymmetrical positions. The reduction of this tension assumes adding some additional constraints to the model – in particular, a constraint that prohibits definitively attaching a certain condition of worth to people, treating it as if it were essential to them.

This model aims not only to account for the arguments deployed by people in the course of their disputes, but also for the means they employ to seek to leave the dispute behind them and re-establish agreement, without resorting to violence but by relying on reality. We called these means *reality tests*.[28] We considered that people were led to put their claims to the test of reality by confronting them with *objects*, material or symbolic, arranged in situations. With each polity, corresponding to the difference principles of equivalence or justice identified, are thus associated repertoires of objects whose comparison and internal coherent alignment outlines spheres of pertinence.[29]

Thus, for example, particularly associated with industrial worth, which is recognized by effectiveness, are tools of measurement and means of calculation that make it possible to judge the more or less effective character of an object or person (such as standards, tests, accounting forms, and so on). Similarly, associated with domestic worth, which values people according to their position not only in kinship but, more generally, in chains of personal dependence (it was a predominant form of worth in Europe under the ancien régime) are devices, values and objects, such as family feasts, marks of respect, testamentary arrangements and so on, whose combination composes a sphere of pertinence that can be used as a basis for establishing tests and make a judgement as to people's worth.

But these polities are largely incompatible. Although they are all at work in a complex society, they cannot be engaged at the same time in the same situation except by forging a compromise, which is always relatively fragile. In this framework we have analysed the critiques that actors make in the course of disputes. These critiques challenge the modalities of judgement in a particular situation, either by invoking a principle of worth that is different from the one on which other participants are focused, or by showing that the judgement is not in fact based on the principles officially proclaimed but, on the contrary, on different, covert principles.

Take, for example, the challenge to educational exams for allegedly taking into consideration, but in implicit, concealed fashion, the social origin of pupils, their 'good manners' or their 'distinction' – a challenge that was an important element in critical sociology in France in the 1960s and 1970s.[30] In the terms of the model whose main lines I have just rapidly mentioned, this kind of situation – the incriminated examination – can be described as unjust because it *corrupts* a test of an industrial type (the exam is supposed, via standardized procedures, to test the effectiveness of pupils faced with problems of a certain type), by considering forms of worth which, while wholly admissible in a domestic type of test, pervert the proper conduct of the educational test. A possible response to this challenge might then be to seek to make the test *purer*, by preventing forms of worth that are legitimate in the world of domestic relations from manifesting themselves in it and, for example, by making the competition anonymous.

According to this model of the ordinary sense of justice, a test is regarded as unjust by people when it takes account, invariably in implicit or hidden form, of forces that do not pertain to the kind of city in which the test is, in principle, inscribed. Every test is indeed, in a way, a test of strength. But a just test is primarily a test *of something* (the ability to create a work of art, to be a loving father, to resolve a difficult problem in computer software, to help the firm that employs you make a profit, etc.) – that is to say, a test where the strength put to the test is *specified*. By contrast, a pure *test of strength*, therewith escaping the rule of justice, may be defined as a test in which partners can commit any kind of force whatsoever in order to seek, by any means, to prevail over the others.[31]

Finally, let us add that these tests are, to various degrees, *institutionalized*. Whereas some tests are incidental and local, so that their unjust character is difficult to objectify (if formulated, complaints can be met with denials), other tests, because they bear on important points and therefore decidedly do face critique, are subject to a labour of institutionalization – in particular, through the intermediary of the law or other forms of regulation that lay down procedures and establish what can be called a *test format* (we shall return to this idea later). This is the case, in particular, with tests that play an important role in the designation of political representatives and leaders and also in the selection of people for access to sought-after positions or advantages (educational tests, work selection tests, tests providing access to social rights, and so on). It follows that critique can point in two different directions. It can take as its object the way in which a test is conducted locally and show that its conduct did not respect established procedures. Or it can take *the test format itself* as its target, showing that its arrangement does not make it possible to control the set of forces engaged in the test – something that unjustly favours some competitors.

Can Critical Operations be Conducted on the Basis of the Sociology of Critique?

We shall now ask to what extent this sociology *of* critique – applied in what Nicolas Dodier has called 'the laboratory of polities'[32] – can contribute to the redeployment of a critical sociology. We have seen that this articulation assumes the possibility of introducing a *normative difference* into the very core of the conceptual architecture. One possibility presents itself in the framework of the pragmatic sociology of critique. It can make use of several formulas (described above) taken from different sociological traditions – in particular, positions developed by American pragmatist sociology (e.g. the notion of experimentation in Dewey);[33] Durkheimian moral sociology, which roots normativity in the collective; and, finally, certain positions adopted by Anglo-American moral philosophy of communitarian inspiration. One thinks, in particular, of the work of Michael Walzer, who accords great importance to critique, but envisages it above all in so far as it is based on values recognized by a collective. In that author it is regarded as valid when it leads to protest against actions performed within a constituted group and in its name, arguing from the fact that these actions contradict the very values which the members of the group esteem.[34]

In a pragmatist sociology of critique, the metacritical position will therefore consist in *making use of the point of view of the actors* – that is to say, base itself on their moral sense and, in particular, on their ordinary sense of justice, to expose the discrepancy between the social world as it is and as it should be in order to satisfy people's moral expectations. By adopting the viewpoint of the actor, the sociologist can in fact cast a normative glance at the world, without it being guided either by her personal prejudices (bound up, for example, with a cultural affiliation or political commitment or specific religion), or by the adoption of a substantive moral philosophy (e.g. utilitarianism).

Starting out from the model of injustice, established on the basis of investigations, to which I referred above, we can certainly conduct certain critical operations to a successful conclusion. For example, we can, as do actors themselves, challenge certain tests by showing that they result in judgements which are based not solely on an assessment of the forces explicitly integrated into their official format, but also on the implicit consideration of adjacent strengths, with unjust consequences. Take tests associated with looking for a job. Critique will attempt to show that they are distorted by the covert consideration of invalid social properties, as is the case when people denounce the forms of *discrimination* that *handicap* some candidates (women, people whose family name indicates North African origin, people identified as gay, the elderly, etc.). Again – a second example – it can be shown that the requirement of repeating tests is rarely satisfied and criticize the fact that the advantages resulting from a successful test are invariable attached *once and for all* to the person of the beneficiary and that the same applies to those who have failed. This is the case in France when people denounce the incorrigible effects, whether beneficial or prejudicial, of competitions giving access to the *grandes écoles* or major state bodies, but also to leadership positions in large firms. However, one has a clear sense that critical operations of this kind, however legitimate and socially useful, are insufficient to satisfy the ambitions of a critical sociology. Several problems present themselves.

The first stems from the way in which, especially in the course of a dispute, the divergences between the positions adopted by different actors are to be interpreted. The position adopted in *On Justification* consisted in constructing a model that makes it possible to integrate the totality of resources which can be employed by actors to make critiques or provide justifications. It is precisely here that this option is connected to more or less structuralist positions. But this stance is only defensible by reference to two frameworks, the first of them more universalistic, the second more culturalist. The universalistic framework is explicitly rejected, because the polities are treated as historical constructs. As to the culturalist framework, it is displaced from *culture* in the sense of anthropology towards the *political*. The normative supports that critiques and justifications are based on are associated with systems rooted in social reality, which are considered to be the product of the political history of a society. As a result, we observe variations between the contours of different polities and above all between their arrangements in different nation-states.[35] The position adopted can therefore be challenged, for example, from a communitarian standpoint. It can in fact be criticized for over-estimating the integration of different actors and different groups in a state framework. Within one and the same nation-state there can co-exist more or less integrated groups, such that some of them maintain, at least in certain situations among themselves, specific forms of normativity (something the idea of multi-culturalism seeks to capture). It can also be argued, this time referring to the idea of domination, that the normative supports integrated into the system of polities universalize and impose on everyone positions that correspond to the values and interests of dominant groups (dominant class, colonizers, etc.).[36]

However, the main difficulty encountered by such an approach in sustaining its metacritical ambitions is the following. The social actors whose disputes are observed by the sociologist are *realistic*. They do not demand the impossible. Their sense of reality is sustained by the way in which they grasp their social environment. They assess the just or unjust, privileged or disadvantaged character of their condition by comparing their existence with that of people close to them – some particular work colleague, some fellow student whose professional success has been greater than theirs, and so on. Or again, they compare their situation with that of their parents, or their current situation with what it had previously been and so on.

In so doing, ordinary people rarely call into question, at least in the normal course of social life, the general framework in which the situations that provoke their indignation and protest are inscribed – that is, the set of *established* test formats and qualifications. No doubt because, in the absence of totalizing tools, the contours of this general set of tests, and their effects, often escape them. But above all because actors know implicitly that tests based on established formats are stronger than they are, so that it would be utter folly to demand for themselves changes in their life that presuppose a radical transformation of this framework. Actors, at least when grasped in the course of their everyday activities, take reality, and the *real* character of the reality test, seriously. The waiter in a cafeteria knows implicitly that it would not make any sense for him to regard the fact that he is not a university professor as unjust, because he is not unaware of the fact that, put to the test, he would prove incapable of satisfying, for example, the requirements of a trigonometry exam (unless, having completed the relevant studies, he possesses the requisite degrees and can protest that he has been excluded as a result of discrimination – for example, because he is black or on account of his sex or sexual orientation, or other).

Moreover, we might ask if the model of the sense of justice established on the basis of inquiries conducted in the 1980s did not over-do a *meritocratic* conception of justice, as a result of its contextual dependence on a moment of history characterized by the defeat of attempts made in previous decades to validate a collective conception of justice, conceived as *social justice*.

A just society in the meritocratic sense is one where all actors occupy positions that correspond to their personal capacities, because reality tests and tested reality are completely superimposed. It follows that not only would critique of the tests no longer have a rationale, but also the tests themselves would take the form of simple routines and gradually become pointless.[37] Everything leads us to think that not only has a society of this type never existed, but also that it is probably not realizable for various reasons. One of them stems from the unstable and concealed character of the personal capacities that the test is supposed to disclose. Since tests cannot be constantly repeated, the tendency would certainly be to seek to root these powers in the innermost being of actors – that is, in their biological substrate. A society intent on being meritocratic is easily threatened by some form or other of racism or, at least, by a biologizing naturalism. A second reason is that it is impossible to conceive test formats that make it possible to arrange each test conducted locally in such a way as to restrict the respect in which the person must be assessed or to neutralize contextual effects completely. It follows that the conduct of genuinely 'just' tests, from a meritocratic point of view, presupposes establishing a particular test format for each particular test to which a particular person is subjected in a particular situation – something that would obviously result in removing any comparative capacity from tests and thus strip them of the power of justifying social hierarchies. They would therefore no longer have any utility.

It remains the case that one has a strong sense that, even in the utopian case of a society where the relationship between reality tests and reality was perfectly adjusted, the social world would not cease to be a potential target of critique. At least of the kind of critique which can be characterized as *radical*, in the sense that, based on a complex exteriority, it opens up the possibility not only of a critique of the way – correct or incorrect – *reality tests* are applied, but also of a critique of *reality itself*.

The Degree of Reality of Reality

We must therefore ask on what conditions a metacritical position based on the critiques developed by actors can prove conducive to the development of a critique of reality. We shall say that this is the case when the actors themselves, or at least some of them, differently direct the operations, inherent in the sense of justice, which consist in comparing their condition with that of others. But whereas in a meritocratic optic this comparison readily takes the form of an individual competition leading to maximization of the differences from those who are faced with the same tests – that is to say, necessarily, actors who are relatively proximate, at least in some respects – from the perspective of social justice comparisons that lead to stressing similarities of condition will be favoured. At the same time, the sense of justice will be directed towards consideration of collective injustices and favour the formation of a *sense of the totality*, opening up the possibility of moving back-and-forth between the particular situations of which actors have direct experience and the wider social orders that can only be accessed through the mediation of political constructs.

But this is also to say that the realistic self-limitation of protests, which we have previously emphasized, is not always at the same level. In the first instance, it varies depending on the degree to which social reality succeeds in getting actors to believe in its solidity and internalize their powerlessness to change test formats. Rapidly put, reality is robust or *hangs together* (in Alain Desrosière's phrase), firstly when the instruments of totalization and representation of what is, or at least what is given as relevant for the collective, seem capable of completely covering the field of actual and even potential events. And, secondly, when they succeed in providing descriptions of what happens and perhaps, above all, of what might occur, in the form of a network of *causalities* connecting entities and forces, which are themselves identified and stabilized by means of instruments of categorization compatible with counting operations.

These instruments, be they managerial, accounting, statistical or political in character, which pertain predominantly (but not exclusively) in democratic-capitalist societies to the state (or inter-state organizations), make it possible to organize reality around a central value – i.e. *scarcity* – and, by the same token, to over-determine its representation by reference to *necessity*. Reality is robust or *hangs together* when no event erupts in the public arena with sufficient relief to challenge the pre-established harmony between reality and the presentation of reality, either because such an event does not occur or because it remains *invisible*. As a result, the experience of scarcity everyone has in the course of everyday realities and, in particular, the constraints encountered by one's desires, can be immediately related to the reality constructed by instruments that ensure its order in the domain of representation but also, indissolubly, in that of the facts and causalities whose effects can be experienced by all those who endure its constraint. The *reality of reality* is therefore maintained by 'seriality as a link of impotence'.[38]

However, for the same reasons, the possibility of introducing some give into reality will also depend on the degree to which actors can have access to practical devices and cognitive tools that enable them to break their isolation by comparing situations, whose constraints they suffer, with different situations wherein are immersed actors endowed with properties that are also different, but with which a comparison or approximation can be made. These tools, whether those that make it possible to go back to test formats (most often, very concretely, regulations that have been subject to a legal type of inscription to various degrees), or those which favour the approximation of conditions faced with tests, are necessarily constructs that themselves adopt the point of view of the totality.

The self-restriction of protests is thus at its greatest in atomized social situations where individuals can only rely on their own forces, and it diminishes in periods when collective action seems possible and, in particular, in exceptional situations – revolutionary or insurrectional. These historical situations are characterized precisely by a serial disorganization of the constraining frameworks of social life which, by opening up the field of possibilities, liberates expectations and aspirations that were hitherto inaudible, either because they were repressed or because they were deemed inadmissible or even crazy. If they were expressed in ordinary situations by isolated individuals, speaking in their own name and with no authority but their own, such demands would seem sheer madness, including in the psychiatric sense of the term. They would most probably be interpreted as the symptom of a loss of the sense of reality, which is precisely the external sign of madness.

I have previously devoted a study to the public denunciation of injustices – in particular, by means of letters to newspapers – in which I asked a panel of people with no particular psychiatric competence to read a sample of 300 letters sent to the newspaper *Le Monde*, featuring an account of an injustice suffered, and to mark the author of each letter in such a way as to express a judgement on their mental state synthetically (this could range from a mark of one, awarded to the authors of letters deemed completely sound of mind, to a mark of ten, given to authors deemed completely mentally deranged). This work made it possible to sketch what might be called a *grammar of normality*. On the one hand, it revealed the important role played by the *ordinary sense of normality* in the judgements facing people in everyday life and, particularly in this instance, when they engage in protest and seek to get it endorsed in the public arena. On the other hand, it showed that the chances of protests against injustice being received as normal (if not necessarily justified) largely depended on the extent to which those who made them public succeeded in connecting, in credible fashion, with a collective (an association for the defence of liberties or human rights) capable of corroborating their complaint and offering it backing.[39]

What we understand by *collective* must be clarified here. Obviously, as sociologies that start out from the individual (e.g. in France, Raymond Boudon with 'methodological individualism') always have done, one can regard the formula which makes collectives (groups, classes, nations, ethnic groups, and so on) the subject of verbs of action as deceptive and obscure, in as much as it consists in treating these disembodied collective beings as if they were people. This happens when one confers on a collective the possibility of having a will, calculating, implementing strategies, assessing outcomes, applying rules and so on. This viewpoint demands that we abandon invoking *communities* to account for social phenomena and assimilates these communities to *fictions*. That communities and collectives in general, taken in this sense, are fictions, is undeniable. But the issue becomes complicated when we consider the fact that reference to communities (or collectives) is far from being a monopoly of sociologists; and that, in this, they are merely adopting in their attempts to theorize society a kind of construction that is constantly employed by actors themselves in the course of their social activity. It would unquestionably be difficult to find examples of societies where this way of construing the re-flexibility of social action is absent. It follows that a sociology whose object is modelling the way in which social actors fashion society can indeed regard communities (or, in general, collectives) as fictions, but on condition of recognizing that these fictions seemingly have a necessary character and must therefore, at least by this token, find a place in sociological theory. (We shall return to this theme and seek to clarify it when we broach the issue of *institutions*.)

Let us at once note that the relationship between this issue and what we have called – in connection with work on denunciations of injustice – the sense of normality as manifestation of the sense of reality. The way reality presents itself to everyone makes it possible to understand why the level of acceptability of a public denunciation of injustice or a demand is very low when they are expressed by an isolated person (to the point of risking being charged with madness), but increases when this denunciation or demand is echoed by others – to the point of assuming a character of self-evidence when it seems to have become acceptable to apply the qualification 'collective' to them. In effect, it is as if, for each person taken in isolation, the import of reality had an uncertain character.[40] In this the relationship to reality is a little like the relationship everyone has to their own desire according to René Girard.[41] Everyone recognizes reality (or recognizes what, in their experience, clearly pertains to reality) only because others designate it to them as such. Reality suffers from a species of inherent fragility, such that *the reality of reality* must incessantly be reinforced in order to endure. And it is doubtless a process of this kind that must be invoked to understand the role played, not for the sociologist but the actors themselves, by the reference to collectives. Later, we shall see how this radical uncertainty is necessary, at least at an analytical level, to understand what are usually called institutions and the role, central in my view, they play in the course of social life, but also to identify the contradictions they contain (and which confer on sociality in its entirety a paradoxical, fragile character).

Always the Same Who . . .

Pursuing the example of denunciations of injustice, we can say that the level of constraint exercised by the sense of reality on judgements about actors' claims and demands largely depends on the extent to which the latter are presented or (which comes down to the same thing) interpreted as being individual or even local or, on the contrary, as being collective in kind and capable of claiming general validity. A *rise towards generality* is therefore a necessary condition for the success of public protests, on condition that it is effected in credible fashion.

That is why situations which can (to be brief) be characterized as revolutionary are favourable to an expansion in the scope of protests, which is itself the result of a reduction in the constraints exercised by the sense of reality on demands in the ordinary situations of social life. In these historical situations, characterized by the collective formulation of individual complaints, attention to difference is not abolished. But it is shifted from attention to the individual differences between those who are proximate to differences which, at a distance, separate collectives or groups. It is nevertheless necessary to add that this process can take a pathological form when general category differences are imported from without, and not drawn from the experience of actors, who can tend to give them material form, to project them onto the space of proximity. They will then identify those who enjoy advantages locally slightly superior to their own as representatives of those external, harmful forces about which people have spoken to them, to the extent that the process of comparison can backfire and take the form of a mechanism of fragmentation and violent struggle of all against all. Thus it is that revolutions degenerate when they are monopolized by vanguards which set about projecting onto lived spaces dogmatic instruments of identification and categorization.[42]

In situations where the process of comparison is rooted in actors' experience, however, the question of why the value of some particular person was recognized in the test emerges, and whether it is just, is replaced by a different question, which immediately takes a collective turn. This question, which can be formulated in deliberately naive terms – that is to say, in terms where it develops out of common sense – consists in asking why it is always *the same people* who pass all or most tests, whatever their nature, and, on the other hand, why it is always *the same people* who, confronted with all tests (or virtually all), prove mediocre (*unworthy people*, in the language of *Of Justification*). It cannot be said that this question is foreign to actors' sense of justice. If such were the case, it would be utterly inaccessible to a pragmatic sociology of critique. But it presents itself to them differently depending on the condition of the social tools – and especially forms of classification – available to construct collective entities and inscribe them in a totality, so as to make such notions as domination or exploitation meaningful.

This is clear from two contrasting developments that have affected French society (and doubtless, more generally, Western societies) in the last thirty years. On the one hand, there is the dynamic of individualization of the relationship to work and, on the other, the developing collectivization of relations between the genders. Without going into detail, we can show how the sense of belonging to a social group, and especially a social class, which was still very present in the 1980s, went hand-in-hand with the internalization by actors of forms of classification that took account of the position occupied in relations of domination. In particular, we are thinking of a managerial tool of the organizational state – socio-professional categories – that was put in place, in the wake of protest movements, roughly between the mid 1930s and the mid 1950s. Relayed through very different mediations (collective agreements, polling organizations, pension systems), these classifications were soon integrated into the cognitive devices possessed by actors to situate themselves in social space, identify others and identify themselves.[43] We know that this sense of belonging to collectives has been highly attenuated and especially disorientated over the last twenty years, in a period nevertheless marked by a significant increase in inequalities and a reduction in social mobility – that is, by a strengthening of the barriers between classes. This development, while not a direct consequence of it, followed hard on the heels of the dismantling of semantic instruments of identification and classification of social groups and social antagonisms that had been forged under the pressure of the labour movement,[44] and, in part, integrated into the tools of governance used by the state.[45] The sense of injustice has not thereby disappeared, but it has long been expressed in the register of resentment, like a bout of bad temper or an unease, difficult to objectify in the absence of tools that make it possible to compare tests pertaining to different spheres and actors who are unequally and differently disadvantaged.

By contrast, in the same period inequalities between the genders resulting from male domination have certainly not disappeared. But they have been subjected to a collective assumption of responsibility and served as a basis for the development of specific demands and struggles. This shift would have been impossible without the construction by the feminist movement of a semantics on whose basis the oppression suffered by women in general (for example, sexual harassment at work, which for a long time could not be heard or spoken of in trade-union milieus) has become the object of specific descriptions, enabling a movement back-and-forth between the experience of each woman in particular and the *female condition* considered in its generality.

In the instance to which we have just referred, the issue of the just appraisal of individual merits, and the just distribution of material and symbolic goods between individuals according to their merits, is replaced by a different question: what is meant by *the same* and how is the demonstration to be conducted in order to unmask the fact that it is for *the same* people that reality is always satisfying, whereas for others, who are also – in this unfavourable respect – *the same*, reality is always gruelling? Putting the idea of class, of social class (but also gender, ethnic group), at the heart of critique is not easy to do and maintain, since this idea has to surmount the undeniable obstacle of individual differences and singularities. The latter must in fact be flattened out by using instruments for establishing equivalence that facilitate comparison between people in a respect constituted as preferential – something that tends to obscure other possible relations under which different people might be subsumed and which must then be treated as secondary.

I have previously tried to show this by taking the subject of the formation in France, between roughly the mid 1930s and mid 1950s, of the category of *cadres* (with the intention of suggesting an alternative to the naturalism or substantialism that characterized the way in which structuralist Marxism posed the issue of social classes at the time).[46] This study consisted in tracking closely the considerable work, cognitive, political and institutional, that accompanied the formation of this category, which is incomprehensible prior to the 1930s but whose existence is regarded as self-evident and undeniable from the 1960s (before being called into question in the 1990s). But it also showed how other possible modes of grouping, based on different principles of equivalence, had been put to the test in the same period without ending up taking form in credible, lasting fashion (the case, for instance, in France with the category of 'middle class', which, at least until recently, never succeeded in achieving institutional recognition).

Let us pursue the example of social classes. In a way, it is quite right to regard them as mere fictions. This fictional character emerges in particularly clear fashion when a substantive definition of classes is given, as if the categories that arise from the work of categorization were rooted from the beginning of time in the reified fabric of the social.[47] This reification foregrounds quasi-legal operations of definition and classification and creates a number of problems, which are merely artificial – for example, that of 'class boundaries' which occupied generations of Marxist sociologists. But, from another angle, we can regard reference to social classes as the necessary pendant of a social order that makes regulated competition between individuals its foremost value.[48] Assigning itself the (unrealizable) ideal of a just distribution of individual abilities, it *inspects reality itself* by formatting it through the intermediary of reality tests. The latter are mutually adjusted so that weakness in one respect, sanctioned by a certain type of test, is more than likely to affect the way actors will have to face other kinds of test. In fact, although they are supposed to be addressed to people considered in different respects, the fact that they involve the same people gives this separation a formal character, and success and failure tend to be contaminated in accordance with the familiar logic of the accumulation of handicaps and disadvantages.

Critical Sociology as a Critique of Reality

If it is acknowledged that actors are generally endowed, on the one hand, with the cognitive capacity to make comparisons, so that it does not escape them that *the same* succeed and *the same* fail (always or nearly always); and, on the other, with a sense of justice involving the idea of a *common humanity*, and hence equality between human beings in principle (even if the latter can come into conflict with exclusivist, nationalist or even racist conceptions of the collective), why do they accept the factual existence of inequalities, which are so obvious and, above all, so persistent that they are difficult to justify, even in a meritocratic logic? Reworking the Marxist idea of *alienation*, critical sociology has often sought to interpret the paradox of apparent submission to this state of affairs by stressing actors' *beliefs* and the *illusions* of which they are allegedly the victims, because they

40

find themselves under the sway of *dominant ideologies* whose category structures they have *internalized*. While not challenging the idea that something like dominant ideologies does indeed exist, seeking both to underestimate and justify inequalities, we can nevertheless show that these constructs are directed in the first instance to disciplining the dominant classes themselves, whose members, especially when they reach the threshold separating the status of child from that of autonomous, responsible adult, also encounter the tension between an egalitarian ideal and a massively unequal reality.[49] The social function of dominant ideologies is therefore above all to maintain a relative cohesion between the different factions that make up these classes and to reinforce (as is indicated by Raymond Aron's interpretation of Pareto)[50] their members' confidence in the validity of their privileges. But when it comes to the dominated classes, different interpretations have to be constructed, taking account of the relationship between the condition of the systems that ensure the running of reality – which can be more or less robust – and the condition of the collective systems actors can rely on to extricate themselves from reality, challenge its validity and, above all, reduce its powers.

This is clear when we examine the current state of critical forces in capitalist democracies. What critique as a collective enterprise currently lacks is doubtless not so much critical energy, present among a large number of people, as a *background* against which it could break loose and take *form* (to borrow an image from *Gestaltspsychologie*), as if it has no sooner been formulated than it is integrated into the formats that give material substance to reality in its public dimensions. It is the difficulty in breaking free of what (to borrow a Sartrean metaphor) we can call the *seriality* and *viscosity* of the real[51] – that is, if you like, its excess reality – which discourages critique and not (as is often said) the absence of a 'project' or an 'alternative' to the present situation. As is clearly indicated, for example, by the social history of the labour movement, past revolts have never put off their dramatic expression until an 'alternative' is presented to them, drawn up in all its details, on the model of the literary and philosophical genre called 'utopia'. On the contrary, it can be said that it is always on the basis of revolt that something like an 'alternative' has been able to emerge, not vice versa. But revolt – in the sense of insurrection – whose manifestation, fairly exceptional, is itself often a response to the 'state of exception',[52] is only one means among others of distancing oneself from reality or, if you like, *relativizing* it. This process of distance-taking is facilitated, as we shall now argue, by sociological enterprises directed toward a metacritique of the social order, in as much as the project of challenging a social order in its totality assumes the adoption of a standpoint situated *apart* from reality. By this token, it will readily be granted that it pertains to a thought experiment or even that it assumes a fictional character. But it is by basing itself on this external lever that reality can be partially stripped of the necessity it lays claim to and treated as if it were relatively *arbitrary*.

This is also why a theory of domination cannot dispense with reference to *collectives* and forms of collective action. In fact, underlying the denunciation of domination – in its most minimal formulation – there is always the question of *number*. To speak of one person's domination over another, each of them being considered (something that is obviously never the case in reality) by identifying her in purely individual fashion, would strictly speaking make no sense. In the condition of a monad, no one can (as Hobbes had posited) dominate anyone. To pose the question of domination therefore consists in asking how actors *small in number* can establish enduring power over actors *large in number*, *dominate* them by exercising semantic control over the determination of *what is*, and subject them to some form or other of *exploitation*. As in the example of the visual metaphor that serves as a frontispiece to Hobbes's *Leviathan* – where the figure of the sovereign is drawn through the accumulation of bodies over which he exercises his power – the question of number, when it takes a critical turn, consists in asking how a small number of human beings can increase their force by combining in such a way as to generate the illusion that they act *as one*. But when it comes to the greater number who endure the domination of a smaller number, the question becomes that of the conditions conducive to the *fragmentation* of those who are dominated. If, in fact, a small number of actors can rise to a dominant position because each of them has increased the necessarily limited force at his disposal by combining with others, it follows that the state of subjection of the dominated must have its origin in the very fact of their separation, which is such that each of them can mobilize nothing but his own strength as an isolated individual. By the same token, the possibility of struggling against domination by getting the dominated to make the transition from a *fragmentary condition* to a *collective condition* constitutes one of the main objectives of the work of *liberation* proposed by critique. And this even if (as is clear in the case of the Enlightenment) this work goes through an initial phase that consists in detaching actors from their old collective attachments, by determining them as *autonomous* individuals. But this initial move towards autonomy is only compatible with a theory of domination if, without halting at the moment of individualization, it poses the question of how autonomy can be preserved and even reinforced by coming to terms with the formation of collectives of a new kind.

Making Critical Sociology and Sociology of Critique Compatible?

To conclude this talk, let us go back to the distinction between critical sociology and pragmatic sociology of critique that has served us as a guiding principle, taking as our subject in particular the possibilities offered by these two programmes for joining up with actors' critical activities and supporting them – that is to say, for constructing a compromise between sociology and social critique. Let us say at once that we find ourselves confronting a sort of paradox.

The main criticism we have made of critical sociology is, briefly put, its overarching character and the distance at which it holds itself from the critical capacities developed by actors in the situations of everyday life. The pragmatic sociology of critique, by contrast, fully acknowledges actors' critical capacities and the creativity with which they engage in interpretation and action *en situation*. But it nevertheless seems difficult, pursuing this programme, to realize all the ambitions connected with a metacritical orientation. We therefore find ourselves confronted, on the side of critical sociology, with a construct that paves the way for candidly critical possibilities, but furnishes itself with *agents* subjected to structures that escape them and skips over the critical capacities of actors; and, on the side of the pragmatist sociology of critique, with a sociology that is genuinely attentive to the critical actions developed by *actors*, but whose own critical potentialities seem rather limited.

This paradox, identified from an investigation of the contribution of sociology to social critique, has as its corollary a tricky problem encountered by sociology, which, more generally, concerns the instruments of description and totalization at its disposal. Description of the social can in fact be undertaken from two different positions. The first consists in starting from an *already made social world*. In this case, sociologists assign themselves the objective of creating a picture of the social environment a new human being finds herself immersed in, despite herself, when she comes into the world. For this newcomer, society is *already there* and she finds herself cast into a particular place in it. In this optic, the description can be carried out in overarching fashion, more or less bracketing human persons envisaged in so far as they act (as *actors*). The description will tend towards cartography, metrology and social morphology (it will employ statistics), and finally towards history (since the world that is already there is a product of the past). It will therefore employ instruments of totalization that have been fashioned to manage society and ensure its governance (most often in the framework of states). But these managerial instruments, on which social reflexivity is based when it is governed from above, are (as we have seen) employed by sociology as tools, whereas, taken from a different angle, they constitute its *objects*, since they are themselves socially constructed for the exercise of a form of power.

The second position consists in starting from the *social world in the process of being made*. In this case, the sociologist will base herself on observation of people in action and stress will be laid on the way they make or (to adopt an Anglo-American term) 'perform' it. Here description will be carried out 'from below' and will take situations as its object, since it is in this framework that action makes itself visible. It will prioritize actors' interactive and interpretative competence. But it will have problems in totalizing the effects of these actions.

The problem is that these two approaches, both of them equally legitimate, will yield results that are different and even difficult to reconcile. In the first case, stress will be placed on the constraints and forces that influence *agents*. In the second, it will instead be put on the creativity and interpretative capacities of *actors* who not only adapt to their environment, but also constantly alter it.

Given their lack of attention to actors' critical capacities, why do overarching critical sociologies seem, despite everything, to generate a critical power superior to that of pragmatic sociologies of critique which, by contrast, fully acknowledge them? There are perhaps two main reasons. The first is that, adopting the standpoint of the totality, overarching sociologies provide disadvantaged actors with collective tools and, in particular, modes of classification, which help them to contradict the individualizing meritocratic representations that contribute to their fragmentation and hence domination. The instruments of classification that overarching sociologies help diffuse (whether they concern social classes, genders, ethnic groups or generations) thus provide the disadvantaged with tools to increase their critical capacities – that is to say, to struggle against the forces which contribute to their fragmentation and to identify by what (or whom) they are dominated.

A second, less obvious reason is that, in clearly adopting the standpoint of the totality – something which (as we have seen) already

44

assumes the prior adoption of a position of exteriority (simple exteriority) – overarching sociologies open up the possibility of a *relativization* of reality (since to describe the social order in its totality presupposes doing it as if there existed a position from which this particular social order can be compared with other possible orders). Relativization is critique's first move. By contrast, pragmatic sociology, precisely because it is rooted in proximity and set on starting out from reality as it presents itself both to the actors and the observer, tends to produce an effect of closure of reality on itself.

Nevertheless, comparison between these two sociological programmes is far from assigning all critical advantage to overarching sociologies. Several problems arise.

The first problem encountered by overarching sociologies precisely concerns the location of the overarching position from which totalization can be both sociologically relevant and effective at the level of social critique. Briefly put, we cannot ignore the fact that this position has been associated in the past with the different nation-states, especially in the case of the critical sociologies that developed after the Second World War and found themselves dealing with the development of the welfare state. In the Western capitalist democracies, this period was marked in particular by a reinforcement in the *nationalization* of social classes – that is to say, not only of the middle classes, who had benefited since the nineteenth century from their participation in the efforts undertaken by the state to increase what Michael Mann calls its 'infrastructural power' over society,[53] but also of the popular classes, who long remained more or less excluded from this enterprise, and even of the dominant classes, whose supra- or transnational character in the nineteenth century and first third of the twentieth century Mann has clearly demonstrated. To a large extent, it was the organizations of the nation-state and especially those of the welfare state that supplied the documentary frameworks on which critical sociologies were based. Obviously, this applies to the socio-professional categories of France's National Institute of Statistics and Economic Studies – a tool which, associated with the functioning of national accounting and the Plan, was used by sociology for describing social classes, but also, for example, for the sociology of work, whose chosen terrain (as is well known) was nationalized firms. Today, critique must confront a different situation, marked by an explosion of power centres in part situated below or beyond the level of the nation-state. It must also take account of the current dynamic of *denationalization* of social classes, with the increase in the number of migrant workers – with or without legal documents – compelled by political or economic necessities to flee their countries in the South; and also with the emancipation of part of the dominant classes from the national space, enabled by the changes in capitalism and financial globalization to revive a supra-national mode of existence that had been impeded by the world wars of the twentieth century and the retreat of economies into national territories. The issue of the identity of the instances sociology must base itself on to effect totalizations, and in what forms, is therefore sharply posed, not to mention the difficulty encountered by sociologists today in gaining access to documentary sources held by organizations that are much less favourable to the social sciences (with the exception of economics) than were the organizations of the welfare state. It follows that critical reference to justice is scarcely sufficient to define not only the wholes within which asymmetries are to be unmasked,[54] but also the beings whom it is pertinent to take into account, be they human or non-human.[55]

The way in which the balance is struck in critical sociology's pictures of reality between description of the forces of domination and description of the actions performed by actors to escape it is an even trickier problem. By underestimating actors' critical capacities and offering them an image of themselves that stresses their dependency, passivity and illusions, overarching sociologies of domination tend to have an effect of demoralization and, in some sense, dispossession of self, which – especially in historical contexts where reality seems particularly robust – can transform relativism into nihilism and realism into fatalism. Because they over-emphasize the implacable character of domination, the pre-eminence in all circumstances, including the most minor situations of interaction, of vertical relations at the expense of horizontal relations (also, moreover, within critical collectives), overarching theories are not only discouraging at the level of political action, but also unsatisfying from the angle of sociological description. They make it hard to differentiate different degrees of subjection and to understand how actors can open up roads to liberation, if only by establishing necessarily local *temporary zones of autonomy* and, further, by coordinating their actions in such a way as to challenge the necessity of a social order. Yet history provides us with numerous examples of conjunctures of this kind. By dint of seeing domination everywhere, the way is paved for those who do not want to see it anywhere.

This problem of the appropriate extension to be given to the meta-critical orientation is rather comparable to that posed to Herbert Marcuse in *Eros and Civilization*, when, having extended the Freudian problematic of repression to all known forms of society,

46

he ends up constructing the concept of *surplus repression* to describe the American society of his time and submit it to a radical critique.[56] Similarly, if we want to impart some meaning to the concept of domination, it must be constructed in such a way that it cannot be completely identified with the totality of social systems and, in particular (as we shall see), of institutional operations for determining what is, which are inherent in the very course of life in society. As in the case of repression and surplus repression, we must therefore be in a position to make a distinction between constraints, identifiable in a very large number of societies (if not all), which do not accord with an ideal of the subject's absolute autonomy or a total liberation of desire, but whose very generality tends to shield them from critique (because it is acknowledged, at least tacitly, that in their absence there would simply be no society at all), and forms of oppression that are superimposed on ordinary constraints, are parasitic on them, or exploit them to shore up the extreme power which certain *dominant* groups impose upon *dominated* groups. This problem can also be compared with that posed to Durkheim (in a spirit which, on this point, is not very far removed from Freud and also, as has often been remarked, Saussure), when, defining society by the constraint exercised by collective norms over individual desires and behaviour – constraints whose transgression is accompanied by collective sanctions – he nevertheless seeks to distinguish a normal functioning of these constraints from one he characterizes as 'pathological'. Or again, closer to us, the way in which Axel Honneth and his team undertake to identify what they call the 'pathologies of capitalism', in particular by employing a reinterpretation of the Lukácsian concept of reification.[57]

Finally, it must be added that, out of a spirit of systematicity, overarching theories of domination tend to reduce all asymmetries to one basic asymmetry (depending on the case, social class, sex, ethnicity, etc.) and, more generally, to ignore both the disseminated nature of power (stressed by Michel Foucault) and the pluralistic character of the modes of assessment and attachments operative in social life (which we sought to model with the concept of polity in *On Justification*). The last point not only affects the validity of the sociological description. It also contradicts the critical expectations of actors who, in democratic-capitalist societies, have learnt not to confuse the work of emancipation with adherence to world-views that present themselves as absolute, and who even seem to have acquired the kind of tolerance for contradiction that is the main bulwark against the various forms of fundamentalism.

The relationship to pluralism and to its opposite – absolutism – is therefore one of the stumbling blocks of overarching theories of domination. In effect, one of the weapons of these critical constructions of domination consists in showing how, in the social orders under challenge, an alignment occurs between different domains – such as religious beliefs, moral and aesthetic orientations, symbolic repertoires, ways of establishing the truth and so on – on a central axis, determined by this token as the dominant ideology and itself adjusted to the specific interests of a group, be it a social class, a national or ethnic group, a gender or whatever. But this denunciation of absolutism should divert critical theories in their turn from the temptation to reduce all dimensions of social life to a factor deemed determinant 'in the last instance', and instead commit them to pluralism. The need to acknowledge pluralism often seems to escape overarching theories of domination, which tend to identify recognition of plurality with liberal individualism.

To be credible today, sociologies directed towards a metacritique of domination should draw the lessons of past failures and, taking heed of the different arguments that have just been developed, equip themselves with an analytical framework that makes it possible to integrate the contributions of what we have called the *overarching programme*, on the one hand, and the *pragmatic programme*, on the other. From the overarching programme this framework would take the possibility, obtained by the stance of *exteriority*, of challenging reality, of providing the dominated with tools for resisting fragmentation – and this by offering them a picture of the social order and also principles of equivalence on which they could seize to make comparisons between them and increase their strength by combining into collectives. But from the pragmatic programme such a framework should pay attention to the activities and critical competences of actors and acknowledgement of the pluralistic expectations which, in contemporary democratic-capitalist societies, seem to occupy a central position in the critical sense of actors, including the most dominated among them.

Thus, for example, the kind of collectives critical actors today seem disposed to combine in are those established *in one particular respect*, which does not prevent each of the participants from connecting, *in other respects*, with different kinds of collective. Here we can follow the analyses (developed, for example, by Zygmunt Bauman or Malcolm Bull)[58] that have recognized the valorization of *ambivalence* as a feature of the critical ensembles established in democratic-capitalist societies. They thereby come into opposition,

48

even conflict, with other tendencies, which can also in their way be called critical, seeking to reduce all dimensions of existence to a preferential relationship (religious, ethnic, sexual, social class) embodied in a group defined substantively and often associated with a territory, real or virtual – tendencies that by this token can be characterized as *fundamentalist*.

But the attempt to render the overarching programme and the programme of pragmatic inspiration[59] compatible cannot be satisfied with a kind of collage. It assumes a continuation of the specifically sociological work that aims to analyse, with the same methods and in the same framework, the social operations which give reality its contours and the social operations that aim to challenge it. We shall sketch it in the following talks by comparing what *institutions* do and what *critique* does when they are at work in society.

── 3 ──

THE POWER OF INSTITUTIONS

One of the lessons to be drawn from an *examination* of the different ways in which the relationship between sociology and social critique is established – the subject of our first talk – was to emphasize an analytical distinction between metacritical theories and critiques that might be called *ordinary*. The former, based on sociological pictures, unmask and challenge the forms of domination in a certain social order from a position of exteriority. The second are carried out from within, by actors involved in disputes, and inserted into sequences of critique and justification, of highly variable levels of generality. But I have also underscored the interdependence between these two types of critique: metacritical theories cannot ignore the dissatisfactions expressed by actors and their ultimate aim is to refocus them in such a way as to give them a robust form; as for the actors, they often look to metacritical theories for resources to fuel their grievances.

The second talk examined two programmes that are faced with the problems posed by the relationship between metacritique and ordinary critiques. The first – critical sociology – is based on compromise formations between overarching sociological descriptions and normative stances and its primary aim is to enlighten actors about the domination they are subject to without realizing it and to provide them with resources to develop their critical potential. By contrast, the second – the pragmatic sociology of critique – starts out from actors' critical capacities and initially aims to use the means supplied by sociology to make them explicit. Next it seeks to establish normative positions – consequently, of a metacritical kind – by basing itself on the modelling of these ordinary critiques and the *moral sense* or *sense of justice* expressed in them. Notwithstanding the significant differences between these two sociological programmes, especially

50

as regards the kind of contribution they can make to social critique, it must be clearly registered that they are both articulated with the *means* by which, in the very course of social life, ordinary actors and, in particular, those subject to exploitation and domination seek to get a grip on what is happening – that is, to overcome their powerlessness.

This talk and the following will be devoted to identifying those *means*, at least in their formal dimensions. I would like, with the tools of sociology, to review the way in which we can interpret the fact that something like *critique* exists in the social world – and this by, as it were, bracketing the very real contributions made by metacritical theories to the deployment of critique in its most everyday, ordinary forms. To pose the question of the very possibility of critique assumes recognizing that social activity is not and doubtless cannot be constantly critical. The *critical form* stands out against a *background* which, far from being critical, can on the contrary be characterized by a sort of tacit adherence to reality as it presents itself in the course of ordinary activities; or by a taken-for-granted world that has been strongly stressed by sociology and, in particular (in the terms employed here), sociology inspired by phenomenology – for example, the work of Alfred Schutz. The argument I am going to develop is that, to account for the pregnancy of this background, we must return to the sociology of *institutions*. The question of critique seems to me inextricably bound up with that of the institutions it leans on. I shall therefore now recall some elements of the sociology of institutions considered from the perspective of a sociology of critique.

In Search of 'Institutions'

If we pursue the preceding discussion dealing with the appropriate extension of metacritical theories of domination, we encounter an especially tricky problem concerning what sociology calls *institutions*. In sociology the notion of institution occupies, as John Searle indicates in his book on the 'social construction of reality', a rather strange position.[1] On the one hand, the concept of institution is one of the discipline's founding concepts: one of those it is virtually impossible to ignore. And in most sociological writings the term institution recurs, often incidentally, as if it were both necessary and obvious. On the other hand, however, the concept is rarely the object of an attempt at definition or even specification. It is used as if it were self-evident, although in very different senses depending on the context.[2] Sometimes the institutional and the social are pretty much identified: the marker by which 'social facts' are recognized is that they are 'instituted' and thereby contrast with 'natural' facts (this is more or less the position of Durkheim and also, in part, Searle).[3] Sometimes it is assimilated to the state, in its legal (constitutional) dimension, and the systems whose 'legitimacy' is ultimately based on the state. In a Hobbesian spirit, the institution is then presented as the instrument that makes it possible to curb the unbridled appetites of human beings and thus check violence (a theme that sometimes resurfaces in Durkheim's analyses). Sometimes institution is used to refer to an empirical object, inscribed in the world of things, like a building with an iron gate and doorman – for example, the headquarters of a bank or a trade union. Sometimes the instituted is associated with what is enduring and necessary, by contrast with that which is labile and contingent (what is institutional is then contrasted with what is situational, conjunctural or contextual). Sometimes constraint is foregrounded and the ideal type of the institution is then recognized in places of imprisonment possessing a total character (the 'total institution' in Goffman),[4] and so on.

In the two sociological programmes we examined in the previous talk, the notion of institution occupies a different position, but one which in both instances has a rather negative connotation, assigning it more or less the role of a repellent. The paradigm of critical sociology acknowledges the existence of something like institutions as a result, in particular, of its Durkheimian filiations and structuralist links. However, in the course of empirical analyses (if not explicitly in theoretical expositions), there is a tendency – shared by many French critical authors of the 1960s and 1970s – to describe institutions predominantly with regard to their effects of domination. In this framework, unlike the Durkheimian position, the notion of institution is therefore negatively connoted and it can be said that critical sociology is largely a *critique of institutions*. The conjunction between, on the one hand, recognizing the ubiquity of institutions and the central role they play in the unfolding of social life in the spirit of Durkheim and, on the other – contrary to Durkheim – regarding them predominantly as instruments of domination, contributes to an indefinite extension of the diagnosis of domination: it is because there are institutions everywhere that there is domination everywhere.

In the pragmatic paradigm, especially in the form given it in France over the last twenty years, the institution and the order of instituted facts are either ignored or, as in the case of critical sociology, connoted rather negatively. In effect, the contemporary currents often referred to by the term *pragmatic sociology* developed in France, at least in part, in reaction against the structuralist-inspired sociology of the 1960s and 1970s – that is, also, by signalling their distance from structuralist interpretations of Durkheim (who had himself expressed his opposition to pragmatism). The tendency to ignore institutions is particularly clear when descriptions identified with the pragmatist programme involve judgements which, most often implicitly, tend to hierarchize the objects described. The primacy given to pragmatism over structuralism then assumes the form of a quasi-ethics (often identifying with the second Wittgenstein).[5] It contrasts *bad* structuralism – macro, holistic, totalizing (even totalitarian), marred by 'legalism', ignoring the humanity of human beings and the modalities of their engagement in action – with *good* pragmatism, respectful of persons and the situations in which they interact, in the 'here and now', where they commit their capacities for invention, experimentation and interpretation to the search for a form of 'living together'. This contrast is deployed, in particular, in connection with the issue of the meaning of statements which, from the standpoint of the second of these two options, is always contextual, local, situated, improvised, and never independent of the act of enunciation – something that leads to challenging the semantic tools with which institutions are equipped (among which legal tools take first place).

In this optic, reference – which is infrequent – to what would be the domain of the institutional therefore invariably serves to draw attention to the constraints imposed on actors from without, impeding their ability to interpret, negotiate, repair situations threatened with discredit, or to use their common sense to find local solutions to new problems. From these theoretical positions marked by a radical pragmatism, sociologies that invoke more or less stable semantics and strive to describe the devices – in particular, the institutional devices – through which entities might preserve their identity by moving between situations (be it actors between conjunctures of events or statements between contexts of enunciation) are subject to different accusations. The most frequent is doubtless that of a simplistic substantialism, whose corollary is the accusation of idealism and 'Platonism'. These sociologies are criticized for ignoring the subtle interplay established by usage between objects and their reference – that is to say, the very logic of language. They allegedly proceed directly from the 'substantive' to 'substance' or deal with statements without concerning themselves with enunciation, thus falling into the error of believing that the permanence of the words used in different contexts has as its corollary an identity in the things referred to. And, following directly on from these critiques, such sociologies are accused of a naive belief in the existence of eternal entities (such as 'the state', 'social classes', the 'family', etc.), which, in the mode of essence, would be in an overarching position vis-à-vis the objects collected by empirical observation of concrete situations.

The Illusion of a 'Common Sense'

In my view, the main defect of the full pragmatic position – at least when, abandoning the terrain of the description of segments of interactions, it is engaged in a quasi-normative perspective – is that it does not follow the highly promising road it has itself mapped out to a conclusion. The main contribution of the pragmatic standpoint to sociology has been to underline the *uncertainty* that threatens social arrangements and hence the fragility of reality. But it stops half-way when it places too much confidence in the ability of actors to reduce this uncertainty. In some currents more or less derived from this paradigm (as sometimes in Goffman or works pertaining to ethnomethodology), this leads to investing actors with a sort of tacit will to cooperate so that something hangs together. It is as if people in society were necessarily inhabited by a desire to protect (local) social arrangements, to preserve links in good condition, to restore adherence to reality, thereby making horror of a social vacuum the main drive of *homo sociologicus*. This overestimation of the capacities possessed by actors to create meaning or repair it, and to create links or restore them, perhaps stems, at least in part, from the excessive significance attributed to a *common sense* supposedly deposited in some way in the interiority of each actor taken individually.

Reference to something like a common sense is present, in various formulations referring to different theoretical justifications, in a large number of constructions in sociology and social anthropology, which count on the existence of a 'set of generally shared self-evident truths' serving as a basis for agreements. One of the ambiguities of the notion of common sense derives from its capacity to lean sometimes towards sense data, sometimes towards the 'dispositions' and 'formal requirements' of the 'rational subject', sometimes towards the categories deposited in ordinary language, or sometimes towards the a prioris bound up with belonging to the same tradition, whether the term is taken in the sense of oeuvres inherited from the past identified with by those who claim to belong to a certain civilization valued as such, or in the less ethnocentric sense of cultural anthropology.[6] In these different cases, agreement is treated as if it emerged by itself through interaction, either because the participants share the same experience of meanings, or because they have the same recourse to reason, or because they are immersed in the same linguistic universe, or finally because their imaginative capacities are structured by the same resources. But whatever the optic, the possibility of a *radical uncertainty*, and the *unease* it creates, is, in my view, reduced too rapidly. More generally, radical uncertainty about *the whatness of what is* [*ce qu'il en est de ce qui est*] occupies a rather ambiguous position in the social sciences. On the one hand, it can be said that it is at the root of the questions to which these disciplines aim to offer an answer. But on the other, it can be stressed that it has been more or less neglected, with primacy being given to explanations based on the phenomenal appearance of an agreement, treated as a kind of necessity. These explanations assume different forms in different currents, which it would take too long to examine in detail here – whether they invoke, for example, socialization by means of experience in the course of education in early childhood (as is the case in culturalist anthropology),[7] shared rationality (as in micro-economic models, whether or not they give themselves a biological basis),[8] processes of self-emergence on the basis of repeated interaction (as in some versions of conventionalism),[9] the convergence of points of view by means of the inter-subjective relationship (as in sociologies inspired by phenomenology),[10] or again those that foreground communication and discussion treated as both empirical realities and ethical requirements.[11]

Without entering into a discussion of the different variants of the idea of common sense – something that would lead us far too far! – I should like to suggest that it has constituted an obstacle to the sociology of critical operations. In effect, it has led to primacy being assigned to descriptions (and explanations) based on the phenomenal appearance of an agreement, while underplaying the uncertainty and 'unease' (the term is Laurent Thévenot's) which, tacitly, continually haunt social life and that become clear in situations of dispute when critique is deployed. It has even been argued (e.g. by Laurent Jaffro) that invocation of a common sense has often had a 'reactive' character, especially as regards morality, to counteract theoretical positions which, taking the form of scepticism or relativism, allegedly pave the way for critique (as was the case, for example, with Shaftesbury's 'moral realism', developed against the radicalizing scepticism of Cartesian propositions or even, 200 years later, the positions adopted by G.E. Moore to block the road to idealism of Hegelian inspiration).[12] The appeal to moral realism, *supervenience* and *common sense* leads to stress being placed on what *everyone would arrive at an agreement* about. Ultimately, culturalist versions of the same paradigm lead to the same result when they aim to show how – albeit, this time, not universally but within a certain group whose members share the same *culture* – everything conspires to fashion situations of agreement, whether implicit or actual. But this move, while it does indeed have the effect of accounting for processes that reduce uncertainty, nevertheless tends to minimize the significance of the disagreement, dispute and, with it, uncertainty which constantly threaten the course of social life.

It was to escape this absolutism of agreement, treated as a 'primitive' phenomenon, that we sought in *On Justification* to construct a pluralist framework making it possible to account for both agreement and dispute, acquiescence and critique, and above all of the often very rapid shifts that can be observed between these two alternatives. In that work the pluralist viewpoint – inherited from Nietzsche and Weber but perhaps even more, in this instance, from Vico – is all the more firmly asserted in as much as the pluralism *internal* to the proposed model of the sense of injustice is extended by an *external* pluralism. Action geared to justice is presented in it as pertaining to one *regime of action* among a multiplicity of other regimes – a position I have sketched, in connection with love, in *L'amour et la justice comme compétences*,[13] and which has subsequently been developed at greater length by Laurent Thévenot.[14] And yet, with nearly twenty years hindsight, it must be admitted that these pluralist positions were not expressed with sufficient force (and were perhaps insufficiently clarified at a conceptual level) to prevent the framework presented in *On Justification* giving rise to re-appropriations which tend to employ it as if it made it possible to effect a closure on reality and hence render it in some sense calculable.

In the rest of this talk, I shall bracket the self-evidence of a common sense in order to pose the question of the consistency of the social world from an *original position* where a *radical uncertainty* prevails (this is a thought experiment akin to the state of nature in the contractualist hypothesis, which in *Leviathan* contains a comparison between 'what was lost with the Tower of Babel' and the threat of generalized hostility).[15] This uncertainty is both semantic and deontic in kind. It concerns *the whatness of what is* and, inextricably, what matters, what has value, what it is right to respect and look at twice. It is obvious when actors, drawn into a *dispute*, disconnect themselves from the practical commitments that preserved a more or less shared course of action, coordinated around reference points, whose provenance must be examined. My intention is therefore to take seriously the constant *unease* about what is and what is valid, which, latent in situations where order seemingly obtains, is forcefully expressed in moments of dispute – and this without resorting either to the hypothesis of a 'collective intentionality' treated as a 'primitive phenomenon' (to which John Searle, for example, gives a biological foundation) or to the untenable exigencies of methodological individualism. I thereby hope to grasp the relationship – which has nothing dialectical about it, in the sense of concluding in a synthesis – between order and critique. I shall maintain that critique only becomes meaningful with respect to the order that it puts in crisis, but also, reciprocally, that the systems which ensure something like the preservation of an order only become fully meaningful when one realizes that they are based on the constant threat, albeit unequally depending on epochs and societies, represented by the possibility of critique.

The Question of Uncertainty: Reality and World

The issue of the relationship between what hangs together and what is stamped with uncertainty, thereby paving the way for critique, cannot be fully developed if it is situated on a single level, which would be that of *reality*. In effect, in a space of two-dimensional coordinates, reality tends to coincide with what appears to hang together, in a sense by its own strength – that is, with order – and nothing makes it possible to understand challenges to this order, at least in their most radical forms. This intuition has supplied backing for sociologies – destined to enjoy great success – that have stressed the *social construction of reality*.[16] But to speak of reality in these terms comes down to relativizing its significance and thereby suggesting that it stands out against a background into which it cannot be absorbed.[17] This background, which we shall call *the world*, is regarded as being (to adopt Wittgenstein's formula) 'everything that is the case'. To make this distinction between *reality* and *world* palpable,[18] we might draw an analogy with the way in which Frank Knight distinguishes risk from uncertainty.[19] In as much as it is probabilizable, risk constitutes one of the instruments for constructing reality invented in the eighteenth century, and is connected (as Michael Foucault has shown)[20] with the liberal mode of governance established at the time. But in the logic of risk not every event is controllable, so that there remains an unknown portion of uncertainty which Knight calls 'radical'. Similarly, while we can construct the project of knowing and representing reality, the design of describing the world, in what would be its entirety, is not within anyone's grasp. However, something of the world precisely manifests itself every time that events or experiences whose possibility – or, in the language of modern governance, 'probability' – had not been integrated into the pattern of reality, make themselves present in speech and/or accede to the register of action, whether individual or collective.

Let us add that reality is invariably orientated towards permanence (or, if you prefer, the preservation of order), in the sense that the elements it takes charge of are sustained by *tests* (which can precisely be said to be 'of reality'), and by more or less established *qualifications* which, through circular effects, tend to produce and reproduce it. But this permanence is difficult to guarantee. The power exercised by the world over reality stems precisely from the fact that the world is subject to incessant changes, which are far from being exclusively 'social' in kind, so that it never offers itself up to the imagination as well as it does in the logic of *metamorphosis* – something Ovid's poetry, for example, helps us to grasp by populating it with gods. However, the world has nothing transcendent about it. Contrary to reality, which is often the object of pictures (particularly statistical ones) claiming an overarching authority, it is immanence itself – what everyone finds herself caught in, immersed in the *flux of life*, but without necessarily causing the experiences rooted in it to attain the register of speech, still less that of deliberated action.

The distinction I have just made between reality and the world, far from having a metaphysical character, can be put directly in touch with empirical research. It underlies, for example, the research I have carried out on conception and abortion (*La Condition foetale*), a summary of which I shall spare you. On the one hand, analysis makes it possible to identify immanent *contradictions* (possessing, in this case, an anthropological character) between different components of the act of conceiving human beings – that is to say, bringing newcomers into the world. These contradictions only emerge, obviously, on condition that these components are compared by a reflexive anticipation (which essentially comes down to mothers), capable of placing them in tension in the field of reality. But it can hardly be otherwise in so far as these beings, if they come into the world, also have the vocation of finding themselves cast into a sociality. These contradictions therefore always threaten conception with failure – at least on a symbolic level. On the other hand, documentary research and field work make it possible to identify *arrangements* that frame conception in certain historical conditions. These arrangements are structured by explicit rules and implicit (or even denied) norms, which can be described in the form of *grammars* (a notion the pragmatic sociology of critique makes great use of). They do not enable supersession of the contradictions they take in hand – something that is impossible – but help circumvent them and tone them down in such a way as to make them tolerable. These grammars thereby play a role somewhat akin to that assigned myth by Claude Lévi-Strauss.[21] Nevertheless, these arrangements, which constitute and organize *reality*, are fragile because critique can always draw events from the *world* that contradict its logic and furnish ingredients for unmasking its 'arbitrary' or 'hypocritical' character, or for 'deconstructing' them – something that paves the way for making arrangements of a new kind. Formally similar processes can take different directions, particularly when the contradictions targeted possess a more historical character. Suffice it for now to underline that critique, although not lacking in objects that can be denounced and challenged in the framework of reality, nevertheless attains its most radical expressions in accommodating events or experiences extracted from the world.

A second argument leads to particular relief being given to critique and the disputes in which it manifests itself. It concerns the difficulty of conceiving and achieving an *agreement* between human beings, all of whom are immersed, albeit differently in each case, in the flow of life. I shall associate this difficulty with the simple fact that human beings *possess a body*. Having a body, each individual is, of necessity, situated – first of all, as the phenomenology of perception teaches, in as much as she is located in a moment of time and a position in a point of space where events appear to her – but also, as we learn from sociology and economics, in that she occupies a social position and has interests; finally, if we follow psychoanalysis, in that she has desires, drives, dislikes, an experience of her own body, and so forth. It follows that each individual can only have one *point of view* on the world. A priori, there is nothing that permits us to conceive these points of view as shared or capable of converging unproblematically. No individual (I shall return to this in more detail shortly) is in a position to say to others – to all the others – *the whatness of what is* and, even when she seems to have this power, does not have the requisite authority to do so. Thus, in the position we have posited as original, no participant possesses the resources that make it possible to reduce uncertainty and dispel the unease it creates. Extending this argument, it can be suggested that different people featuring in what might be regarded as the same *context* – if we define it exclusively by spatial and temporal coordinates – are not thereby immersed in the same *situation*, because they interpret what happens differently and make different uses of the available resources.

For these various reasons, perspectives of a pragmatic variety, while they clearly bring out the characteristics of a certain register of action (what I shall call *practice*), do not seem to me to take sufficient account of the constant threat that critique, in seizing hold of mundane uncertainty, brings to bear on systems for maintaining order. That is why, on its own, this kind of approach seems to me insufficient to identify the procedures whereby something like a reality ends up persisting, despite the extraordinary difficulty presented by the task of more or less agreeing about what is and making beings who are subject to change endure in time. In particular, this applies to entities lacking stable corporeal existence, about which it is therefore impossible to establish an agreement of meaning by referring to them both by a term and a wave of the hand. By this token, we can quite correctly characterize these entities – as does, for example, Frédéric Nef – as *non-existent beings*.[22] And yet it is hard for sociology to ignore them in so far as its principal objects pertain to this class of entities, be they societies, collectives, groups, social classes, sexes, age groups, or nations, countries, churches, peoples, ethnicities, political parties and so on. Their existence is problematic not only – as heavily underscored by methodological individualism – because they refer to sets, only the elements of which really exist: that is, flesh-and-blood human beings. It is also, or especially, problematic because the latter are themselves highly unstable: a disparate set composed of mortal beings who are destined to die and newcomers who have arrived from who knows where, not to mention the dead who, in a number of societies and possibly all, play a highly active role in the course of social life (an idea dear to Auguste Comte, as Bruno Karsenti has stressed in his book on him).[23] And yet, in giving credence to these entities, sociology is simply following what is done by actors themselves, who are incapable, without reference to these non-existent beings, of providing themselves with a representation of the reality in which they are immersed and above all of seeking to bond with one another lastingly (an enterprise which is so difficult that it is nearly always doomed to fail).

On the basis of the preceding remarks, we can outline two strategies for grasping the role played by uncertainty in the course of social life. The first consists in taking as its object *critique* and the disputes in which actors oppose their divergent points of view, when they do not resort to violence, if only of a verbal kind. Such situations are moments when uncertainty makes itself visible in its most direct forms, since each of the protagonists presents not only a different interpretation of what has 'really' occurred, but also different facts in support of her truth claim. But adopting a second strategy – this time indirect – we can also seek to reach uncertainty, *a contrario* as it were, by taking as our object the considerable means that it seems necessary to employ to reduce it, or at least to diminish the unease it creates, and to get something to hold together even minimally – that is to say, for there to be *some reality*. This second road passes via analysis of the institutional function. However, in both cases, the position adopted is the same. It involves abandoning the idea of an implicit agreement, which would somehow be immanent in the functioning of social life, to put *dispute* and, with it, the divergence of points of view, interpretations and usages at the heart of social bonds, so as to return from this position to the issue of agreement, to examine its problematic, fragile and possibly exceptional character.

The Structure of the Framework Presented Here

The attempt to refocus critique and agreement around the issue of uncertainty is based on two major contrasts. The first distinguishes between *practical* moments – in which *pragmatic* approaches, stressing *usages* in a certain *context*, are particularly interested – and moments of *reflexivity*, demanding from actors the employment of procedures that might be characterized as *metapragmatic*. Let us state at once that in practical moments people actively combine to remove a menacing uncertainty by ignoring differences of interpretation of what is happening and, above all, by closing their eyes to the differences of conduct that might introduce factors of uncertainty.

The second contrast exclusively concerns the register of action I have just called metapragmatic. Within this second register, it distinguishes between two different modalities of metapragmatic intervention which issue in different forms.

The first is forms that make it possible, by making a selection in the continuous flow of what occurs, to establish *what is* and to preserve it as *being* despite the passage of time. In their case, I shall speak of systems of *confirmation*, for (as I shall try to show) what is at stake in them is excluding uncertainty by confirming that what is *Is* in the sense of *really Is* – as it were, 'in the absolute'. I think that these systems also sustain, albeit according to different modalities, what might be said to be *official* assumptions and those which are

61

contained in the expressions of what is called *common sense*, conceived as a minimal agreement about what is, capable of being in its turn engaged in the practical modalities of action.

The second are forms associated with systems that depend on factors of uncertainty to create unease, by challenging the reality of what presents itself as being, either in official expressions or in manifestations of common sense. In their case, we shall speak of *critical* forms.

These two kinds of form and the systems with which they are associated are generally treated as involving antagonistic positions. From each of these positions, incompatible points of view are adopted on the world and sociological constructs that are difficult to reconcile develop (to be brief, let us say of pragmatic inspiration in the first case and institutionalist in the other).[24] However, I shall seek to make them symmetrical, study their relations and integrate them into a single framework. In this framework, confirmation and critique become meaningful only when conceived in their *dialogical* relationship. Thus, the main orientation of confirmation is to prevent critique. As for critique, it would lose any point of application and lapse (as will become clearer later) into a sort of nihilism if it did not base itself on experience of what happens in the world to challenge the confirmed assertions on which reality rests.

Practical Moments

To characterize briefly the modalities of practical action and the moments when these forms of action are preponderant, I shall rely on one of Pierre Bourdieu's first books, *Outline of a Theory of Practice*,[25] but also on certain approaches and results of pragmatic sociology.

Actions in common pertaining to this first register unite people in the performance of a task. One of their important characteristics is that the people involved in the course of action act as if they more or less knew what was going on – what they are in the process of doing – and/or as if the others, or some others, in whom one can have confidence, knew it (and this even if the definition of the task performed in common is rather vague). And also as if all could more or less, with more or less success, converge, cooperate and be coordinated in performing the task in hand. This is what can be interpreted (obviously from without, since from within the question does not even arise) as a tacit agreement not to create unease about what is occurring and not to bother about the issue of agreement – a tacit agreement that has often been interpreted in the sociological literature, and especially in currents inspired by phenomenology, as a convergence accepting what is happening as if it were *taken for granted*. In this first register, action in common is therefore primarily directed towards something 'to be done', a task to be performed, with the concern of 'getting by'. This does not necessarily signify fulfilling an unequivocally predefined 'objective', still less following a plan,[26] but only aiming at the end of a sequence of actions, most often simply so that it is possible to move on to something else. Action is therefore directed *towards the future*, often with a greater or lesser sense of urgency.

Although there are no predefined plans or procedures, action is not thereby unconstrained. It can be orientated by reference to *salient* points or reference points,[27] external and internal, variably marked depending on the situation. These *reference points* provide footholds for more or less *coordinating* actions and directing them towards something to be done together, whose interpretation can vary somewhat among the different people involved without this harming their relations, at least as long as no one remarks it. External reference points are systems and objects, material or symbolic. Internal reference points are habits or dispositions – that is to say, systems inscribed in the body (in Bourdieu *habitus*). But they can also be more or less stable states of mind, capable of giving rise to qualification and even, in public relations, of being extended into justifications. Finally, they can involve non-temporal configurations pertaining to psychic life (of the order referred to by the term 'unconscious'). In positioning themselves with respect to these reference points, actors learn as they proceed to make or remake the requisite gestures. Habits are formed. It follows that one can describe the moves of actors in a practical register without the concept of *rule* – in the sense of explicit instructions both technical and deontic in character – and this even if observation, from an external standpoint, makes it possible to identify *regularities*.[28] This is to say that action in a practical register is always *situated*, as is underlined by *pragmatic* sociology, which is a tool particularly well adapted to exploring this kind of situation.

In these practical moments there generally prevails a certain *tolerance* – more or less great depending on the case – of behavioural differences within a fairly flexible general framework, as if the need to do together something that none of the participants could do on their own played a pacifying role. To speak of tolerance means, roughly, that for as long as possible people turn a blind eye to the diversity of usages, to the differences between different ways of doing. These differences can be seen and known without being registered ('seen but not noticed', as Goffman puts it). People act as if they were not relevant. The tolerance that prevails in this kind of situation must be related to the issue of *sanctions*. To speak of tolerance means that the actors avoid putting themselves in a situation where they have to enforce – or demand that a third party enforce – a sanction, at least explicitly, since tacit and vague sanctions can exist, like 'giving a dirty look' or 'sulking' or performing a task 'with bad grace'.

The difference between explicit sanction and tacit sanction is easy to establish. In the case of an explicit sanction, the one who promulgates it must take public responsibility for a judgement and a request for a sanction. She thus puts herself in a position of being judged by others, who might consider, for example, that the sanction demanded is unjustified or excessive. In the case of a tacit sanction, on the contrary, it falls to the person subject to it to complain if necessary. She must then give explicit form to what was implicit, at the risk of seeing the one whom she accuses, and the observers present, deny the real character of the sanction evoked and consider her to be the victim of a kind of 'persecution complex'. Tolerance and the unavailability of sanctions can stem simply from the fact that none of those present wants to run the risk of punishing, often simply because no one has sufficient authority to do it. More generally, however, tolerance and the exclusion of sanctions are tacitly motivated by a shared concern to prevent or defer the dispute that would be bound to develop if differences in behaviour were registered. (That is why practical tolerance, when envisaged from an ethical point of view that is completely alien to it, can be lauded as wisdom – it enables activity to follow its course with a minimum of hitches – or, on the contrary, denounced as 'hypocrisy'.)

Tolerance, which is therefore one of the distinguishing features of this register, is bound up with a low level of reflexivity. Repairs (as Goffman puts it) and adjustments intervene constantly, but possess a local character.[29] The absence of an overarching position, the low use of devices of memorization external to the body proper, of category tools making it possible to construct equivalences and give explicit form to tacit comparisons and, more generally, of calculating instruments, make the transformation of dissatisfaction and unrest into explicit demands difficult. Above all, however, as Jack Goody has stressed in his research on the anthropology of writing,[30] without the support of graphic tools of totalization and, in particular, lists, diagrams and tables, it is difficult to transform the differences, divergences and discrepancies that intervene at different points in the course of action, which are spread out in time, into patent tensions or well-known contradictions (except by employing 'arts of memory' specifically designed for the purpose). Moreover, the maintenance of this limited reflexivity (to speak like economists) can be given a functional interpretation, stressing the fact that, at least up to a certain degree of dispersion of practices, a sub-optimal level of coordination facilitates the pursuit of an action in common that would be threatened by the transformation of differences in ways of doing into divergences over the way in which they *must* be performed, created by explicit attempts to increase the level of coordination between participants.

One of the advantages of a practical regime is thus that it enables actors not to linger unduly over not only *their contradictions*, but also the contradictions between reality and the world. It is thereby possible to preserve the appearance of an agreement that would risk unravelling if these contradictions were objectified and became explicit. This low level of reflexivity, which is a condition of tolerance and the unavailability of sanctions, makes it possible to maintain a minimal level of coordination without risking a dispute or demanding authoritarian interventions based on a form of power – which would be the case if the most minor differences of usage or interpretation were immediately registered from an overarching system. A self-limitation of disputes follows, at least when antagonisms remain below a certain *threshold of tolerance* (whose identification in each concrete situation should be an essential task for ground-level sociology).

Some of the most interesting properties of the practical register for our framework involve language. Immersed in a practical register, people obviously use language. But on the one hand the use they make of language has a highly indexical character and the production or reception of statements is based on context and can be accompanied by demonstrative gestures (as, for example, when one says with a wave of the hand: 'give me that thing there'; 'you mean the pen?'; 'yeah, sure, the thing for writing – hurry. . .'). The categories incorporated in language, which in this instance can correctly be characterized as *ordinary*, present themselves for description in the form not of homogenous spaces defined by boundaries, but of focal points around which is established a space with fluid edges, whose activation is constantly modalized by the practical relationship to objects of enunciation.[31]

On the other hand – and this is of particular importance for the rest of the argument – language is employed as if it were joined to what it refers (as if it were the same thing to name or to show by pointing with a finger). It does not serve, or only rarely, to make a report on the action that is temporally separated from its course, as is the case when one describes in detail an as yet unperformed action – for example, *getting something done* by someone else – or, on the contrary, when one explains a past action to someone else (e.g. to *justify* its adequacy). More generally, the relationship between *symbolic forms* and *states of affairs* is not envisaged in its own right, whether to compare them or contrast them. By the same token, one avoids rendering the relationship between qualifications and objects, or between types and tokens, problematic. For these different reasons, the practical register is unfavourable to the development of critique. This is also to say that, in this register, the question of the *truth* of statements is rarely in the foreground. Not that the possibility of lying is excluded. But if the claims revealed by words, or even by ways of doing, do arouse suspicion, it is in a sense *repressed*, as if out of tacit respect for the collective effort to keep disputes at bay.

The mode of existence in a practical register no doubt assumes unequal importance depending on the society (in *Outline of a Theory of Practice*, Bourdieu seems to associate it in particular with traditional peasant societies). But there is doubtless no social formation where the possibility of flipping over into this regime is absent. We can approach it in different ways. In the theoretical architecture that underlies Bourdieu's sociological work, *practice* is constructed in opposition to *scholastics* (this is what grounds his critique of structuralism, assimilated to a legalism, and makes it possible to construct a link between data derived from social anthropology and the notion of *praxis* as developed in Marx). To take a different example, in my work on the contrast between a *regime of justice* and a *regime of unconditional love* [*amour en agapè*] (published in the book entitled *L'amour et la justice comme compétences*),[32] the features associated with a regime of love – in particular, preference for the present and renunciation of the calculating tools which, by contrast, cannot be dispensed with in a regime of justice – suggest that this regime might constitute a sort of boundary point towards which practical logic tends.[33]

The frequency of moments when the practical register is predominant is such that we have all had experience of the possibilities it contains and the advantages it brings. But the argument defended here is nevertheless that it is impossible to conceive of a complete social life with the practical register as the sole framework of action in common. Several problems arise. The first is the *references points* required for preserving a minimal framework of action. Obviously, it might be thought that they are created by an effect of self-emergence or self-organization on the basis of interaction and its repetition; and that they are based on the regularities ensured by habits. But according to us, this explanation is insufficient, in particular because it does not account for the normative dimension of these reference points and the deontic force they contain.

A second problem is *disputes*. Because it is unreflexive and non-cumulative, the practical register allows for the maintenance of tacit disagreements that do not extend to disputes, but only (as has been said) up to a certain *threshold of tolerance*. When this threshold is crossed, action in common, even at an undemanding level of coordination, cannot be maintained exclusively by the means available in this register. In a dispute, divergent and often incompatible *points of view* are opposed. Several claims to truth, bound up with different ways of going to the root of things, find themselves in competition. The very idea of an absolute truth – that is to say, a truth which would have no need for confirmation or justification because it would in some sense be established in and of itself (the kind of truth G.E. Moore sometimes seems to refer to) – is imperilled. In consequence, the differential between reality and the world, which in a practical register is more or less absorbed in the course of action, grows significantly wider, since it is the very texture of reality that is put in question and shattered by the projection of elements extracted from the world into the polemical field.

Alongside the practical register, it is therefore necessary to conceive the possibility of a different register: the one we shall call *metapragmatic*, freely borrowing this term from linguistic anthropology.[34]

The Metapragmatic Register

To distinguish them from moments that form part of a practical register, I propose to call *metapragmatic* moments those that are marked by an *increase in the level of reflexivity* during which the attention of participants shifts from the task to be performed to the question of how it is appropriate to *characterize* what is happening. The attention of the participants is then directed towards the action in common itself, its modalities, its conditions of possibility, the forms it is inscribed in. What people are in the process of doing, as if they were doing it together, no longer seems self-evident. And even if, as we shall see, the appearance of an agreement might not be called into question, expectations and energies are diverted from what is to be done to confront the emergencies of reality, and are directed towards the question – self-referential, if you like – of knowing *exactly* what one is doing and how it would be necessary to act so that what one is doing is done *in very truth*.

Take, for example, a situation we are familiar with: a meeting of teachers to examine student profiles. Everyone participates, but with a covert concern for saving time: not to tire oneself out; not to get into a conflict with colleagues; to finish before 6 o'clock because it is necessary to go and collect the kid from school, and so on. Ten files have already been examined and twenty remain. No coffee break, you go on, it is necessary to finish the work, and so on. But at a certain point a colleague starts to speak, with a serious air, and raises the question of whether we are actually following the same rules and the same procedures for each file. We then stop examining the files and everyone is coordinated in this new regime. We ask: 'but what in fact are the procedures?' Are there even any procedures? And what are we doing? What is the collective we form? Does it merit the name of jury? Or is it a bunch of tired teachers, lax and disposed to look with favour on anything that might distract them from the task they are performing or, rather, 'botching' (as a critic observing them from without would say), by conducting a test that is very important for those who will suffer the consequences with the utmost arbitrariness?

Whereas up to then, when the activity was being pursued in the practical mode, no one seemed to be concerned to follow a rule, in moments of this kind the issue of *rules* comes to the fore. The participants will examine whether a rule exists that might limit their confusion and lift the threat of a disagreement. Some, boasting of their authority in the matter (e.g. the President/Chair), can invoke a rule if an object of this kind has previously been constructed and stored, and if someone knows where to go to find it. The participants can also exploit deposits of semantic forms (in particular, forms which are legal in style) pertaining to common competence and, by analogy, derive formulas from them that make it possible to say what the action in hand consists in and, above all, what it *should* consist in.

The Question of Qualification

What does 'are we a genuine jury' mean? This question, which would have no relevance in a practical register, but which by contrast typically signals engagement in a metapragmatic register, concerns the relationship between a *type situation* (the *genuine* jury) and a *token situation* (what we are in the process of doing).[35] Moreover, it is the relationship between what is happening here and what, in a normative optic, should happen, that makes it possible to clarify the way we shall use the term *situation*. The situation is identified, on the one hand, by reference to a certain context in which the action occurs and, on the other, by the meaning given to this context by relating it to a determinate type of action. One and the same context can therefore be the site of different situations, at successive moments, but even, particularly in the case of disputes, at the same time for different actors. But it can also be said, more formally, that the issue of knowing what we are really doing and hence, inextricably, what we are, concerns the relationship between a *state of affairs* and a *symbolic form* whose features are logically arranged and laden with values. The attention given to the terms whereby reference is made to the objects of which reality is composed (this can extend to an obsession with the 'right word') stems then from the fact that reference to types renders their place in a hierarchy of values salient (is it not to insult a 'research seminar' to refer to it, e.g. by the term 'class' or to devalue a 'château' by applying the term 'villa' to it?).[36]

To designate the process that interests us in its specifically social dimension, I shall use the term *qualification* (which was suggested in *On Justification*), whose origin is legal, but altering the denotation in such a way as also to invest it with the treatment that cognitive anthropology inspired by Humboldt makes of notions like categorization or classification.[37] Taken in this sense,[38] qualification possesses at least three relevant properties. (a) It fixes the relationship between a symbolic form capable of being associated, on the one hand, with a state of affairs and roles in a *type situation* and, on the other hand, with a state of affairs and performances in a *token situation*. Therewith it aims to control *reference* by relating it to what Frédéric Nef calles 'schematic formations', or (as Irène Rosier puts it in her history of mediaeval intentionalist grammars) to take in hand the relationship between 'the properties originally conferred on nouns and those manifested by their utilization, their utterance'.[39] (b) It associates with the situation or object in question not only various predicates, but also relations to other objects, making it possible to invest them with a *value*.[40] (c) Finally, it points towards *consequences* in reality, particularly at the level of usage, in such a way as to posit an alternative between correct usage and incorrect usage, and thereby open up the possibility of a sanction. The process of qualification is therefore indissolubly *descriptive* and *normative*.

It can be viewed from two different angles depending on whether it concerns the operation of establishing or fixing types; or the operation of comparing case by case, on the one hand, already established and more or less stable types and, on the other, tokens. Finally, let us add that the requirement of qualification is far from being imposed with equal force in connection with all beings, objects, facts or situations. It mainly concerns objects that matter – that is to say, especially, but not exclusively, those which in our societies are taken charge of by the law or other forms of regulation not dependent on the state.

To clarify what is to be understood by being, object, fact, situation and so on that *matters*, we can use the term *respect*, metaphorically exploiting one of its possible etymologies, which refers to the idea of *looking twice*. We shall then say that a state of affairs is treated with respect when it is looked at once in its indexical or contextual mode of being and a second time in as much as it is related to a type. That is to say, also when, in a single move and by means of a sort of flash-back, the type is made to return to the token, as if to cover the latter, in such a way that symbolic form and state of affairs, whose relation was put in crisis by critique or risked being, are made to coincide completely once again. Taken in this sense, respect therefore comes down to assigning relevance and hence a value. Whereas a state of affairs that is only considered once, and which is therefore purely contextual, could be treated as contingent (its relevance depends solely on the context or usage in the here and now), a state of affairs considered twice, and related to its type, is endowed with value, with significance. It must, however, be noted that this value can be positive or negative; and as a result that it can be said of objects deemed detestable that they merit respect, in the sense we have just stated, but expressed this time by opprobrium.

Metapragmatic Registers and Natural Metalanguage

It has been said that in a practical register everything happens as if language, employed in predominantly instrumental fashion, was treated as if it coincided with the world. In a metapragmatic register, by contrast, it is the relationship between symbolic forms and states of affairs and, as a result, the space that separates them (or can), their possible gaps, their potential distance, which is placed at the centre of common preoccupations. Uncertainty, which is at the heart of social life, is transferred from an unease about the possibility of a failure

70

of the beings who make up the environment (is the motor going to work? will the horse obey?, etc.) and focused primarily on the question of *qualification*. What are we doing exactly? What situation are we immersed in? What is it (e.g. a 'referendum' or a 'plebiscite'? A 'crime' or an 'act of love' or an 'act of courage'? etc.)? Presented as a borsch, does this soup actually merit the name? And this watch, which has all the external appearances of a Rolex, is it a real Rolex or a fake one? Or again, a 'fake Rolex' or an 'imitation Rolex'? And even, is it really a watch? And so on. As we can see from these examples, the problem does not only concern the designation of the object in its descriptive and functional properties (as if, in a practical register, I had created an ambiguity by calling 'wooden chisel' what other participants usually call an 'adze', to the point where my partner would not have handed me the right tool). First and foremost, it concerns the value to be assigned to the object in question with the deontic consequences this presupposes.[41] Let us also note that, on the level of categorial functioning, the flipping of the practical register into metapragmatic registers is often associated with an alteration in the way in which the categories incorporated in language are employed. It is associated with the transition from a categorial usage which (as we have seen in connection with the use made of language in a practical register) activates vague ensembles polarized around focal points or prototypes (something that facilitates indexical variability), to a categorial usage established by reference to homogenous semantic spaces limited by boundaries, stabilized by definitions and associated with rules.[42]

But the most striking feature of metapragmatic registers is the use we find in them of the possibility possessed by natural languages – the only ones to possess it, in contrast to artificial languages – of speaking about language itself without changing language. This is the case – a classical (macho) example – when people refer, for example, to 'a man in the full sense of the word'.[43] While remaining immersed in natural language, the speaker acts as if he could place himself in a position from which he could put his discourse, and himself as subject of the enunciation, at a distance. In fact, recourse to metalanguage as a 'language instrument that serves to speak of a language object' (as Josette Rey-Debove writes in her book on the subject)[44] is the only thing which makes it possible to turn attention to the relationship between symbolic forms and states of affairs – a relationship that remains opaque or irrelevant in a practical register. This recourse to the possibilities afforded by metalanguage is particularly clear in the case of the one of the metapragmatic registers which interests us – that where certain modalities of critique are manifested. Take, for example, a seminar. The professor is dreaming, the Ph.D. student giving the paper is mumbling, the students are sleeping, chattering or playing electronic games on their mobile phones and so on. A participant who is rather more demanding than the others can then get up and ask inconveniently, 'you call this a seminar?' A statement of this kind consists in criticizing the token situation by reference to a type situation – that is to say, in pointing to the fact that the state of affairs in the here and now does not warrant being designated by the symbolic form (seminar) that indexes the properties of the type situation. Formally, it resorts to the metalinguistic possibilities of natural language as signalled by the formula 'you call this a'[45] (which can, moreover, be implicit).[46]

The Metapragmatic Register of Confirmation

Let us leave the register of critique to one side for a moment in order to broach another metapragmatic register – *confirmation* – which seems to me to possess properties that are symmetrical and converse from that of critique.

We shall start from another statement of a metalinguistic type, which consists in saying something like: 'a seminar is a seminar' – which can be translated as follows: "<what you call> a seminar is <indeed, in fact> a seminar'. If we bracket the specifically metalinguistic part of the statement (which is not explicit in empirical examples), the formula is a tautology. A tautology of this kind can obviously possess two referential orientations. In the first case, the two terms refer to the type (to the seminar type situation). In the second, one of the terms refers to the seminar type situation and the other to the token situation. In the first case, the qualification of what a seminar is, in its type, is marked by reduplication (and we are in the presence of a genuine tautology). In the second, a state of affairs is qualified as a seminar by reference to the established type of the seminar and the two are identified with one another.[47] At stake in such operations is consolidating what is by confirming that what *is* (in a certain context) *Is*, in all possible worlds or, if you prefer, *sub specie aeternitatis*. In fact, one of the formal properties of tautological statements is that they present themselves as 'true for anyone and independently of the circumstances of enunciation'.[48] Now, it seems to me that operations of this kind play an essential role in establishing social reality and that it is perhaps precisely their everyday banality which accounts for the lack of attention paid them, except for occasional scoffing at their platitudinous character.

To grasp the way in which the register of confirmation operates, we can take the example of what Aristotle in the *Rhetoric* calls epideictic discourse[49] (more or less adopted in Bourdieu's sociology under the term 'discourse of celebration'). Epideictic discourse is a discourse of praise or blame which, consequently, inextricably discloses both *the being of what is* and its *value*. In Aristotle's description of it, it has remarkable characteristics – in particular, that of being a discourse performed in public but not possessing, strictly speaking, any informative content, because it deals (so Aristotle says) 'with what does not give rise to controversy; with what is known by everyone'. This type of discourse, which, in disclosing what is and what is valuable, aims to fix it, as it were, for good, achieves its consummation in the funeral oration. In effect, given that the person who is the object of the description is dead, she will not be able to alter the list of predicates with which the celebration credits her by new actions. A discourse of this type may be regarded as a means of assuaging unease about what is, and this in particular to confront the constant threat, although variable depending on the situation, historical context and society, represented by critique when it poses the question: 'you call that a . . .?' (e.g. in the case of epideictic discourse: 'You call that a hero? a saint? a scholar? an artist?', etc.).

As the example of epideictic discourse indicates, operations of a metapragmatic type, be they of the order of confirmation or critique, must have a more or less *public* character. Being public, epideictic discourse helps stabilize interpretation and limit subsequent possible alterations. In effect, it transforms the opinion that everyone can have 'in their possession' into a *common knowledge*, such that everyone henceforth knows that what he knows (or is supposed to know) the others also know and know that he knows it, in accordance with the logic of common knowledge on which game theory establishes the possibility of epistemic equilibria[50] (but treating them as the result of interactive mechanisms, without raising the question of the bodies authorized to give the judgement the character of an attested public fact). This signifies that performances of this kind must not only be realized with others, but also in front of others, placed in the position of witnesses, and whose presence, far from being restricted to being physically actual in a certain place at a certain time, must be associated with some form or other of engagement, if only that of memorizing what has occurred – that is to say, being in a position, if necessary, to recall its factual character to a contradictor.[51]

The Bodiless Being of the Institution

The question of what is, as raised not by philosophers but by the actors who perform the social world, when they are led to pose it to themselves – no doubt often, when the situation is infested by dispute and violence threatens – is not that of knowing what is for Pierre, Paul or Jack, or what is in Lyon or Paris, but what is for everyone, of what is here as well as there. It therefore cannot be the object of an individual response. As indicated by the example of epideictic discourse, she who pronounces it does not present herself as if she was expressing a *point of view* on the object of her discourse. At the risk of seeming to return to supposedly obsolete issues, we can say that she speaks to make manifest what is 'in itself' or 'essentially'. And yet, as suggested above, no individual possesses the requisite authority to say to others, all the others, the whatness of what is, for the simple reason that she has a body and, having a body, is necessarily situated both in an external space and time and an internal space and time. In ordinary situations of interaction, all that anyone can do, as is quite rightly said, is 'give her point of view'. But especially when a dispute becomes explicit and escalates, and it is necessary to put an end to disagreements that threaten to spill over into violence, the expression of a point of view is insufficient.

As Olivier Cayla (referring to Austin) correctly observes,[52] in connection with statements that fall within the provisions of a legal assessment, 'each speaker', however 'sincere' and 'serious', 'is never capable on her own of successfully directing her speech towards agreement with the other', because 'an unbridgeable gap always separates the literal meaning of the statements she utters from the intentional power that her act of enunciation deploys over her interlocutor'. In fact, 'it is never in the text of the statements that the intention actually harboured can be read by the interlocutor'. It follows that the interlocutor cannot do without an *interpretation*, 'in as much as he always has to ask for what obscure, hidden, secret, shameful . . . purpose the speaker said what she said to him'.[53] From this Olivier Cayla deduces – particularly in the case of law, but his thinking can be extended – the necessity of installing what he calls 'the device of a third party' to whom is accorded, 'by agreement', the prerogative of 'having the last word' – that is, a monopoly on correct interpretation. This third party usually presents itself in the form of a character (e.g., in the case Cayla is dealing with, a constitutional judge). But one does not expect this character to express his 'point of view', as an ordinary person engaged in a body might give hers. To hear him it is necessary to ignore his body.

The only conceivable solution is therefore to delegate the task of saying the whatness of what is to a *bodiless being*. Only a bodiless being can stop 'see[ing] objects as it were from the midst of them', and 'view [them] *sub specie aeternitatis* from outside', to borrow a formulation used by Wittgenstein in the 1914–16 *Notebooks*.[54]

This bodiless being, which haunts sociology, is obviously the *institution*. An institution is a bodiless being to which is delegated the task of stating the whatness of what is. It is therefore first of all in its *semantic* functions that the institution must be considered (as does John Searle). To institutions falls the task of saying and confirming what matters. This operation assumes the establishment of types, which must be fixed and memorized in one way or another (memory of elders, written legal codes, narratives, tales, examples, images, rituals, etc.) and often stored in definitions,[55] so as to be available, when the need arises, to qualify, in a situation of uncertainty, states of affairs that are the object of ambiguous or contradictory usages and interpretations. In particular, institutions must sort out what is to be *respected* from what cannot be; what can only be considered once, in association with a context and as if it were accidental, and this by comparison with what it is appropriate to look at twice. This also means sorting out what is, here and now, from what is elsewhere in space, before in the past and later in an indeterminate future. That is why the phenomenology of institutions attributes to them as an essential property their capacity to establish enduring or even, in a sense, eternal entities. Unlike the individual bodies of those who give them a voice, serve them, or simply live and die in spheres of reality that they help to cohere and to last, they seem removed from the corruption of time.

On the other hand, let us add that, being themselves bodiless beings, institutions alone are truly capable of endowing non-existent beings with content. Whereas corporeal persons can make the relevance of material objects manifest simply by entering into inter-action with them, or with one another in connection with them (by touching them, showing them, moving them, exchanging them), non-existent beings can only be inscribed in reality through institutions. Institutions provide these beings, often maligned by linguistic logi-cians, for whom they derive from '"the fatal tendency of language" to form proper names that no objects correspond to and which threaten "to undermine the reliability of thinking"',[56] with the possibility of acceding to a form of existence that is far from illusory (did not mil-lions of men die in the First World War to defend their 'fatherland', a non-existent being if ever there was one?).

The semantic functions of institutions far exceed specifically linguistic forms, since they have responsibility for the supervision of the very wide range of symbolic expressions studied by semiotics (ranging from body language to icons or music, as is clear from the case of rituals where these different mediums are more or less coordinated and, in some cases, strictly defined by explicit rules). Nevertheless, to give a sense of what is involved, we might take the example of the way in which specifically linguistic institutions fashion languages and, for example, in the case of events resulting in the division of a political body into several entities, how they slice up a continuum of patois in such a way as to create different national languages. (A classic example is that of the formation of Norwegian after the separation from Sweden, but the same remarks could be made about linguistic processes subsequent to the break-up of ex-Yugoslavia.)[57] The construction of a language, like that of a nation and even a 'people' (by contrast with a 'gang'),[58] is based on an enormous labour of homogenization of vocabularies and syntaxes and definition of good and bad usage, in such a way as to impose them on a determinate territory. This homogenization, which is often based on a dominant dialect (in the case of France, that of the Parisian region), can be accompanied by real violence towards peripheral speaking subjects, as has been clearly shown by Michel de Certeau, Dominique Julia and Jacques Revel in their work on the linguistic policy of the French Revolution.[59] So-called national languages are distinct in this from 'patois', which tend to become different bit by bit, from community to community, over a certain area. The variations can affect only features that are initially secondary, but their composition tends to render communication increasingly difficult as the spatial distance between 'dialects' increases. From the standpoint of the national language, the latter are then virtually reduced to the state of *jargons* or even *private languages*, rather like those invented by children to understand one another and shield their exchanges from adult ears, or those sometimes fashioned by writers with a view to conveying their uniqueness in a text, at the risk of rendering it inaccessible to most readers, if not all.[60]

To institutions thus fall all the tasks that consist in *fixing reference*, especially when it bears on objects whose value is important and whose predicates must be stabilized by definitions. Without these tasks – studied, in particular, by the economics of conventions[61] – something like capitalism would simply be impossible. In fact, as Hernando de Soto has shown, the transformation of de facto possessions into capital assumes a change in the forms of determining property, such that assets can be maintained without the guarantee of personal testimony and circulate free of the body of the people who both possess them and are possessed by them.[62] This is clear from the case of the law of windfall [*droit d'aubaine*], studied by Simon Cerutti, whereby the public power was able to seize goods on the death of their holder when he was a foreigner, if no one came forward to demand their inheritance. Detached from their holder in his corporeal factuality, these goods could then be regarded as being 'without a master'.[63]

Institutional operations are necessary not only to affix things – material or immaterial, like titles – to persons or organizations, in such a way that they can be transmitted, but also to define their properties – which transforms them into *products* or *goods* and enables the establishment of markets.[64] For supply and demand to be able to coincide, and a market then to be established and operate (more or less), information about goods must be concentrated in prices. But for this process itself to be possible, the goods must previously have been subject to a labour of definition, or rather the relations between goods and the words that designate them, or the names given to them, must have been stabilized by a *determinate description*.[65] This task of *fixing reference* is what is performed by brands,[66] and, more generally, institutions of normalization (e.g. ISO norms) or quality control, which prevent objects losing their identity in the course of the multiple uses made of them.[67] All these institutions guarantee, as is said in the case of wine, '*appellations contrôlées*'. Operations of the same kind are involved, for example, in the appraisal of firms to the extent that it depends on the constraints set by underlying accounting frameworks, themselves highly variable from one epoch to another or between countries.[68]

We might equally take the case, in which I interested myself in *La Condition foetale*,[69] of the determination of the moment of gestation after which abortion is no longer permitted by law. The determination of this moment can be established in two ways. The first consists in fixing on the being in gestation and considering that from a certain stage of development the latter makes the transition from the condition of 'thing' to that of 'person' – which would open up the possibility of regarding it as a subject of right. But this would then require pursuing the work of medical categorization, which distinguishes gametes, pre-embryo, embryo, foetus, viable foetus and so on, in such a way as to endow it with an ontological status that can be transformed into a legal status, by introducing and justifying radical discontinuities in a process of continuous maturation. It is in order to get round this difficulty that, in numerous countries, the legislation prefers to take as its rationale the fact that abortion contains a danger for the mother after a certain stage of development of the pregnancy. In the latter case, the break established by law, while it can be criticized for its arbitrary character (especially given the fact that it is highly variable depending on the legislation considered), nevertheless does not assume an ontological discontinuity – leaving it less exposed to becoming the focal point for disputes over the legitimacy of abortion.

Semantic Security and/or Symbolic Violence

In considering such operations from the point of view of critique, it is quite correct to regard them (as does, e.g. Pierre Bourdieu) as pertaining to 'symbolic violence'. Following Austin, one will then latch on to the performative character of institutional acts which, by means of declarative sentences, *create reality*, but while stressing the link between illocutionary force and the force, of a quite different order, supplied by the availability of policing instruments and, as a result, the *arbitrary* character of constitutive acts.[70] The more or less arbitrary character of institutional acts is undeniable, in as much as they invariably consist in *slicing up* (a term that evokes violence) – that is to say, replacing the *continuous* by the *discontinuous*. This is particularly clear in the case of the formation of borders between nation-states, amply documented by the work of geographers.[71] But thousands of other examples might be given, like the border between the last to pass and the first to fail in a competition for a Grande Ecole, who, although they have obtained virtually identical marks, will experience a very different fate. In cases of this kind the logic of marking and demarcation operated by institutions therefore has a powerful multiplier effect, by transforming small gaps into distances that are all the more significant for being attached to people for good. Far from being limited to confirming a value, in large measure they help create it.[72]

But the problem is that, by looking at them from a different angle, we can also detect a role of *semantic security* in these operations. It is in fact operations of the same kind that enable the re-identification of beings and, in particular, abstract beings – those whom one cannot point to or touch – in different contexts and hence, also, their stability through time and space. They also make it possible to transform concrete beings – which is the case with human beings in as much as they are flesh and blood – into stable abstract beings, like, for example, the subjects of liberalism. *Constant properties* are thereby attached to beings whose life is highly fleeting and changing, as is that of human beings and especially those who – as is clearly brought out by approaches of a pragmatic type – see the contours of their identity alter depending on the situation in which they are immersed.[73] Take the classic example of slavery. In certain contexts the masters of slaves might well appreciate them, be attached to them, listen to them recite their poetry and so on. But come a change in circumstances and they are sold: friend one day, commodity the next.[74] This is rather how we act today towards our pets. The slave is therefore a being without semantic security, even if he can be the object of personal, contextual protection.

To assign institutions a predominantly semantic role, consisting in stabilizing reference by taking the least possible account of the context of usage, enables us not to confuse them with two other types of entity with which they are invariably associated, but from which they are to be distinguished analytically: on the one hand, *administrations*, which perform *policing* functions;[75] and on the other, *organizations*, which perform *coordinating* functions. These two kinds of entity refer, if you like, to the means with which institutions must be equipped in order to act in the world of bodies. Moreover, it is their deeply embodied aspect that makes it easy to suspect them of being nothing but weapons in the service of special interests and hence so fragile when faced with the fire of critique. However, if the articulation between organizations and institutions can be indirect (thus, capitalist firms have no institutional authority of their own, so that capitalism is always associated with the state), it remains the case that institutions cannot be completely uncoupled from administrations because their semantic role has an immediately deontic character. They do not make do with establishing dictionaries. They prescribe *definitions*, ignorance of which entails *sanctions*. In their case, semantic work and police work go together.

Even so, it must be noted that the conceptual distinction we have just made between institutions, organizations and administrations becomes blurred when the term institution is employed – as is the case in its current usages, for example, when a school or hospital is referred to as an 'institution' – in a quasi-reified fashion, where stress is placed on the simultaneously regulatory, accounting and material framework (buildings, credit lines, etc.). In fact, a number of situations inscribed in these frameworks can, when considered in detail, assume highly diverse aspects, more of the order of administrative or organizational work. Everything that occurs in 'institutions', construed in this sense, is therefore far from being of a specifically institutional order, with a large number of situations even unfolding in the register that has been characterized as *practical*. It is only when hiccups prevent routines from being followed that the institutional dimension of the institution takes priority. This is also to say that 'institutions' themselves must continually be subject to a process of re-institutionalization, if they do not want to lose their shape and, as it were, unravel. In the course of these reparative processes, actors, or some of them – usually those who regard themselves as invested with a form of authority – strive to restore the (fictional) presence of the bodiless being by recalling the requirement to act *in the correct forms*, in such a way as to check its dilution into the composite forms of organization of corporeal persons who are (wrongly) said to be its 'members' or to compose it.[76]

At the intersection of semantic controls and physical constraints we find *tests* and *rules*. We shall return to the question of tests in the next talk. Suffice it for now to note that the *formats* of reality tests are subject to institutional guarantees and often regulatory texts defining the procedures that must be followed if the test is to be deemed valid. This especially applies in the case of selection tests that play an important role in people's access to desirable positions (educational examinations, sporting tests,[77] electoral consultations, in some cases employment exams, etc.). These definitions claim to stabilize and clarify the components of the test, so as not to leave the specific qualities being submitted to the test unclear (an operation which, as we have seen, is necessarily incomplete, paving the way for critique). To be judged valid, the reality test must be presented as a *test of something*, in order to be distinguished from another kind of test – which we shall not deal with in these talks – which is the test of strength involving violence and where people will do whatever it takes to win.

It is doubtful whether institutions, in the sense in which the term is used here, can derive exclusively from a process of self-emergence set off by interactions and their repetition in the course of action. Such processes, while wholly credible when it comes to accounting for the formation of habits and, with them, so-called 'objective' regularities, or even the establishment of tacit conventions enabling actions to converge on focal points treated as *arbitrary* (everyone conforms to the behaviour she believes the other will adopt, the classic example being, as we have seen, driving on the right or left), do not seem capable of rendering the way in which institutions support the qualification of beings intelligible. On the one hand, because these mechanical processes can largely skip over the determination of the properties of objects, but above all because they do not make it possible to generate a value and sustain the specifically *normative* character of the norm – if we might put it like this – with its deontic consequences. We can readily concede that observance of habits and positioning based on regularities – or rather, invariably, on signs in which they are deposited (e.g. train timetables) – might be sufficient to guide action on all those occasions that can correctly be described as *routine*. In fact, one of the characteristics of this kind of situation is precisely that the issue of whether the reference points are arbitrary is excluded. Typically, one does not ask if the fact that the train arrives in the station at 7.45 rather than 7.34 is really well-founded. But the same is not true in situations of *dispute* (as would be the case, for example, if the arrival of the train at a particular time advantaged some actors and penalized others). The prescribed rule must then be *justified*, so as to prevent the possibility of it being challenged by critique charging it with arbitrariness. But justification rarely has an occasional character, which would not be the case if it was immediately accepted by everyone as self-evident. Each of the good reasons suggested is invariably inscribed in the course of a process, characterized by a sequence of justifications, critiques and justifications in response, which tends to shift the justification, to disseminate it in accordance with a process we have called a *rise towards generality*. It is precisely because dispute and critique occupy a central position in the course of social life that normativity can never be completely absorbed into regularity.

Institutionalization and Ritualization

The compulsive character of institutional interventions and the iterative character of rituals have often led the intuition of an affinity between these two forms being ascribed to repetition. And yet, as we have just suggested, repetitions exist, of the order of regularity, which have little in common with ritualization[78] (I shave every morning because my beard grows back every night – a routine, rather tedious activity – but it would not occur to anyone to think that in doing so I have performed a ritual.) It is therefore necessary to look elsewhere for the principle of the relationship between institutionalization and ritualization. According to me, it has to do with the constraints that weigh on metapragmatic operations of confirmation. A pertinent feature of ritualization consists in prioritizing requirements about the way of making (or saying) over consideration of the functional consequences of what is done (or said), at least if they are considered in respect of an action that aims to make an alteration in the state of affairs – an alteration that can be achieved in different ways. If, for example, during a fly-fishing trip I am more concerned with the perfection of my casting off than with whether I will catch a trout (one can catch a fish when casting off badly and not catch one when casting off well), we can then say that I have a tendency to *ritualize* my gesture. Here ritualization reveals its objective intention, which is to abolish the distance that on the ordinary occasions of existence always separates the *type situation* from the *token situation* and, as a result, to act as if they could coincide in a synthetic act through which symbolic forms and states of affairs would be indissolubly superimposed. This on condition, however, of closing one's eyes to the effects of selecting certain features, deemed pertinent, at the expense of others, rejected as incidental, necessarily operated by *stylization*. Reality is thereby confirmed as being not only what it is, but – indissolubly – what it must be to be what it is and, as a result, as not being able to be other than it is.

Such operations, often associated by anthropology with dramatization,[79] especially when (as is invariably the case) they are carried out in public (but even if the person who performs them is alone, she will tend to split into two as if *to see herself acting*), and when they succeed (which, as we shall see, is not always the case), ensure the coordination of actors and spectators in the same course of action. And this, precisely, in such a way that the differential between activity and passivity (and between leaders and led), which is never altogether abolished, is reduced to the point where they are rendered as indistinct as possible.[80] Some human beings, hitherto dispersed in a multiplicity of states, internal and external, then find themselves plunged together into the certainty that what is really is, in incontestable and often (as is clear in the case of rites of passage) definitive fashion. No one is any longer entitled to doubt that the new-born is highborn, that the son or daughter has indeed left childhood to enter into adulthood, that the single person is now married, that he (hitherto one man among others)[81] who has been made chief, is indeed chief, that the dead man is indeed dead and so on. And yet it happens that doubt is introduced and critique erupts.

In the next talk, I shall seek to clarify the way in which critique emerges from the very contradictions contained by the tasks, at once necessary and chimerical, entrusted to institutions.

— 4 —

THE NECESSITY OF CRITIQUE

In the preceding talk I emphasized the uncertainty that permeates social life and identified the different registers of action on which actors can base themselves, if not to reduce this uncertainty, then at least to make it bearable. Thus, I distinguished a practical register, marked in particular by a low level of reflexivity and a certain tolerance for differences, from registers I have called metapragmatic, which, by contrast, are characterized by a high level of reflexivity. I suggested that we can identify at least two metapragmatic registers: confirmation and critique. By confirmation I mean, above all, the kind of tasks that are carried out by institutions when they have responsibility for constructing reality, which is thus set apart against the background constituted by the world. Finally, I sought, as it were, to justify institutions by pointing out the necessity of appealing to a bodiless being to establish a minimum semantic agreement, which cannot derive from an exchange of points of view between people bound up in bodies. But this enterprise of justification did not lead me to ignore the validity of a different, clearly critical position on institutions: the one that denounces their power, regarding them as the manifestation of a symbolic violence. This second position assumes the necessity of critique. I shall now try to justify this necessity. I shall do so, first of all, by developing the argument that the possibility of critique is inscribed, in some sense latently, in the tensions contained in the very functioning of institutions. I shall then proceed to a fuller examination of the critical register in its relations with the register of confirmation, so as to make clear the fact that critique is the only bulwark against the domination liable to be practised by institutions. It is indeed the indispensable role played by critique in social life that explains the importance sociology has always accorded it.

Hermeneutic Contradiction 1: Embodiment in a Spokesperson

The problem with institutions is that they are at once necessary and fragile, beneficial and abusive. In so far as they are necessary and beneficial, we have to believe in their existence. But their fragility stems in the first instance from the fact that it is difficult not to question the reality of this existence and doubt about them becomes especially pervasive when their abusive character makes itself most obviously felt. Two problems in particular prevent institutions from holding. The first, which is the more often invoked and which we shall not stress, concerns the issue of their foundation. In so far as they found an authority, institutions must themselves be founded and inscribed in a sequence of authorizations which, in modern societies, usually do not stretch back beyond the state. Whatever its length, however, this chain of authorizations comes up against an issue which is especially tricky now that the theologico-political has become obsolete – namely, which being is capable of ensuring an ultimate foundation[1] – and even if the endeavour to find a foundation for the authority claimed by institutions is not simply futile (an issue rather similar to the paradox encountered by speculations that explain the origin of language by an explicit convention, since it would then be necessary to possess a language to establish the conventional agreement on which language is based).[2]

The factor of fragility confronting institutions that will more specifically concern us here involves, in the first instance, their embodiment in spokespersons. It will next lead us to a yet more radical query, which will focus not only on the tension between the bodiless being of the institution and the flesh-and-blood being of the one who speaks in its name, but also on the limits of institutional speech itself when faced with the requirements of action – that is to say, with the means it possesses for being realized in situations.

It was suggested above that a *bodiless* being could escape the constraint of the *point of view* and state the whatness of what is by viewing the world '*sub specie aeternitatis*'. But the problem is that, when it has no body, this being cannot speak, at least other than by expressing itself through the intermediary of *spokespersons* – i.e. flesh-and-blood beings like all the rest of us – such as judges, magistrates, priests, teachers and so on. Even when they are *officially mandated and authorized*, the latter are nevertheless mere ordinary corporeal beings – situated, self-interested, libidinous and so on – and hence condemned, like all of us, to the ineluctability of the point of view, at least when they are not assumed to be expressing themselves as the delegates of an institution. That is why they are often endowed with specific symbolic signs (such as uniforms, established rhetorical phrases, etc.) to make clear the occasions on which they are expressing themselves not in their own name and from their own body, but precisely in the name of an institution that is supposed to invest their corporeality with the properties of an incorporeal body (in accordance with the logic of the 'two bodies' made famous by Ernst Kantorowicz). It remains the case that, since the external appearance of these spokespersons can only alter slightly (if not by costume, tone of voice, deportment, etc.), depending on whether they present themselves in their ordinary being or their institutional modality, we have no sign facilitating sufficiently sure access to their interiority to be certain that they are not mistaken and that the one we see and hear is indeed the embodied institution, and not merely a mere mortal like you and me.

Hence a profound ambivalence as regards institutions, which is no doubt inherent in all social life, especially when the size of the entities concerned no longer makes it possible to repair ruptures through a continuous adjustment of relations, which assumes reciprocal knowledge and proximity. And even in the case of small groups, of which certain Amerindian societies (called a-cephalous) are a classic example, disputes, when they escalate, find an issue solely in the removal of certain members, kinship groups or neighbourhood groups, who leave to settle further off, in accordance with a process of division-fusion (analysed in the case of the Yanomami of the Amazon Forest by Catherine Alès)[3] – something that is possible only in ecological contexts characterized by a small population disposing of a vast territory with abundant natural resources.

On the one hand, therefore, people have confidence in institutions, 'believe' in them. How can they do otherwise, since without their intervention *unease* about what is could only increase at the same time as disagreements? On the other hand, however, everyone knows full well that these institutions are mere *fictions* and that the only real things are the human beings who make them up, who speak in their name and who, being endowed with a body, desires, drives and so forth, do not possess any particular quality that would enable us to have confidence in them. So people swing between 'it's a decision of the local council' and 'you're talking my old friend! It's the mayor, that bastard who wants to sell the dump he inherited from his aunt, that mean old biddy, at an inflated price'. But there again, belief in the institution and critique of the institution form an indissoluble couple because, if no one took the trouble to say what is, what would there be to criticize?

I propose to regard this tension as a contradiction, which is in a sense inscribed at the heart of common social life, and which it is appropriate to broach by regarding it, at this level of analysis, as insurmountable. I shall call it *hermeneutic contradiction*. It poses the following dilemma. On the one hand, it consists in abandoning the task of stating *the whatness of what is* (in itself, for us, etc.), in favour of an exchange of *points of view*, entailing a risk that goes beyond not achieving a closure, if only provisional, of the discussion. The danger is above all that of reviving uncertainty about the determination and stability of the beings whose environment constitutes the basis for action, and thereby creating a fear of fragmentation that actors can seek to protect themselves from by falling back on interpretative microcosms – something which is bound to entail a fragmentation of collectives and ultimately contains a risk of violence. The other branch of this alternative is to delegate the task of stating *the whatness of what is* to the bodiless beings that are *institutions*, but at the price of another kind of *unease*, which is no less constant than unease about what is. This time it focuses on the issue of whether the spokespersons who enable the institution to express itself clearly convey the will of this bodiless being or, under the guise of lending it their voice, simply impose their own will, with the hidden design of satisfying their egotistical desires – those of corporeal and hence self-interested and situated beings like the rest of us.

What is designated here by the term 'hermeneutic contradiction' is therefore not merely an analytical device. This contradiction is constantly in the consciousness of actors or, at least, on its edges, and liable to be resuscitated every time an incident – be it a dispute or a simple maladjustment between the elements that make up the environment – reawakens doubt about the content of reality. But it would be a mistake to confine this unease to the psychological register of belief. It is above all in the domain of action that it manifests itself. The main question confronting people in society is not, in fact, so much knowing what is to be believed (a question that only really exists for those whose power is based on the control they exercise over institutions), as knowing how to act and above all what it is possible to do – that is to say, the issue of the *ability to act*. The latter assumes an assessment of the limits that the constraints imposed by powers which are not those of the person acting exercise over her – an assessment which (it has been suggested) could, depending on historical conditions, rest on realistic bases (socially constructed

86

reality) or, on the contrary, explore the lateral possibilities offered by the experience of the world (everything that happens). This is to say that manifestations of hermeneutic contradiction are to be sought less in the interiority of beings (who, to protect against it, allegedly allow themselves to be deceived by beliefs or ideologies), than in their relationship to action, as a function in particular of their assessment of the opportunities afforded them to act in a specific way without having to pay an exorbitant price for it.

Hermeneutic Contradiction 2: Semantics versus Pragmatics

But the kind of unease that can be created by the articulation between the bodiless being of the institution and the corporeal being which gives it a voice is merely the tangible manifestation of a difficulty rooted in the relationship between language and the situations of enunciation wherein it is realized. In fact, this unease could easily be reduced if the speech that presents itself as the institution's was always as proximate as possible to practice – that is to say, if the semantic function of the institution genuinely had the power wholly to cover the field of experience and, as a result, abolish the multiplicity of points of view in favour of a single perspective that would end up saturating the field of significations. But this presupposes that the diversity of concrete situations could be surmounted, in such a way as to dissolve them all into a continuous, seamless situational web. Now, such an operation is simply impracticable, because it would come into contradiction with the very logic of action which, operative in the world of bodies, cannot liberate itself from the changing context it is realized in, so that it necessarily finds itself associated with interpretations. However, there does exist a kind of situation that seems to represent an exception, which is especially illuminating for our argument: that established by rituals.

In fact, a problem of this kind is what is confronted by ritual (and, in degraded form, by what I shall later call *truth tests*). One of its most specific features, whereby it is often identified, is that it establishes a situation which presents itself, when viewed in a teleological optic, as if it had been organized in such a way as to maintain two kinds of correspondence as intimately as possible. That is to say, on the one hand, a correspondence between different registers of manifestation of action – especially between what is done by words and what is done by deeds; and, on the other hand, a correspondence between human actions and the disposition of other, neighbouring beings – or a set of predefined objects (which can serve only for this occasion), determinate places in space, dates, selected, repetitive moments and so on. Thus, each of these elements intervening in the situation operates a constraint on all the others, in such a way that the set of the system is stabilized self-referentially. The very idea of *context*, in the sense of conditions relatively independent of actions performed or words spoken, to which these actions and words should therefore be adjusted, at the price of variations based on interpretations, is, at least in principle, quite foreign to ritual. For each of the registers of manifestation is pre-established in such a way as to be adjusted to the others – for example, in the dialogical form of questions and answers – and the set of manifestations, organized in sequences whose unfolding is predefined and hence predictable, is (as far as possible) adjusted to the surrounding system, which is itself specified and stabilized. As we know, particularly following Austin's research, it is enough for one of the elements to be absent or not in accordance with expectations, for a necessary word not to be spoken, or not at the right moment, or not by the right person, or for the performance of a gesture to find itself inopportunely blocked or diverted, and the correspondence unravels and the ritual fails.

But we must still ask what is meant by this. To say a ritual fails means that the world has ended up imposing its untimely presence, and forced it to be acknowledged, in an environment entirely constituted to incorporate it and, hence, reduce the very possibility of its manifestation. Or, alternatively put, that it has manifested itself precisely in so far as it is distinguished from reality – something that reduces the ritualistic situation to its artefactual mode of being and, in a sense, denounces it, by making it but one constructed reality among other possibilities, whereas its orientation is completely geared to the objective intention of reducing the differential between reality and the world. Thus, the slightest gap, even the most contingent,[4] is the equivalent of a critique. And, similarly, it is enough for some people, present in the same *context*, pointedly to refuse to enter into the *situation* for the ritual action to be shattered and, in a certain way, denounced. (We often see this today, for example, with funerals, which assemble for an hour in the same church the relatives of the dead person, anxious that the remains of their dearly departed should be accompanied religiously, and his friends, unbelieving or hostile, who do not know what to do with themselves in this context or what gestures they can publicly perform without disavowing themselves in front of the others.)

88

Now, this reduction of the differential between the world and reality is the only imaginable way of making a bodiless being genuinely exist in the world of bodies. A bodiless being cannot manifest itself in the way normal to bodies, be they animate or inanimate. For this way of being consists in persisting in being, but only at the price of a series of adjustments to an environment that is itself changing. That is to say, by means of a continuous play based on the difference between the world and a reality which must be constantly *repaired* to be maintained as such and hence put to the test of what challenges, precisely as reality. But to act in this way, it is necessary to possess a body. That is obviously why religions, which justify themselves by their capacity to establish arrangements enabling human beings to address gods and, less frequently, gods to answer them, have gone as far as is possible in inventing such a system. The presence of the bodiless being is revealed in them, in particular, by the constraint that the sequence of the ritual imposes on all the participants. Each of them can be assured of her own state by adjusting to the state that she assumes the others likewise find themselves in – something which enables the conjunction of bodies, speaking the same words and making the same gestures,[5] to realize a virtual, yet material, analogue of the bodiless being, which is not only evoked (as when an orator mentions the name of Napoleon in a speech), but presented.

This kind of system has thus constituted, as it were, a stock or hoard of paradigmatic practice that other functionalities drew on every time they had to rely on reference to bodiless beings – in particular, functionalities of a political type – but encountering problems which the specificities of the religious sphere make it possible, to a certain extent (whose limits we shall shortly note), to circumvent. In fact, gods are endowed with capacities, comparable to those of the joker in card games, which are very difficult to transpose into the political order. One of these, at least in religions of salvation, is their acknowledged potential to act by intervening directly in the innermost being of people – in their 'hearts' – and this invisibly. Now 'hearts', understood in this sense, are precisely located at the point of non-differentiation between reality and the world. Another joker, seemingly more difficult to use, and which is often regarded with a certain suspicion by religious authorities (at least in the case of Christianity), consists in the possibility of miracles – that is to say, in an untimely irruption of the bodiless being into the world of bodies, where it intervenes in the manner of bodies. This solution, which can be characterized as hybrid, has the advantage of imparting a tangible reality to the action of the bodiless being, but the defect of causing the tension between reality and the world to resurface in the form of an opposition between this world – which will then be characterized as 'mundane' – and the other world – which will then be characterized as 'divine'.

It is also to be noted that, even in the case of rituals which are usually attached to the religious sphere – especially if they are envisaged not in isolation, but in their sequence in ritual itineraries of a certain duration fulfilled in a plurality of different spaces – the semantic dimension is constantly threatened by alterations affecting the performance. In particular, they accompany changes in the context of action, control of which can never be ensured to exclude the unpredictable. For an observer, the pragmatic dimension, which manifests itself in the interaction between the actors and in their relationship to objects, tends then to take priority over the semantic dimension. Symbolism itself reveals its 'ambiguity', its 'indeterminacy', its 'superabundance' and its 'paradoxes'.[6] But it is precisely because ritual itineraries exploit the available symbolic repertoire in a relatively under-determined fashion that they are capable of incorporating, en route, actors whose properties, life-stories and expectations are different, unforeseen events, failures and disclaimers, whose interpretation permits of varying degrees of plasticity, depending on the authority of institutional representatives charged with dogmatic control. It is precisely by virtue of this plasticity that the non-distinction between reality and the world can be maintained, since everything that happens, or virtually everything, is capable of 'assuming a meaning', when the correspondences linking these disparate beings and events to the entities which intervene in ritual, and also to one another, are disclosed.[7]

The kind of issues faced by religious rituals in affixing themselves to a semantics are posed particularly sharply when these forms are transposed into the political order. The problem of politics when based, as has nearly always hitherto been the case, on institutions, treated as bodiless beings, is that it must at once be entirely located in reality, while claiming to be representative of something more fundamental and more permanent than reality – that is to say, something which is not merely *constructed*. And this, as if to bind as tightly as possible a power – authority – which no human being really possesses, condemned as they all are to the ineluctability of the point of view, in such a way as to confer on some people, acting like one person, an exorbitant power over others, condemned to fragmentation. But such an operation is practically never realizable in truly convincing fashion, except perhaps in special moments like ceremonies or feasts and, more generally, those moments defined by Durkheim as 'effervescent'. This stems quite simply from the fact that it pertains to politics, if it wishes to be realistic, to recognize the existence of a context that partly escapes it, even if it assigns itself the mission of dominating it.

The borderline example of ritual, and mention of the problems posed by its transposition into the political order to found its authority, can help us achieve a better grasp not only of the meaning of the distinction proposed above between *reality* and the *world*, but also of the relative fragility of reality as *constructed* reality. It has been suggested that reality was constituted by the relationship between elements extracted from the world and test formats, qualifications, principles of categorization, modes of totalization – whatever form they are incorporated into, be it legal, scientific, customary and so on – possessing the dual character of descriptive tools (which say how things stand with what really is) and deontic powers that generate prescriptions and prohibitions. These formats, determined under the pressure of an institutional power, are treated not only as if they were capable of incorporating and stabilizing fragments of world, but as if the possibility (and the mission) of seizing the world in its entirety belonged to them.

This is to say in passing that – as will become clearer later – the distinction we have posited between the world and reality cannot be grasped by an actor who positions herself completely from the point of view of reality and still less by a spokesperson when she expresses herself in her institutional capacity. For the objective aim of reality is orientated in the direction of the totality – and this even if it does not appeal to technical tools of totalization, of the kind, for example, afforded by statistics. It is only by presenting itself in the place of the whole that reality can seek to ensure its solidity and defend itself against the forces which aim to relativize it – that is, challenge it. Viewed from within, it has no exteriority. It follows that the distinction between the world and reality is rooted in a particular optic which is already that of critique.

Viewed from this angle, reality, as reality constructed under the power of institutions, is positioned as a continuation of ritual. Or, rather, it constitutes an attempt, necessarily doomed to failure, to push ritualization beyond the limits, which are very narrow, where it remains possible, in order to implant it everywhere or virtually everywhere. That is, where it inevitably encounters the contingency and uncertainty inherent in situations, in as much as they are *also* in the world, and, by the same token, the requirements of the action that must be deployed by *actors* to face up to them – that is to say, by each of us when we leave behind the rare ritual situations for situations that are called 'ordinary', where the main business of life is conducted. For institutional formatting, in so far as it is realistic, cannot be exclusively directed towards aligning forms of behaviour by subjecting them to rules, but also necessarily stabilizes, in and through the same operation, the contexts where this behaviour unfolds, so that the rules encounter conditions of execution corresponding to them. But this is to ask too much of what it is wholly appropriate, in this instance, to call *providence*; and it is only rarely, at the cost of duress and violence rendering human action practically impossible, that such an adjustment is actually achieved.

A reality where the institution really is *total* (to adopt Goffman's term)[8] – that is to say (as we shall see), a reality excluding the possibility of critique – would in fact be a reality offering no purchase for *interpretation*. *Semantics*, which is the domain *par excellence* of institutions, would then completely prevail over *pragmatics*. But if, as was suggested above, a world where pragmatics always wins out over semantics is difficult to conceive, because it would generate an infinite fragmentation of significations, a reality entirely subject to a semantics stabilized from institutional positions would also be one where action either became impossible, or was condemned to be performed by severing the links that relate it to language or even to any other type of semiotics. However, it is indeed towards this limit that the institutional use of language tends, when it endeavours to fix vocabulary and syntax in *formulas* that are correctly called *stereotyped*, to signify that they longer refer to anything but the language itself, because they operate as if it was possible to stabilize reference once and for all, whatever the context in which the words are used.

As indicated by the example of 'wooden language', be it that of a state, a party, a church or the one in which the functionaries of international organizations readily express themselves, not to mention the most ordinary of institutional jargons – whose paradigm is the language of law – this use of language, founded on a catalogue of prescriptions and prohibitions – that is, on the basis of a semantic violence – no longer makes it possible to say much and, in any event, not anything adjusted to the concrete situations where speech must be linked to action. Forms of 'wooden language' therefore no longer say anything, at least nothing genuinely related to speech situations, as if, having become wholly self-referential, they can do nothing but speak themselves.

It is thus the very fact of the inadequacy of official formulations to the situations in which actors must practically engage and act – that is to say, confront other human beings and also a multiplicity of non-human beings (animals, things, artefacts, 'forces of nature', etc.) – that introduces interpretative games paving the way for a challenge to, or, at least, a relativization of, institutional qualifications.

This tension is not ignored by spokespersons. There does indeed exist a way for them to seek to protect themselves against the de-realizing effect of the institutional performance, and try to attenuate its violence, by incorporating it – that is to say, by adjusting to the situations as if they were plunged into them as ordinary individuals. They will then endeavour slightly to alter the vocabulary, syntax and even the corporeal *exis* of the speaking subject in such a way as to make institutional speech more 'natural' and 'alive' (as people say), as if it was their own speech (this is the 'plain speaking' of politicians). But this stratagem, by giving more weight to the corporeal presence of the one who speaks on behalf of the bodiless being, always risks having the opposite effect from the one sought – that is to say, not diminishing unease about the validity of what is said, but on the contrary increasing doubt as to whether it is indeed the bodiless being who is saying what is being said, or an embodied, banal being with its determinations, interests, libido and so on.

Institutional Violence

The issue of the tension between semantics and pragmatics I have just mentioned refers to the question of violence, around which hermeneutic contradiction revolves. The possibility of metapragmatic registers and, in particular, a metapragmatic register of confirmation entrusted to institutions, had been derived from the risks actors find themselves confronting when the pursuit of their activity in common, conducted in a practical register, has to confront an escalation in the level of dispute. Ascription to an institution of the requisite *authority* to say the whatness of what is has therefore been envisaged, in the first instance, in its pacifying role. But, as suggested by the preceding analyses, the power institutional language is invested with cannot itself be manifested without also betraying the violence that inhabits it, and which is invariably denied by inserting responsibility for the measures adopted into a chain of authorizations leading to the non-existent being that the institution claims to represent – a denial which is consubstantial with the *afterwardsness* of confirmation. In effect, to be exercised without violence, at least without physical violence,

93

institutional language would have to be in a position to prevent, *by its very existence* as it were, the possibility of actors engaging in different behaviour and divergent interpretations of what occurs – and this as if the institution was genuinely capable of supplying the only possible point of view on the world and thereby furnishing the norm of truth. Now, we have seen that this objective, which doubtless is indeed contained at the heart of the institution-form, is impossible to achieve, in particular on account of the variability of the contexts of action.

Moreover, were such a project possible, institutions would in fact be pure semantic systems, whose words would have only to be uttered for practices to find themselves automatically homogenized and aligned, as if there were no distance separating saying from doing. But then institutions would have no need to be linked to *organizations*, whose task is to govern actors so as to coordinate their activities, or, still less, with *administrations* exercising a policing function. Now, this is never (or virtually never) the case. For the reasons we have just outlined, the semantic violence inflicted on the texture of language to fix its usages and stabilize its references is not sufficient to achieve conformity of conduct, so that it is always necessary (or virtually always) to combine it with physical violence, or at least the threat of it, to stabilize interpretations and hence remove the risk of an open dispute. To the violence, verbal or physical, that is said to be *unleashed* when a dispute escalates, the institution thus counter-poses a violence *chained* to the semantic and administrative systems which justify its existence: 'When the consciousness of the latent presence of violence in a legal institution disappears' (writes Walter Benjamin) 'the institution falls into decay.'[9] This violence – shown by Benjamin to be, for example, inherent in law – can take the form of a sort of hidden hoard, whose existence is invariably denied, for 'law-making',[10] or manifest itself, but justifying itself by reference to legitimacy as 'law-preserving'.

But critiques of this kind are not limited to the law, whose repressive function is obvious and even accepted. They also extend to rituals, whose immutable staging is not only denounced as formalism, empty of any content and foreign to the dynamic flow of 'real life', and hence often as 'inauthentic' (as when, for instance, the formal character of marriage is contrasted with the spontaneity of true love constantly confronted with the risk of evanescence). Their determination to coordinate the participants in celebrating what is, as if it could not be otherwise, is interpreted – correctly, but only from a certain point of view, that of critique – in the register of domination, in ways, highly active in profane critique, which anthropology can also echo.[11]

As we shall see more clearly when we examine the resources

of critique, violence is tacitly present in institutions because they must struggle against the unmasking of hermeneutic contradiction. This unmasking is intolerable to them, to the extent that it consists in revealing the contradiction between the overarching position, superior to points of view associated with interests, occupied by the bodiless being and the self-interested character of the corporeal beings who occupy it and speak for it; or, if you like, particularly in democratic-capitalist societies whose principle of legitimacy is the *Rechtsstaat*, between the legal order and the social order.

Institutions are therefore interdependent with systems aiming to repress or circumvent hermeneutic contradiction, in the absence of being able to transcend it, as if they were able to assert their real existence and (which in their case comes down to the same thing) posit themselves at each moment of time by suspending the possibility that they might come to an end, only by linking themselves to an *absolute*. The absolutist temptation is inherent in the claim to occupy an overarching position, which would in some sense be situated at a higher *logical level* than the one in which actors are placed when they express their divergent points of view. A position where disputes between actors could not reach the institutional instances and whence their interventions would have the power to resolve these disputes – that is to say, not only increase the force of one of the parties in such a way that it prevails over the others, but to cut through them *without remainder*. The horizon of pacification without residues, or victory without losers, is indeed what is contained, for example, in the idea of *common good*, conceived as a good superior in rank to the different forms of determination of relatively incompatible goods that actors invoke when they endeavour to support their critiques or justifications by a rise towards generality.

To be fully satisfied, however, such an orientation presupposes that the losers stop complaining and give up challenging the validity of the tests which have been unfavourable to them. Now, institutions in their semantic dimensions do not have the means to achieve this objective, which can only be realized by depriving the *malcontents*, through an action on bodies, of speech, or (which in practice comes down to the same thing) by obstructing their efforts to coordinate themselves so as to get dispersed discontents to converge in a collective action. Those whom the tests disadvantage are led, first, to suspect the way each test detrimental to them was applied locally; and then, when they have collected evidence from other actors disadvantaged by what are deemed similar tests, to challenge the format which, at the most general level, governs the procedures followed by these tests. Suspicion can focus in the first instance on particular individuals accused of having abused their duties or misinterpreted the directives, as if to shield the institutions themselves from critique by directing the protest at flesh-and-blood individuals without challenging the bodiless being, whose sovereignty is not impeached. The works of historians of critique are thus full of examples of rebellious movements directed in the first instance against the *bad* counsellors of the *good* prince, adjudged ignorant of what is done *in his name*, like the rioters in pre-revolutionary France (referred to by Charles Tilly)[12] who chained their lord to a wagon placed at the head of the procession of protesters, as if to make it clear that he remained the embodiment of the value system in whose name they were rebelling.

But when the revolt escalates and the malcontents come to compare and share the motives that inspire them, it becomes increasingly difficult to maintain the fiction of a radical separation between the pure will of the bodiless being and the wills embodied in the corporeal person of those who make themselves its spokespersons. Added to this is the fact that protest action itself, while first of all being rooted in what we have called a *practical register*, is directed, as it unfolds, towards reflexivity. Now, as the malcontents develop their movement, coordinate their action and exchange views, the gap goes on growing between the semantic qualification of the situation provided by official instances and interpretations that seek to articulate what is in the process of occurring in words, by going back to a causal explanation of the reasons which have brought people to this pass – the fact, for example, that 'they have come to blows'. This dynamic, which tends, on the one hand, to lead to the reappearance of the beings who materialize the institution precisely in their corporeal determination bound up with particular interests (e.g. class interests) and, on the other, to prioritize the pragmatics of action over institutional qualification, has the effect of voiding the bodiless being of any content, thus tipping it over into fiction. The emperor has no clothes.

Through the same operation, the semantic security guaranteed by institutional power is abruptly converted into its opposite: symbolic violence. The existence of such violence is the main justification of critique, whose first move is to unmask and denounce the violence concealed in the folds and interstices of the systems of pacification associated with institutions. It is then applied to re-describing the work of institutional confirmation in the register of violence and, for example, to unmasking 'power relations' under 'legal relations'. And it empowers itself with this re-description to justify the forms of violence – if only verbal – that it itself employs. For critique, especially when engaged on the terrain of justice, finds it hard to maintain itself in an order of protests made in vague fashion – 'in the abstract', as we say (e.g. in connection with the abstract entity that is 'society') – without extending itself by means of *accusations* against people. Now, an accusation does not only generate violence. It is in itself already a form of violence.[13] This is no doubt why, when carried out in appropriate forms, denunciation of injustice is accompanied by rhetorical means geared to a *rise towards generality*, in such a way that the accuser can base her act, including in her own eyes, on defence of the common good – as if she were herself the spokesperson for a potential institution – and not on that of specific interests. And this requirement, intended to reduce the violence of the accusation, imposes itself all the more strongly to the extent that she is the victim of the injustice she denounces.[14]

Accordingly, in the first instance it is by this means that the *reality of reality* can be challenged. Far from being definitively excluded, dispute thus regains the upper hand over the systems of confirmation that were supposed to get its closure accepted. But, compared with the disputes that emerge in a practical register, and which move along the track of serial chains, it has changed form because it is polarized by the resistance mounted against it by reality, qua constructed reality whose greater or lesser robustness stems in particular from the condition of the institutional forces enrolled in the service of its conservation. It is because reality holds and institutional systems make it hold; because spokespersons certify its necessity and maintain that there is nothing other than the world as it is, such that it cannot be otherwise, that critique can assign itself objects, fix objectives and unite (invariably temporarily) around these salient points – themselves provisional and fragile – different actors in so many respects that their links would otherwise be constantly redistributed in the course of a multitude of local disputes.

The Possibility of Critique

It cannot be denied that the institutional work of determination and qualification of what is and what is valid has, regardless of the kind of society in which it is carried out, the effect of constructing an official truth and also what is usually subsumed under the term 'common sense' (in particular, a common sense of the behaviour judged normal or abnormal, in the sense understood by psychiatry). The power of institutions thereby has a powerful effect on what we have called the construction of *reality* and, correlatively, contributes significantly to ensuring the exclusion of lateral possibilities – that is to say, putting the *world* at a distance. However necessary, institutions therefore do indeed – as frequently charged by the critical sociology of the 1970s – exercise an *effect of domination*. Does this mean that domination cannot be surmounted?

The domination exercised by institutions would effectively be unlimited if they ended up occupying the whole social space, without the slightest element of critique being able to be introduced into it. I would now like to show that nothing of the sort is true. My main argument is that the tension incorporated by institutions harbours the possibility of critique, so that the formal genesis of institutions is inextricably a formal genesis of critique.

In fact, hermeneutic contradiction opens a breach that critique can rush into. Without it, people would forever be under the sway of the forms of confirmation dependent on institutions and, as a result, completely immersed in a world treated as self-evident, without being in a position to adopt a position of relative exteriority vis-à-vis these forms, so as to challenge them. But we can perhaps also imagine another alternative where they would constantly be in a state of the utmost scepticism about everything. Unlike these absolute and never (or virtually never) attested positions, the existence of critique is precisely based on the possibility of *giving one's adherence* and *doubting* and also, often in connection with the same objects, oscillating between these two positions or even adopting them simultaneously – so many moves whose principle consists in the uncertainty that derives from the impossibility of putting an end, once and for all, to hermeneutic contradiction.

It follows that to observe that social life generally appeals, when faced with disputes or the threat of them, to instances capable of stating the whatness of what is, does not necessarily lead to regarding sociality as totalitarian or 'fascist' in its very essence (in the sense that Roland Barthes could say in 1977, in his inaugural lecture at the Collège de France, that language is 'fascist', not because it prevents people from saying things, but because it 'compels to say'). For, confronting the institutions that say what is, stands *critique*, which is no doubt also present, but to different degrees and in different forms, in all societies. Addressing objects or events that matter, those it is right to respect and where the link between symbolic forms and states of affairs has been soldered by operations of confirmation and celebrated, critique explicitly challenges this link and therefore opens up a gap between what is and what is said about what is – a gesture invariably accompanied by an attempt to halt the course of action. It thus begins by confronting (supposedly) respectable objects in their instantiations in context – be it mundane contexts in the case of concrete objects or propositional contexts in the case of abstract objects – with the types that identify them, before challenging the value of these types themselves.

Let us add that if they were as sure of themselves as is often claimed, institutions could save themselves a lot of work by saying what they have to say once – that is, once and for all. However, as has been shown by the study of ritual or ceremonial forms, but also that of law and all other modalities of normalization, institutions are trapped in the task of incessantly re-saying what they mean, as if the most peremptory and seemingly irrefutable assertions were always faced with the threat of refutation, or as if the possibility of critique could never be completely excluded. Moreover, that is why we call institutions, considered in their semantic dimensions, *instances of confirmation*.

Thus, institutions not only have to state the whatness of what is and what is valid, but also endlessly *re-confirm* it, in order to try to protect a certain state of the relationship between symbolic forms and states of affairs – a certain state of reality – from the attacks of critique. To put it figuratively, institutional confirmation places reality in a preserve as if to remove it from the ravages of time, on which, by contrast, critique bases itself when it inspects the changes that have occurred in the world to make them serve the contestation of a reality regarded as being, 'in fact', no more than a certain *state* of reality and hence open to being transformed. Moreover, it is this suspension of time that justifies the use of the term *confirmation* to refer to the operations in question here. For one can only confirm what *has already occurred*. As if to get around the vicious circle of the founding moment, institutions act as if what they establish had *already* been produced. They are always in *afterwardsness* (*Nachträglichkeit*, in Freud's terminology).[15] This authority is rarely sufficiently assured for them to be able to take the risk of affirming that there is something new – something done by revolutionary moments, precisely because they are located at the moment of juncture where old institutions are overthrown but new ones have not yet been constructed.

Two Different Forms of Reflexivity

Confirmation and critique must therefore be regarded as two mutually inter-defined functions, which only exist through one another.

99

Nevertheless, there are important differences between these two metapragmatic registers, involving, in particular, modes of reflexivity.

In the case of critique, reflexivity has an obvious character because it takes a personal form. This applies both to the critical actor and to those whom she asks to follow her. The critical actor is defined by the specific form of reflexivity called 'lucidity'. This lucidity is what gives her the strength to challenge institutionally confirmed truths and the truths of common sense (which are invariably the same thing). This challenge takes the form of a transgression, in speech and/or action. The critic engages, and must engage personally, in the transgressive public action she undertakes. She cannot make do, for example, with spreading a rumour, in the sense of a statement that everyone can simply pass on to others without engaging in its enunciation. On the contrary, she takes personal responsibility for what she asserts, with the risks this action might entail in prompting disapproval and anger on the part of defenders of the established order. She thus posits herself as spokesperson for a potential future community.[16] Certainly, she asks to be followed by others, real individuals, who are her contemporaries. But this also contains a risk, for, if she finds no one to follow her; if a group is not formed around the cause whose advocate she makes herself, her words and deeds can be disqualified as eccentricity or madness (paranoia).

As evidence of this, take the work I have done on the public denunciation of injustices in the form of letters sent to newspapers. I asked a panel of people with no particular psychiatric competence to read a sample of 300 letters sent to a major evening paper, featuring the exposure of an injustice suffered, and to award a mark (from 1 to 10) to the author of each letter, depending on how they assessed his mental state (perfectly sane or completely deranged). This made it possible to outline what might be called a *grammar of normality*. On the one hand, it revealed the important role played by the *ordinary sense of normality* in the judgements people face in everyday life and, in particular in this instance, when they engage in critiques and protests. On the other hand, it showed that the chances of protests against injustice being accepted as normal (if not necessarily justified) largely depended on the extent to which those who publicized them succeeded in making a credible link with an already established collective, capable of corroborating their complaint and supporting it. For a sociologist, the actors labelled 'paranoid' therefore take the form, in the first instance, of critics who ask others to adhere to their cause and yet whom no one follows:[17] critics facing failure and opprobrium.

The risks faced by critical speech are especially clear in the case of the figure of the *pamphleteer* who, while forming part of a French tradition whose genealogy runs through the period of the Ligue,[18] and that of the Fronde in the seventeenth century,[19] and then the numerous satires that accompanied the birth of the form of the 'affair' in the eighteenth century (studied by Elisabeth Claverie),[20] developed above all in the last third of the nineteenth century and the first half of the twentieth. As has been well analysed by Marc Angenot,[21] the pamphleteer presents himself as a solitary figure who addresses everyone and 'casts his bottle into the sea'. Let us note that what he has in common with the critical theorist is that he assails the social order as a whole. But, unlike the latter, he does not seek to reach a compromise with a sociological description that can lay claim to *objectivity*. On the contrary, he legitimates himself exclusively with the rights of *subjectivity* to insult, ridicule and deploy a verbal violence that make him an *imprecator*. But this borderline figure, whose most remarkable examples are shared between left and right (often with an orientation that will bring them close to fascism) clearly reveals one of the requirements weighing on actors foreign to the social sciences – especially writers – when they undertake to engage publicly in social critique: that of rooting their words in a personal existential experience. In effect, it is on the basis of this personal experience, which underlies their commitment, that they can claim access to a particular lucidity, because it is from this that they derive (as will become clearer shortly) an access to the *world* whence *the reality of reality* can be challenged.

Things are quite different in the case of the metapragmatic register of confirmation. In the case of confirmation, we also find ourselves in the presence of operations of a reflexive character, at least in the sense the term is used in here by articulating the question of reflexivity with that of metalanguage. Taken in this sense, 'reflexive' means that the relationship between symbolic forms and states of affairs and, radically, between language and the world is no longer treated as a matter of indifference or rather, if you like, as innocent (as is the case in a practical register). On the contrary, it creates an unease that is the motor of action in a critical register and which confirmation seeks to assuage or prevent. Operations of confirmation therefore likewise possess a reflexive character, since their object is the relationship between symbolic forms and states of affairs – and this in order to bring them closer together or prevent the threat of a challenge from critique. However, in this case, unlike what we observe in the case of critique, it is the *system* as such that has a reflexive character, not the

actors themselves, who are in the position of spokespersons or officiants of the bodiless being of the institution. They are not supposed
to engage on a *personal* basis in their action. For example, we do
not ask – at least when the act is performed in normal conditions – if
the spokesperson for an institution or the officiant at a ritual really,
personally, 'believes' in what she is saying or doing. That is not the
point. What matters is simply that she does what is expected of her
in the prescribed forms, so that it is done and done properly. Hence,
moreover, the discomfort often created by figures awkwardly positioned between critical speech and institutional service, as are (and
above all were) spokespersons for revolutionary parties – what have
been called 'apparatchiks' – whose critical language was tainted with
inauthenticity as a result of its compromise with a quasi-established
collective whose 'directives' they applied – something that earned it
denunciation as 'wooden language'.

What has just been said of spokespersons (or officiants) also applies
to those who are in the position of witnesses of a ritual (e.g. a religious one) or ceremony (e.g. a national one). Whether they watch
passively or participate actively, they are not expected to develop a
personal reflexivity. On the contrary, what is asked of them is the
kind of renunciation that expresses the way in which they acknowledge the reflexivity of the system as a whole and its capacity to make
manifest what is. Moreover, it is this renunciation that is often interpreted as *emotion*.[22] Emotion, which in this case might correctly be
called 'collective', even if it takes form in individual, separate bodies,
has its source in the experience of a kind of plenitude of meaning, of
the order of *bedazzlement*, that is to say, in assuagement of the unease
about the existence of what is and what has value – of what one is
attached to, in the affective sense of the word. It is testimony to the
always disappointed expectation of a reconciled world from which
critique would be absent, one to whose possibility the fact that no one
speaks up to derail the demonstration underway seems to point. We
can therefore say, without exaggeration, that emotion is the form, at
an individual level, taken by reflexivity in the register of confirmation.
And this especially when people gather to *celebrate* not so much their
fusion or communion – as in the moments of collective effervescence
that fascinated Durkheim – of whose illusory character they are never
completely unaware, as the possibility that there could exist something like an agreement about what is. And hence these moments are
no doubt virtually the only ones when the bodiless being succeeds in
embodying itself in the world of bodies and thus getting people to
believe that it exists. But it is also necessary to add that, correlatively,

it is enough for a significant number of those present (and perhaps a single person) not to be engaged in the requisite state for the ritual or ceremony to fail. Their physical presence, distant or ironic, even when it remains silent, is the tacit equivalent of a critique. Ritual is then 'demotivated', to use François Héran's term,[23] not – as is nearly always the case – because the participants have forgotten the principles that accompanied its foundation (which are invariably illusory or reconstructed retrospectively), but because the effect of *bedazzlement* has vanished.

Let us add that the different forms of reflexivity, just described, go hand-in-hand with what might be called different forms of unconsciousness. The instances of confirmation, vigilant about the risk critique makes them run, shut their eyes to the evanescent character of what holds the place of foundation for them, to which critique counter-poses its lucidity. But critique ignores – and this is the form of unconsciousness peculiar to it – what it owes to the labour of confirmation that supplies it with the axis without which it would be condemned to drift aimlessly.

The Distinction between Three Kinds of Test

In a construction of the type I have just outlined the social world is subject to three kinds of test. Thus, on the one hand, we shall distinguish a kind of test employed by institutions, understood in the broad sense – that is to say, instances of confirmation endowed with a semantic function. We shall call tests of this kind *truth tests*. On the other hand, we shall posit the possibility of two other kinds of test exploited by critique. We shall call the first *reality tests*, whose performance is placed at the service of a critique that can, to be brief, be called *reformist*. We shall call the second *existential tests*. When critique seizes on them, it instead makes them serve a critique that can be called *radical*. Let us now give a provisional description of these three kinds of test, starting with truth tests.

Truth tests are employed by instances of confirmation. They strive to deploy in stylized fashion, with a view to consistency and saturation, a certain pre-established state of the relationship between symbolic forms and states of affairs, in such a way as to constantly reconfirm it. The state of affairs whose reality and value are to be confirmed is established in token situations which, to the maximum extent, possess the properties of the type situations that correspond to them, with which they are supposed to coincide. This assumes strict

103

control of the context in which the performance occurs. Repetition plays an essential role here, but one that has nothing to do either with technical requirements (for example, filling one's fountain pen whenever it is empty), or with the regularities deriving from habit. The only role of repetition is *to make visible the fact that there is a norm*, by deploying it in a sense for its own sake, without it being given any external function – something that has an effect of reflexivity. We can thus regard a number of ceremonies (for instance the ceremonials of the Ancien Régime, on which there is a rich historical literature)[24] as truth tests during which a social order is deployed via the connection of disparate elements that – as Marcel Hénaff writes of the way in which structuralism treats symbolic systems – 'are thought out between them'.[25] The work of confirmation, whose main operator (as has already been noted) is tautology, thus takes the form (to be brief) of a reapplication of forms of codification, which are duplicated, deployed and transformed (depending on orders or structures). In the course of ceremonies, operations of confirmation feature in this way, aiming to *make visible* the relationship between the order of symbolic propositions and the order of the states of affairs whose image they are – and hence to confirm and stabilize it – and this, in particular, by conjugating several modes of representation, such as statements, performances (in the theatrical sense), icons and gestures, between which correspondences are established.[26] The statements state nothing other than quasi-tautologies – for example, 'God is great' (it would make no sense to ask 'Yes, great, but roughly what size?'); 'the king is the monarch'; 'the Republic is the Republic' and so on. And that is why truth tests indicate a preference for the genre of the *formula*, a statement without a subject of the enunciation, since the one who makes it merely realizes a saying that precedes her and which, possessing no informative character, is at the antipodes of *argument*.[27] But these tautologies are charged with power when duplicated in different mediums.

The interplay of correspondences and quasi-tautological relations closes the totality on itself in such a way that its signification is entirely given in each of its elements. Thus, if by chance some new beings come along, they are either not acknowledged as such and are integrated into the already established set at the cost of a series of reinterpretations, or they are rejected. This is clear, in particular, in the seemingly paradoxical case of transgressive rituals – for example, periodic festive events wherein prohibitions are temporarily lifted or inversion is even prescribed. Far from representing critical operations, transgressive rituals have no objective aim apart from defusing critique and, more generally, of integrating (negating) negativity by deploying it in a formula which is isomorphic with that employed to celebrate the world in its respectability.

These formalizations and representations of a coherent world fully warrant the name of *test*, for the simple reason that they can always fail, as is attested by the unease that presides over their preparation. Even in the absence of a critical volition, they can in fact fail, because the world can manifest itself in an inopportune, anarchic fashion during the course of the demonstration and defeat the order sought. This particularly applies to non-human beings – objects, machines, animals – which, being insensitive to the beauty and grandeur of the orders realized and made palpable in their symbolic dimensions, can simply escape the expectations placed in them and not act correctly – either because they are, as is the case with animals, inspired by their own will and drives (they can be hungry, on heat, afraid, etc.), which prevents them containing themselves; or because, as objects and (in particular) artefacts and other machines, they are subject to operational constraints unrelated to the significance of what is played out in the course of representation.

By covering with the same semantic fabric all the states of affairs whose representation is dramatized, this deployment creates an effect of coherence and closure – of necessity – which satisfies expectations of *truth* and even saturates them. This coherence makes manifest an underlying intentionality whose strength is imposed even on those who are ignorant of its content or do not grasp its 'meaning'. Such operations no doubt play an important role in what might be called the *maintenance* of reality. When they succeed, their effect is not only to make reality accepted. It is *to make it loved* – but without it being directly *put to the test*. The reality of reality is not what matters here. In effect, the elements detached from reality that serve as a support for the truth test (e.g. in a major Stalinist ceremony, the hero of labour, the intercontinental ballistic missile, the young pioneer, the old leader whose white head is covered with a fur cap, etc.) are there only as signs. Each of these signs supports the truth of the others. But it matters little whether the hero labour is *in fact* merely a lazy social climber, whether the missile always misses its target, whether the young pioneer is a rich kid thinking only of a laugh, whether the old boss is a senile, criminal dictator and so on.

Reality tests – which we have already had occasion to speak about – are employed to face up to critique in a situation of dispute, always liable to lead to violence. They have the character of tests. They make it possible to put to the test the reality of the claims of beings, especially human beings, by confronting them with their ability to satisfy the corresponding requirements, stabilized by qualifications and formats. To adopt the Aristotelian distinction, we can say that the *powers* of these beings must then be revealed by *acts* performed in specific conditions and in contact with systems of objects. In other cases, it is the test itself that is put to the test, and one then examines whether the way in which it is conducted here and now, in some particular situation, fully conforms to the form and pre-established procedures that should govern its course. Unlike truth tests, which reduce uncertainty, reality tests assign it a significant place. This uncertainty, which essentially focuses on the capacities of beings – that is to say, something which is supposed to remain in their interiority and not be immediately accessible to the senses – must be reduced in action if it is performed under certain conditions.

Reality tests are distinguished in their very construction from truth tests, especially by the fact that they disconnect two kinds of operations: on the one hand, operations exhibiting what creates value (which truth tests do optimally, but at which they stop) and, on the other, operations aiming to recognize whether this value is materialized in the very texture of reality and to attest it by evidence aspiring to general validity. In this sense, whereas truth tests unfold what is desirable as if it were what is, reality tests posit a differential between what should be and what is, between value judgement and factual judgement, and explore it. Hence, in the order of language, their preference is for argumentative devices, unlike truth tests that affirm and confirm what is by repeating formulas (as the pleonasm has it, 'ready-made formulas', as if a formula could only have a single occurrence).

Whereas truth tests always reinforce the existing order, reality tests can proceed in the direction either of confirming the established order or of critique. Their orientation is conservative when they reinforce existing hierarchies by validating a reality that is already in large part pre-adjusted to the test formats (i.e. constructed). But when taken seriously, the reality test can have a disruptive effect, either by unmasking contradictions between various forms of normative expression, or by revealing dimensions of reality that might be called forgotten. In fact, the organization of tests, including the most 'legitimate', is comparable – as Wittgenstein says of language – to an 'ancient city' with its modern districts, its seedy areas, its half-ruined buildings, its forgotten back streets and its cul-de-sacs,[28] so that critique can also find in reality itself elements that facilitate challenges to the confirmed representations of reality.

Critique can therefore take advantage of reality tests – and this in two different ways. It can first of all denounce the fact that some particular person does not have the position corresponding to what she can *in fact* do, or that she is not *recognized* as she merits being. The reality test brings the backing of *evidence* to such claims. Critique can also challenge the illegitimate fashion in which some test is applied in a particular situation (e.g. challenging whether elections have been conducted in conformity with the statutory procedures). It can also identify inconsistencies between the logics governing different tests in different spheres of reality and demand that *compromises* be constructed to reduce these tensions, and so on. But in none of these operations is reality as such challenged and it can even be said that, in some respects, these critical operations can help to reinforce the reality of reality. When a person or group motivated by critical dispositions engages in a reality test, it is indeed to get others (and invariably, in principle, everyone) to recognize the validity of their claims and the factual character of the injustice they have suffered. But, in so doing, the plaintiff acknowledges what might be called *the reality of reality* – that is to say, the validity of the forms of organization that are at once guaranteed, at least in principle, and reproduced by the established test formats, as is the case every time someone appeals to social justice, the rules, respect for established procedures, and so on.

Alongside truth tests and reality tests, room must be made for what we shall call *existential tests*. Unlike the first two, existential tests must not be regarded as having been subject to a process of institutionalization, so that they retain an individual – or, as people say, 'lived' – character even when they affect a large number of people, but each of them taken in isolation. Only their sharing can confer a 'collective' character on them. The latter is liable in its turn to be foregrounded to support demands, criticize existing reality tests and, if necessary, demand that new ones be introduced – and this in order to sanction *acknowledgement* of offensive factors that have hitherto remained unacknowledged, in the sense that they could be *seen* but without being *identified* or integrated into the domain of reality. In the case of existential tests, another of the meanings that can be taken by the word test prevails over the one predominant in the case of the reality test. It refers to what provokes suffering, at least psychic, what *affects*. Existential tests are based on experiences, like those of injustice or humiliation, sometimes with the shame that accompanies them, but also, in other cases, the joy created by transgression when it affords access to some form of authenticity. But these experiences are difficult to formulate or thematize because there exists no pre-established format to frame them, or even because, considered from the standpoint of the existing order, they have an aberrant character. For this reason, they are often called 'subjective', which makes it possible, when the one who experiences them seeks to share them with others, to deny their reality, disqualify them, or ridicule them (e.g. it can then be said of someone who expresses the way an injustice or humiliation has affected her that she is overly 'sensitive', that she has 'misunderstood', even that she is 'paranoid', etc.).

But precisely because they are situated on the margins of *reality* – reality as it is 'constructed' in a certain social order – these existential tests open up a path to the *world*. Hence they are one of the sources from which a form of critique can emerge that might be called *radical*, in order to distinguish it from *reformist* critiques intended to improve existing reality tests. That is why radical critique is frequently based, at least in its early stages, on expressions used in forms of creation – such as poetry, the plastic arts or the novel – where it is socially more or less permissible (at least since Romanticism) to confide to the public personal experiences and feelings, and whose aesthetic orientation makes it possible to bypass the constraints of consistency and legal or moral justification imposed on argumentative discourse. And this is perhaps also why philosophy, when it seeks to release critique from the iron cage of reality, often initially looks for its subject-matter to an analysis of the work performed by writers on language itself, in such a way as to inscribe their uniqueness in it (for example, in the case of Sartre's reading of Jean Genet). But what philosophy does with writers is precisely what the sociology of critique intends to do with ordinary people, by working to make their existential experiences visible and intelligible.

To arrive at a better appreciation of what I mean by existential tests, think of the tests *in themselves* experienced by homosexuals, forced for centuries into a quasi-clandestine existence and faced with insult and opprobrium, whose experience was initially conveyed in literary, dramatic or pictorial works, before taking a collective form paving the way for a movement that could claim public recognition for what had become a *collective*. This gradual recognition (which is far from being complete) went hand-in-hand with a change in the contours of reality and the establishment of tests *for self* – more precisely, reality tests – enabling objectification of the injury, which makes it possible, for example, to establish a crime of homophobia in law.

When critique, by seizing on existential tests, undertakes to share and publicize unhappy experiences like contempt or denial, hitherto lived in solitude and privacy, it assigns itself the task of undoing the generally accepted relations between symbolic forms and states of affairs. It can seek to do so, in particular, by drawing from the world new examples that endanger the completeness of established definitions and cast doubt on the universal character of confirmed relations. In effect, the examples are samples of beings, taken from the world and projected into reality, where the properties that enter into the definition of objects are instantiated. In a way, this is the possibility of giving examples that destroy the risk of circularity faced by definition, by opening it out onto the exterior. But the problem is that the universe of possible examples is itself incomplete and open. The different samples that can be taken as examples must be recoded in terms of the definition of the object. But we can find not only samples that can be coded so as to support the definition of different objects, depending on the properties retained in the coding process, but also samples occupying an unstable position between objects which give rise to contradictory definitions.

This is clear in the case of the processes we have called *affairs*. Take, for example, an event such as an act that has deliberately brought about the death of a person and which is presented by some (but not all) as an act of assisted euthanasia, not a criminal act. In the Humbert affair, a woman, helped by a doctor, injected a lethal dose of poison into her paraplegic, paralyzed son, who, incapable of killing himself, had (she said) insistently requested her to do it. This woman and the doctor who gave her his assistance were charged with a crime. Associations that campaign for the legalization of euthanasia then fixed on this example and, very concretely, this mother's statements, her tear-stained face shown on television screens, the book she has written and so on, to say something like: 'you call her a criminal?' Although she had in fact deliberately performed an act that resulted in death, this did not suffice to justify her being characterized as *criminal* – a negative predicate – because consideration of other properties of the state of affairs to which this act belongs conferred on her, on the contrary, a heroic character. But over and above the particular case of this woman and her son, the object of the affair is to alter the extension of the qualification of criminal – defined by the fact of deliberately causing death – by highlighting the discrepancy between different examples. On the one hand, we have examples of acts that no one hesitates to qualify as criminal (e.g. the act of a man who deliberately kills another to rob him) – examples which occupy the core of the category (in the sense of Eleanor Rosch); on the other, we have borderline examples which, it is demanded, should be qualified by a different term.[29]

What is at stake here therefore concerns the types to which these acts, each taken in its contextual particularity, must be referred; and, as a result, the form of respect to be accorded to them. It is never a question of irrelevant acts that are to be considered only once. But the first, initially considered in their contextual existence, must be related to a type that possesses, among other properties, the normative property of being the object of a highly negative evaluation, which leads to them being accorded negative respect. In contrast, the second must be related to a different type that, while having properties in common with the first (in both cases the act deliberately caused death), contains positive or neutral properties on a normative level, which commits us to adopting a different form of respect for them.

Critical operations, which often take the form of *affairs*, as is the case with the one I have just mentioned, are based on existential tests in the sense that they must be based on lived experiences – experiences that serve to extract from the *world*, or if you prefer, the *flux of life*, elements that can invalidate both the confirmed relations and the established reality tests. 'If that woman is a criminal, then all loving mothers are criminals.' Affairs thus play a very important role in altering the tools that support the operations of qualification used by institutions – in particular, in our societies, instruments of a legal kind. By affording new examples that do not fit with the accepted definitions, they make it possible to challenge the law and, often by adopting a rhetoric of change, to denounce it as a 'dead letter' that no longer corresponds to the present state of affairs, or (which comes down to the same thing) to the alterations in ordinary people's sensitivity to the states of affairs inherited from the past (their 'moral sense'). The law is thus caught out when it calls a man who takes bread (from a rich crook) to save his children from hunger a 'thief'; when it calls a young girl who has had an abortion after being raped by her boss a 'criminal'; when it characterizes this mother who, torn apart by the inhuman suffering of her hemiplegic son, gives him (at his request and with the agreement of a doctor) a lethal injection as a 'murderer', and so on.

The Critical Work of Exploiting Contradictions

Without drawing up a list of the very different routes critique can take, I shall dwell for a moment on the way it exploits the contradictions that run through reality, not only in its realizations but also

110

in its formats. Truth tests are organized in such a way as to render disparate elements consistent. As for reality tests, they are subject to requirements of internal consistency polarized by regulatory principles. However, in both cases, the maintenance of consistency can be more or less satisfied only if the tests are confined to arenas in such a way as not to interfere with one another. Different tests, organized in contexts that are spatially and/or temporally proximate, can be based on divergent and even incompatible principles.[30] And, conversely, the same framework of justification can be invoked in support of positions that are difficult to reconcile. Critique will be able to seek to exploit these disparities by comparing tests or positions involved in different spheres, so as to bring out the contradictions that the actors put to the test are locked into. Thus, for example, in the case of disputes over the issue of abortion, 'pro-choice' critique can legitimately denounce the inconsistency of those who proclaim themselves 'pro-life' while being, in different contexts, in favour of the death penalty. These contradictory attitudes are doubtless generated by the transformation of the same categorial operator based on the analogy between the opposition life/death and the opposition innocence/guilt. But this schema inherited from sacrificial religions – which makes death the ransom of sin – is today wanting in relevance and legitimacy, so that it is difficult for it to be explicitly set to work in a justification, which condemns it to remaining covert.[31]

Other contradictions, which critique can exploit, manifest themselves when the same object of *reference* assumes different, incompatible *meanings* depending on the situation it is involved in. On the propositional context in which reference to an object stabilized by a rigid designator, or even by a definite description, is inserted then depends its relation to different types associated with different modes of assessment. Thus, for example, the same lamb has the property, when considered in the meadow, of being 'affectionate and charming', but, when tasted on the plate, of being 'tender and exquisite'. Depending on the situation in which it is involved, it can be a pet or a piece of meat.[32]

The beings that are subject to manifestly contradictory qualifications when involved in different situations are very often vectors of critique, so that the boundaries between the contexts in which they can be involved must be marked by particularly robust separators. It is in cases of this type, which are very frequent, that the most complex and constraining *grammars* of qualification and action are established. Their objective purpose is to distance critique by suggesting to actors and speakers the paths to take or not to take, in order to avoid dangerous comparisons; or even, in their most sophisticated forms, to propose practical arrangements and rhetorical forms that make it possible, if not to resolve, then at least to blur contradiction. Examples can be given of these grammars drawn from already cited works by the present author. Thus, the grammar of *accusation* blurs the tension between the use of violence and a demand for justice; the grammar of *justification* seeks to reconcile a requirement of common humanity, which presupposes the equality of actors, with their ordering in a hierarchy; the spectator of suffering at a distance (for instance, on the television) is caught up in the tension between a demand that is made to her as if what was shown concerned her, and the fact that she has no means of improving the lot of the unfortunate people whose spectacle is presented to her (which exposes her to the accusation of viewing solely for the purpose of indulging a 'sick' pleasure),[33] and so on.

Let us add that it is largely the inability to handle these complex grammars correctly that indicates mental derangement. The sense of normality, referred to above, is not only based on a knowledge of normative models (or roles), in the sense of culturalist anthropology. It is above all attentive to the way people muddle through difficult situations where they face the risk of contradiction. It therefore knows how to tell the difference between normative transgression, be it of the order of criminality or mere eccentricity, and madness,[34] which manifests itself in the strange way that complex grammars of contradiction are employed, often excessively, as if deranged people could not tolerate the undemanding relationship that normal people maintain with the principles of consistency whose relevance they are supposed to recognize.

The way in which critique undertakes to bring out the contradictions contained in a certain state of social reality often takes the form of *provocation*. A gesture, which might be compared with those of madness were it not made intentionally, even strategically, is publicly performed to get spectators to react – to 'shake them out of their routines', that is to say, to force them to behave in a way that is no longer within the limits of the complex grammars that manage contradictions, whose presence, blurred in the ordinary course of existence, is then *unmasked*. Thus, for example, provocation – this time manifesting itself in acts of violence – can aim to put political orders invoking democracy and human rights in contradiction with the values they claim to adhere to, by forcing them into the repressive violence that is latent in them.[35]

112

The Four Orientations of Unmasking

In the case of the truth test, as in that of the reality test and the existential test, we can speak of *unmasking*, but in different senses. The truth test *unmasks* a universe of signs by exhibiting it in its plenitude and consistency. It makes it *manifest* and gives *lustre* to what, in it, stands behind the feeling of *respect* it inspires. In and through *acts*, the reality test *unmasks* the *powers* concealed in the interiority of beings, so that the treatment accorded them is brought into harmony with what they really are and, in this way, the consistency and cohesion of a *reality* that most closely resembles the representations deployed by truth tests is maintained – that is to say, a reality whose *correctness* is as one with *justice*. As to the existential test, at least when it ends up being formulated and made public, it *unmasks* the *incompleteness* of reality and even its *contingency*, by drawing examples from the *flux of life* that make its bases unstable and challenge it, in such a way as to confront it with the inexhaustible, and hence impossible to *totalize*, reserve represented by *the world*.

To these three directions in which unmasking can proceed we must add a fourth orientation, which represents a temptation and a threat to critique. We shall seek to identify it analytically by signalling what distinguishes it from the forms of unmasking employed in existential tests, which this final orientation can parasite to the point of being confused with them. Like reality tests, existential tests present themselves as tests *of something*, even if, in their case, what is tested has not been subject to official qualification or even explicit characterization, capable of being incorporated into the normative formats that sustain reality. Nevertheless, this something can form the object of an explanation by the actors themselves – or, in the first place, some of them – from the suffering that accompanies its privation, which, in determining it as the *desire* for something, initiates its substantial fulfilment. It is precisely this operation of determining privation and formulating desire that offers the possibility of making them shared and thereby paves the way for the expression of *desiderata* which, if then recognized and adopted by others, will take the form of demands that will be presented as *collective*. This means that in this instance critique cannot be determined solely by its opposition to the established order of reality, considered in its opaque generality, but also, or above all, by its reference to possibilities, already identifiable in the experience of the world, of which suffering and desire are the manifestation in the flux of life.

Conversely, when it has not been possible to carry out this work of determination, the actual experience of suffering and lack can take the concrete form of a general unmasking, which declares itself in the manner of a drive of *suspicion*. In this case, critique can have no other guarantor than recognized truths, without being in a position also to provide itself with an anchorage in desire specified as the desire for something.[36] Critique then tends to exhaust itself through both a lack and an excess of objects. For this critical configuration, it suffices for a truth to be accredited for it to be suspect – and this even without the solidity of the instruments that equip it being clearly put to the test or, at least, without critique finding itself in any way affected by the justifications counter-posed to it and to which it does not feel obliged to respond. The form of critique carried out by the drive of suspicion, which corresponds fairly closely to what is usually intended by the term nihilism, can be called *alienated* in the sense that it is not determined by anything other than the forces that appear to resist it. It remains clearly motivated by a desire. But this desire itself, bereft of objects, is nothing other than the inverted transformation of what oppresses it. Hence its tendency, on the one hand, to generate fictional elaborations that it feeds off and, on the other, to seek satisfaction in the critical gesture itself, and not in what it makes it possible to obtain, with the temptation of an aestheticization of transgressive acts pursued and appreciated as it were for their own sake, as if they were works of art.

No doubt it could be shown that this alienation of critique is, at least in the main, the result of the obstacles it encounters. It is when the relationship between institutional confirmation and critical contestation is highly unbalanced, to the detriment of the latter, that suspicion is generalized. Reality then attains such a degree of consistency, of closure towards what does not enter into established frameworks and, at the same time, of solidity and durability, that those whose expectations constantly meet with tests that discourage them end up endowing it with intentionality and considering it, in its generality, as a *conspiracy*. The affirmation, by recognized authorities with institutional power, of truths treated as absolute, whose impalpable character is protected not only by the doctors of the law, but also by police measures ready to punish any lack of adherence, then – in the logic of blasphemy – makes their contestation, and the performance of gestures intended to make it clear that the norms associated with them can be transgressed, dizzily exciting. From this perspective, the most inflexible situations of domination are not the least vulnerable. This is true even if alienated critique cannot ultimately have any other effect than overturning them in favour of alternative situations of domination. Unless it ends up emancipating itself by restoring the links that might connect it to the experience of actors – that is to say, to the sufferings and desires they have experienced, and also to the moral sense they have applied in order to interpret these tests and seek to weather them by giving them a political orientation, so as to transform sorrows and dreams into demands and expectations.

— 5 —

POLITICAL REGIMES OF DOMINATION

The Incorporation of Hermeneutic Contradiction into Political Regimes

In the previous talk, I presented hermeneutic contradiction in its generic form. From that perspective, it could be interpreted as if it were an inevitable consequence of any political order, forever torn between the necessary character of institutions and the inevitable possibility of critique. But thus conceived, critique would be more or less futile, since it would not be able to free itself from the bonds which, in the very labour of subversion, link it to institutions (realizing the kind of form of conflictual solidarity that combines the 'fort' and the 'buttress').[1] It would thus ultimately help reproduce in different modalities a political order that was essentially equivalent to the one it had taken as its target. This way of seeing things – towards which the Weberian position can be drawn – pretty much comes down to supporting overarching theories of domination which, by unmasking underlying effects of domination in any political order whatsoever – this boils down to regarding domination as ubiquitous – have virtually the same practical consequences (as has already been noted) as positions that definitively exclude the issue of domination.

Now, it must be stressed, on the one hand, that hermeneutic contradiction always manifests itself in specific forms and, on the other, that it is articulated with modes of government which are not only different, but not equally oppressive, when considered with respect to the effects of domination they facilitate. We can use the term *political regime* to refer to the arrangements which, constitutive of different historical societies, are established around hermeneutic contradiction, both to embody it in different forms and to conceal it.[2] It is largely to ensure this work of concealment that modes of domination are established, which are all the more necessary to the extent that institutions themselves are more strongly associated with the perpetuation of the asymmetries and forms of exploitation at work, and/or that the voice of critique makes itself more loudly heard. In effect, as was suggested in the previous talk, no political regime can completely avoid the risk of critique, which is in a sense incorporated, in different forms, in hermeneutic contradiction. By domination – if we really want to take the notion seriously – must therefore be understood not a factual condition that is imposed once and for all, but *processes*. It is through these processes that the instances responsible for the determination of what is, and the maintenance of reality, strive to contain and limit critique, silence it, expel it – that is to say, in a different idiom, to act in such a way that reality has sufficient robustness to conceal the world as completely as possible and prevent it from manifesting itself.

An effect of domination can therefore be characterized by its capacity to restrict, in more or less significant proportions, the field of critique or (which in practice comes down to the same thing) deprive it of any purchase on reality. In a situation of domination, the loops of reflexivity whereby circulation between confirmation and critique is established are broken. The function of confirmation tends to prevail over the critical function, to the point of more or less reducing it to complete silence – something that is manifested by an absolute pre-eminence being accorded truth tests over reality tests and, still more, over existential tests, whose consideration can no longer accede to the order of public communication. But what is manifested in the case of tests is simply the repercussion of mechanisms of *repression* whose main object is hermeneutic contradiction itself. In a historical context where the margin of autonomy required by actors in order to act (i.e. to confront an uncertainty without simply following orders or carrying out an internalized programme) is respected, hermeneutic contradiction is inscribed in the mechanism of the systems supervising social life. People can then either act as if they were unaware of it, or, on the contrary, seize hold of it and restore it to the foreground. Conversely, in a context of domination, it is debarred. It is therefore wholly legitimate, confronted with situations of this kind, to employ a normative language and characterize them as *pathological*.[3] This is also to say that the main indication of a pathological situation is not incoherence or even disagreement (as a conservative interpretation of the position adopted by Durkheim might lead us to believe). For it is part and parcel of the normal course of social life that it is only very partially coherent and yet, despite everything, that it enables the

117

coexistence of beings whose differences and divergences are always stronger than what they can unite around, albeit only sometimes. What should prompt identification of a situation as pathological is therefore, on the contrary, *the maniacal quest for coherence*,[4] as if it were possible for human beings to live in a single world and, all together, always in the same one.[5]

Without taking the description very far, which would require elaboration that exceeds the limits of this little précis, we can nevertheless seek to indicate some of the dimensions which might be taken into account by an analysis of the way hermeneutic contradiction is actualized in different historical situations and political regimes.

An initial dimension might be the form in which hermeneutic contradiction is invested depending on the preponderant politico-semantic regime – that is to say, depending on the nature of the institutions principally entrusted with the tasks of stating the whatness of what is. Later, I shall especially stress the distinction between institutions that claim to represent the 'general will', in whatever form it is supposed to manifest itself, and institutions which are above all based on expertise, with, on the edges, the authority of science.

A second dimension that can clarify the way hermeneutic contradiction fashions a specific political order is represented by consideration of the systems that help to mask it as much as possible. A political regime is defined, at least in part, by the way it treats hermeneutic contradiction – that is to say, most often, by the way systems that aim to circumvent and conceal it are established. Among these systems must be counted all those that help to absolutize institutions. These systems can have a symbolic dimension or, better put, a mythical one – as is the case, for example, with those that undertake to root in a *political philosophy* the fiction which serves as a foundation for institutions and, in particular, the one that remains the most powerful and general of them, on which institutions operating in particular domains rely to ensure their legitimacy: the institution of the *sovereign state*. But alongside the great theologico-political myths, whether they appeal to divine law, the sovereign people, the nation, science and so on, there is a multiplicity of more modest systems, whose role in the everyday functioning of institutional power is nevertheless incontrovertible. Their object is to anoint spokespersons and magistrates in such a way as to detach, as far as is possible, their institutional avatar from their corporeal manifestations in other situations where they act as ordinary people. Among these very numerous and often highly sophisticated systems, we can signal, for example, those supervising *multi-positionality*, which aim to make it difficult to bring together in a synoptic table the different positions that the same person can occupy in different spaces – for example, in our society, in a political space and an economic space.[6]

A third interesting dimension is none other than the articulation of institutional power and critique. Although there is doubtless no kind of society from which critical forms are entirely absent, different political regimes are distinguished by the role they accord critique in the face of the power of institutions. As we shall see later, we can thus distinguish political regimes where institutional power is maintained by crushing critique from political regimes that give it a place, at least in verbal form – which does not necessarily mean that they have excluded every form of domination.

In today's talk I shall sketch the ideal type (so to speak) of two modes of domination that have marked contemporary Western societies. But, taking a broader historical perspective, I shall first of all seek to situate different kinds of possible political regime by examining in broad outline the way that different political metaphysics come to terms with the unavoidable problem posed by the integration of continuous change, gradual or brutal but in any event inevitable, in the established order.

Uncertainty and the Question of Change

The relationship, under the pressure of uncertainty, between institutional forms and forms of critique itself depends on the issue of *change*. In the absurd utopia of an unchangeable world without any history, it might be thought that different people's points of view would tend to converge in quasi-mechanical fashion. By contrast, in the real world, the experience of change – if only, for example, that of ageing – is the most general, incontrovertible experience. But this raw experience cannot be left to itself. It must constantly be counteracted. No human group could yield to it without making life literally impossible and condemning itself to disappear into the multitude of states of affair that follow one another and are superimposed at random. But it must also be constantly resumed and freshly put to work, so as to avoid reality losing any link with the world. The issue of how to overcome change by integrating it into an order capable both of accepting it and reducing it, in order to make reality cohere – an issue that comes down to institutions; and the issue of how to base oneself on change to denounce these orders and undermine these constructed realities – an issue that falls to critique – can both give rise to very different treatments. Among a range of possible solutions, I shall envisage two, which have played (and perhaps still play) a pre-eminent role in Western societies, borrowing categories from Philippe Descola's work on the structural anthropology of metaphysics articulated with what, in our society, we call 'nature'.[7]

The first solution, which can be called *idealist* (or, if you like, Platonist), consists in establishing types or ideals (essences) containing truths that the appearance of things tends endlessly to travesty. Access to knowledge is then defined not by the observation and description of surface appearances, which are associated with shifting, misleading singularities, but by an understanding of the types or ideals that alone have the power to confer form and meaning on empirical reality. In constructions of this kind, the possessors of knowledge – scholars and philosophers – are those to whom authority and, consequently, the legitimate exercise of power falls. It is in them that institutions are embodied. Their main task is to frustrate the fragmentation that threatens the polity when it is prey to confrontation between *points of view* – *opinion* – by guiding, voluntarily or forcibly, the citizens' emotions and actions towards those focal points removed from ordinary perception that are types and ideals. In this sense, whether democratic or authoritarian, they are appeasers, since without their far-sighted intervention the collective would collapse into dispute. This solution can be called *political*, whatever the way – which varies with historical circumstances – in which an invariably precarious compromise is constructed between a popular will, expressed directly or via representatives, and the authority of guides or experts selected for their knowledge. The latter cannot be absolutely blind to change. But their wisdom manifests itself in their ability to resist and *delay* it, as far as is possible, or to interpret it in such a way as to seize hold of it and integrate it *smoothly* into the existing social order (which comes down to removing its revolutionary potentialities).

In contrast, a second solution (what Philippe Descola calls 'analogism') consists in starting from singularities, envisaging them in the multiplicity of the spatial and/or temporal contexts they are involved in, while establishing similarities and differences between them on the basis of empirical properties (such as a colour, a smell, a form), in such a way as to immerse them in a finely woven network of *correspondences* that is never closed (new ones can always be discovered). These correspondences, projected against the background of human beings' experiences which, by virtue of their construction, are incomparable, make it possible to construct comparisons between them which can precisely be characterized as *analogical*, in the sense that, unlike what we observe in the case of classification or categorization based on some form of idealism (with reference to the type that defines the class), comparisons established in this fashion preserve the singularity of the beings between which a relationship is posited. In this case, change is absorbed by being integrated into the heartbeat of the network that constantly takes shape and loses shape. But it would be a mistake to think that this solution proves more favourable to acknowledging change. For, in a construction of this kind, change is always understood locally, in its circumstantial dimensions, without assuming a general form. As a result, in and through the same operation, it is acknowledged and ignored or, at least, underestimated.

In this second solution, which we might call *poetic*, the role of institutions is first and foremost steadfastly to confirm, by deeds or words, by ceremonies, rituals or poems, the play of symbols that enables the establishment of correspondences – and this with particular intensity when events of exceptional force or strangeness seem to challenge the field of singularities as a whole; or when it is necessary to manage the metamorphoses the beings are subject to.[8] This is to say that in societies or historical moments when the second solution prevails over the previous one, institutions, in their external manifestations, become more visible, more active, more present. Whereas idealist institutions are predominantly devoted to often rather obscure tasks of prediction and prevention, as attested by the importance they attach to the *education* of *citizens*, analogical institutions must in a sense constantly be on the alert to intervene in order to repair tears in the fabric of correspondences made by the irruption of unpredictable events.

From this different kinds of critique also follow, based on different actualizations of *hermeneutic contradiction*. Faced with *idealist* institutions, critique, basing itself on an embodied conception of hermeneutic contradiction, will challenge either the representativeness or the integrity of the spokesperson, or the competence of the guide or expert, and will seek to destabilize the types or ideals, sometimes by exhibiting non-qualifiable states of affairs, sometimes by unmasking contradictions between species of category. Confronted with *analogical* institutions, the task of critique consists in emphasizing the inadmissible character of a particular event and the failure of operations, ritual or narrative, aiming to reintegrate it into the framework of correspondences outside of which what happens possesses no meaning. In this case too, hermeneutic contradiction will assume salience but (if you like) of a *performative* kind (in Austin's sense), with critique striving to show that institutional rites were doomed to

121

fail because they were not performed adequately (which, in the case of a ritual, means that it has not been performed at all), thereby provoking trouble in the very order of things. Unease will then focus less on the actual person of the authorities, questioning their integrity or competence, than on the question, no less troubling, of whether the requisite deeds and gestures have been correctly performed, in their smallest details. Now, it is very difficult to pacify unrest of this kind, because, even in cases where a precise procedure exists, set down in writing or preserved in the memory of the wise or the old, the list of rules to be followed can never marry up with the circumstances in all their details, which, by virtue of their involvement in the world, have an unlimited character.

It is tempting to characterize *modernity* by a gradual increase in the place accorded critique, but on condition of realizing that this process corresponds above all, in fact, to a development of idealist critique at the expense of analogical critique. This development in the intensity and visibility of critique is accompanied (as Bruno Latour's works have shown) by a significant restriction of the field of application of critique. On the one hand, this conquest and, indivisibly, this restriction were sustained by a decline in analogical modes of constructing reality, which were still highly active in sixteenth-century Europe. This decline was marked by a reduction in the presence of institutions in their symbolic performances – ritual, ceremonial or linguistic – and, correlatively, a consolidation of less spectacular institutional forms of life, which I have characterized as idealist. But, on the other hand, the increase in the power of critique (and also its containment) went hand-in-hand with the development of what Philippe Descola calls 'naturalism' or what Bruno Latour in his book *We Have Never Been Modern* calls the 'great divide'.[9] To be brief, the latter consisted in dividing the task of ruling on what is, and constantly confirming it, between two very different kinds of institutions, depending on whether what was involved was facts regarded as pertaining to 'nature' or facts regarded as pertaining to the social life of collectives.

This great divide thus distributed the tasks of critique between two kinds of institutions: on the one hand, *scientific institutions* and, on the other, *political institutions*. As Latour has clearly shown, the power assigned science continually grew by seizing hold of facts attributed to the realm of nature and thereby wrested from politics. Thus defined, science made it a point of honour to make critique its main instrument of knowledge. However, in and through this operation, such critique was removed from the overwhelming majority and placed in the hands of scientists and them alone, with the result – strange enough when one thinks about it – that the latter have arrogated to themselves the power to declare non-discussible (by others) the truths that they proclaim at some particular moment, while reserving to themselves the liberty of rejecting them the very next minute. We might reasonably think that it is the (unduly) large role assigned to science which, investing it with the power to stabilize the relationship between symbolic forms and states of affairs as regards most of the objects deemed pertinent, has as a result liberated the possibility of an autonomization of social critique in domains defined as specifically *political* (in order to distinguish them from scientific problems). But the same operation also significantly contributed to narrowly restricting this critique by virtue of the scope of the issues on which science had become the sole instance of authority.

In this landscape, the arrival of the social sciences and, at their head, economics, had the effect of significantly altering the compromise established on the basis of the great divide between a (major) science and a (minor) politics, further reducing the field of the latter. To the critical claim that 'everything is political', which marked our youth (but already with a *reactive* character), came the response – in increasingly vocal fashion with the passage of time – that everything is scientific – that is, reserved to the authority of experts. This slippage from a definition of politics based on a compromise between representatives of the people invested with the role of spokespersons and experts claiming to represent the authority of science, towards a definition of politics almost entirely subordinate to the power of expertise, can be regarded as a genuine change of political regime and a new form of domination.

On the basis of this approach, I shall now try rapidly to characterize two contemporary forms of domination associated with two different ways of repressing hermeneutic contradiction. The first consists in rupturing the relations between truth tests and reality tests – that is to say, ignoring reality (including, or especially, qua reality constructed with reference to confirmed test formats), as if it was possible to dispense with it without anything untoward occurring. In this first scenario, obsessive unease especially concerns change, to which it is necessary to shut one's eyes. The second consists in continually altering the contours of reality as if to inscribe the world in it, as a site of constant change. But it is then the world itself that is the subject of debarment and which, as it were, finds itself abolished. In the first case, I shall speak of an effect of simple domination; in the second, of an effect of complex or managerial domination.

The Effects of Simple Domination and Denial of Reality

We can identify effects of simple domination in two kinds of situation. On the one hand, in borderline situations associated with contexts where people are partially or wholly deprived of basic liberties and where deep asymmetries are maintained or created by employing explicit violence – particularly (but not exclusively) physical violence. It seems to me preferable in cases of this kind, whose paradigm is slavery, to speak of *oppression*. But we can also invoke oppression in numerous, less extreme scenarios, where the maintenance of an *orthodoxy* is obtained by means of violence, particularly police violence, aimed at suffocating critique. In situations of oppression, it is only with great difficulty that people can recognize something in common by regarding themselves in different respects from those considered by official classifications. As is demonstrated by the literature on slavery (not to mention the extreme case of concentration camps), the collective is impossible or very difficult to establish. Fragmentation is complete and, hence, the possibility of critique is simply excluded, as also can be the mere possibility of posing questions about what occurs ('here no questions are asked'). Critique and questioning being evacuated, justification no longer has any rationale. These situations can also practically take the form of ideologies, at least addressed to the dominated if not to the personnel who use violence – a task that is relatively difficult to perform cold and long-term without ideological or even (if I can put it like this) 'moral' support. In this kind of context, one can do without an intense ideological activity directed at the dominated – which is always costly – since the coordination of actions does not appeal to consent, but is secured directly by violence or its threat and the established systems. Likewise, and for similar reasons, instances of confirmation are reduced to a minimum. Given the impossibility of posing questions about what is, there is no need for the presence of instances charged with confirming that what is really is.

On the other hand, we can also refer to effects of simple domination in less extreme situations where critique appears possible to a certain extent (although the actors never know to *what* extent or *how far* they can go without the costs of critique becoming exorbitant), and where justifications are provided by the actors or institutions that realize the effects of domination. In these contexts, the main difference is between *the official* and *the unofficial*. *Official* justifications are not confronted with reality. Something like reality tests related to formats do indeed exist. But no one is in a position to control the conformity of the conduct and result of tests applied locally, here and now, to the format to which they are supposed to correspond. Likewise, requirements of justice (meritocratic or social) can be officially recognized – for example, the reversibility of states of worth ('equality of opportunity') – or of separation between forms of assessment of capacities aiming to curb an 'accumulation of handicaps', but they are confined to declarations without being accompanied by systems that make it possible to implement them.

In this kind of context, critique, when it is possible, remains without any real effects. As to justifications, they degenerate into mere *pretexts* and take the form of *empty words* – as is said by those to whom they are addressed and who, far from always being dupes, invariably develop realistic interpretations – i.e. without illusions – of their condition. In these contexts, an *unofficial* knowledge is constructed on the basis of everyday experience, knowledge that it is forbidden to make public. Existential tests find it difficult to be shared and to issue in demands. Efforts to create or preserve margins of autonomy take the form of individual small-group initiatives. To reduce the constraints that weigh on them, actors thus develop a specific interpretative competence aiming to identify spaces of freedom by exploiting flaws in the apparatuses of control. This is also to say that the 'ordinary' people who suffer these effects of domination lose neither their sense of justice, nor their desire for freedom, nor the correctness of their interpretations of what is happening in reality, or (if you like) their lucidity. But it is made impossible for them to act.

Faced with this lucidity, and in order to try to reduce the incredulity with which they are met, the instances responsible for defending a certain state of what is and what is valid and, hence, with establishing and maintaining profound asymmetries (between genders, social classes, identity groups, etc.), thus hold open the possibility of *exploitation*. They seek to reduce propensities to critique, on the one hand, by regularly reconfirming the established order through a spectacular deployment of truth tests (rituals, ceremonies, parades, award of decorations) and, on the other, when this does not suffice, by appealing to the administrative bodies that possess the means of violence (usually dependent on the state), so as to maintain their domination through *repression*. In a model of simple domination, the instances of confirmation are obsessively orientated towards preserving a ready-made reality, which must be sheltered from disturbances that might be provoked by consideration of experiences in touch with the world. This obviously goes hand-in-hand with the crushing of critique. The objective aimed at can therefore be characterized by *the refusal of change* and the means employed have something to do with *the state of war* against a permanent internal enemy.

Effects of simple domination therefore fit well enough with the various entries in the kind of specifications posited at the beginning of this talk. In this mode of domination, institutions endeavour to contain change. More precisely, their efforts are geared to preserving reality in such a way as to prevent it being outflanked by elements that have emerged from the world, which presupposes that critique is contained not only under the impact of semantic violence but also, if necessary, by physical violence. 'Law-preserving' violence is fused here with 'law-making' violence (this, according to Walter Benjamin, characterizes the 'ignominy' of the police).[10] The masking of hermeneutic contradiction takes the form in it of a socialization of institutions and especially their spokespersons or officiants, in the literal sense when the principle of sovereignty that serves as a foundation for institutions is related to a religious origin (as in the different forms of power of divine law), and in the figurative sense of a secularized quasi-sacralization when the place of the heavenly sovereign is occupied by a terrestrial homologue (such as the Nation, the People, the Party, etc.).[11] As we have seen, truth tests occupy a major role in this kind of regime of domination. The spokespersons and officiants are surrounded by an apparat, as if disguises were sufficient to ensure the manifestation of their glorious body and cause the ordinary and hence situated body (self-interested, libidinous) which serves as its support to be forgotten. Hence, be it said in passing, a preference for the elderly (Pétain, Pinochet, the Pope, Stalin or Brezhnev, de Gaulle, etc.), who are entrusted with the most important responsibilities, in so far as their great age tends to diminish their corporeal presence and, above all, assuage unease about the libidinal drives (necessarily individual) that might inhabit leaders and drown their claim to embody the common good – and this, however expression of the latter is supposed to manifest itself (inspiration, observance of tradition, elections, etc.), in such a way as to be concentrated in a personal or collegiate *will*. This will justifies itself by decreeing or conserving rules (defining procedures, qualifications, test formats, etc.), whose observance enables the maintenance of order – that is to say, of reality such that it cannot be otherwise than it is.

126

Complex or Managerial Effects of Domination

We can, however, identify other forms of domination better adjusted to contemporary *democratic-capitalist* societies. One of the characteristics of these societies in that they have broken with the model of simple or patent domination I have just briefly described. They are precisely defined by the fact that they have proscribed the very idea of domination and, so far as is possible, avoid resorting to repression – at least when it comes to what is made visible to the public, by contrast with what is done *behind the scenes* (to adopt a notion of Goffman's).

In fact, in these societies the deeds and gestures engaged in within the public arena, and the discourses that relate to them, are subject to an *imperative of justification* so that they can be made *discussable* by any recipient (deemed *legitimate*), whatever the properties with which s/he is endowed. Finally, people's antagonistic claims, at least when the disputes that oppose them are transferred into the public arena, are subordinate to the application of *reality tests*. In this type of society, such exigencies are imposed not only on agencies that depend on the state, but also on what can (with Williamson) be called the *institutions of capitalism*.[12] We can say of social systems of this kind that they precisely have as their intentional aim to exclude the possibility of domination, in particular by arranging the relations between institutions and critique, which must be attended to (if not necessarily satisfied), at least when it manifests itself in forms deemed compatible with legitimate conventions. It is therefore precisely the establishment of a new kind of relationship between institutions and critique and, in a sense, the incorporation of critique into the routines of social life that characterizes these systems.

Nevertheless, in the kind of historical context I have just described, we can identify effects of domination of a different kind, compatible with the requirements of a democratic-capitalist society. One of the characteristics of the systems which make possible these effects is to ensure a form of domination that does not preclude change and is even, as we shall see, exercised *via the intermediary of change*, by employing, whenever possible, more or less peaceful means, at least when taken at face value.

In these modalities of domination, which can be called complex (or managerial),[13] the possibility of an exploitation taking advantage of the instrumentalization of differentials in order to generate profit is preserved. These differentials can be various in kind, with, in the forefront, the property differential but also, for example, the mobility differential (as Eve Chiapello and I tried to show in *The New Spirit of*

127

Capitalism). Processes of domination are therefore always combined with the enduring maintenance of one or more profound asymmetries, in the sense that *the same people* benefit from these tests (or virtually always), while for others, always likewise *the same*, the tests always have prejudicial outcomes (or virtually always). But the preservation of these asymmetries is effected unintentionally or in a way that the intention is always denied. Their revelation by critique is supposed to create surprise: people 'examine their conscience'; proceed to 'an agonizing re-examination'; invoke the 'harsh reality' or, in accordance with the rhetoric analysed by Albert Hirschman,[14] the *'effets pervers'* of well-intentioned policies. The validity of critique is therefore acknowledged, at least in particular cases of tests (deemed to have been conducted in unjust or 'excessive' fashion). But the very processes of its incorporation nevertheless finally have the result of restricting its extension. When the preservation or augmentation of asymmetries is challenged by critique, which is what usually ends up happening, justification of the existing order of things gives way to excuses invoking sometimes fortuitous circumstances; sometimes historical developments assigned to an autonomous, neutral space (typically that of science and technology); sometimes the actions of those who, in most tests, do not really display themselves to their advantage – for example, because they are thought to drink or take drugs, or because they do not really want to work. This boils down to 'blaming the victim'[15] – that is to say, in accordance with neoliberal logic, shifting onto 'individual responsibility' the weight of the constraints that operate at a collective level.[16] The main device consists in endowing people with a formal autonomy and, no less formally, an equal access to a range of 'opportunities', such that any failure confronted with the established tests can be assimilated to a shortcoming in the one who, of her own free will, did not want to seize 'the opportunities offered her' or who proved incapable of so doing. As was the case in the nineteenth century, such unfitness is once again increasingly often put down to biological factors: 'they' do not amount to anything because they have not benefited from a truly satisfactory *genetic* endowment and it is no one's fault except the accident of the same name.

One of the characteristics of complex domination effects is therefore that they offer less purchase to critique than a regime of repression. Moreover, it is precisely this feature that was stressed in the critical theory and critical sociology of the 1960s and 1970s. One of the main issues raised by critical sociology at the time was the seemingly more or less passive acceptance of asymmetries by the very people who bore the brunt of them. It was to answer this question that critical thinking focused on a theory of *ideologies* and put the theme of *belief* and *illusion* at the heart of sociology. By contrast, one of the contributions of the pragmatic sociology of critique has been to show that actors are *not* abused (in any event, not to the extent that critical sociology gave it to be understood) and that, as regards everything which concerns real life and the injustices they might suffer in everyday life, they harbour *no illusions*. But it has also shown that this lucidity does not thereby give actors a sense of having the least purchase on reality. To understand the way domination effects of this type are maintained, we must therefore set aside, at least provisionally, the themes of ideology and illusion (e.g. as fostered by the media, etc.) to go and see what happens *in reality*.

Dominating by Change: Necessity as Will and as Representation

This form of domination is based on *systems* that individuals or groups can exploit. But different people can have a grip on these systems at different times, which makes identification by critique of the possessors of potential for action difficult. Embodied in individuals, they nevertheless always retain a more or less impersonal character. The question of knowing *who* the dominant are therefore presents itself as problematic. These systems do not operate by seeking to curb change so as to maintain some orthodoxy at any price, as in so-called 'totalitarian' societies. On the contrary, they intervene by promoting, managing and orientating change. In this sense, they are part and parcel of capitalism as a historical form surviving by the interplay of repetitions and differences, but which advocates change for its own sake as a source of energy.

These systems are therefore not primarily geared towards the preservation of established qualifications and test formats, but intervene to alter sometimes *the test formats*, sometimes *the reality* constructed and validated by the outcome of tests and sometimes *the world*. It is through this *plurality of interventions* that critique finds itself disarmed. In effect, it becomes difficult for it not only to reveal that the reality tests do not conform to their official formats, but above all to draw from the world experiences that elude reality as it is constructed, in such a way as to challenge the validity of established definitions and qualifications. These different interventions can avoid the accusation of deriving from a will to domination, and be conducted in a *relatively irreproachable* fashion, only to the extent that they are incorporated into a process of managing constant *change*, presented as both *unavoidable* and *desirable*.

I shall base myself on an article written thirty years ago, when I was a collaborator of Pierre Bourdieu, 'La production de l'idéologie dominante' (published in 1976, this long text is now available in book form).[17] This article offers an analysis of the literature produced by the political and economic elites in power at the time – that is to say, at a hinge moment between two modes of combining capitalism and the state: the one, more or less dirigiste, which lasted from the 1950s to the 1970s; and the one that was then put in place and which assigned a much greater role to the market economy.

The main characteristic of these leaders (but this also applies to those currently in power) was that they advocated 'change'. These elites wanted to be radically innovatory and modernist. The core of their argument (which we encapsulated in a formula: the 'inevitability of the probable') was as follows: we should want change because it is inevitable. It is therefore necessary to *wish for necessity*. Obviously, change will create victims (those who will not be able to 'keep pace with it' and who some years later were to be called 'the excluded'), but it would be worse if, 'as leaders', we did not manage change; if we did not *want* it.

This assimilation, strange when one thinks about it, between *volition* and *necessity*, which is often associated with totalitarian regimes invoking a determinist philosophy of history, is a commonplace of modes of governance of advanced capitalism. The change in question is not so much an actual change as a heralded change. We do not know it yet, or only incompletely. It is therefore necessary to appeal to *experts* in social science (economics, sociology, statistics, political science, etc.), and to calculation and forecasting centres, so as to conceive now the change that will be imposed on everyone, but later, inevitably. When, twenty years later, this time in collaboration with Eve Chiapello, I undertook to analyse the discourse of neo-management that had been established and diffused during the 1980s and 90s, we rediscovered near enough the same type of rhetoric, of which many examples might be given, taken from the discourse accompanying neo-liberal policies, particularly in England and France.[18]

This stress on necessity is required to render political action legitimate in a framework formally orientated towards the common good when it is given a democratic denotation. In such a framework, an action is illegitimate when it can be said to be *arbitrary*, by showing that it is subject to the will of an individual or group which takes exclusive control of the decision. Invoking impersonal and inexorable forces makes it possible to subordinate the will of actors, as dominant position, to that of laws inscribed in the nature of things – that is to say, indivisibly, in reality and in the world – such as it is modelled by experts, which makes it possible to, as it were, reduce the world by rendering it indistinct from the reality it is consequently incorporated into. But in and through the same operation reality also sees its contours blurred. It is no longer inhabited by the will of a collective embodied in institutions and actors, who are supposed to realize that will because the reality they create and defend against what might threaten it is desirable in itself. With the loss of its ceremonial and fictional dimensions, which cannot be dissociated from the manifestation of desire, reality also eludes the threat of being denounced by critique for not being *real*, this time in the sense that it encompasses everything that can be, but merely *constructed*. Reality is no longer anything but what it is, whether one likes it or not – that is to say, what inevitably is and cannot be other than such. To be what it is, and incapable of being otherwise, is indeed the hallmark of the world. But with this essential difference, by which it is precisely distinguished from reality, that we do not know the world and cannot know it, at least as a totality. In the political metaphysics underlying this form of domination, the world is precisely what we can *now* know through the powers of *Science* – that is to say, indivisibly, the so-called natural sciences and the human or social sciences, which are increasingly closely combined with one another to the point of confusion, as we see, for example, in the case of the alignment biological sciences > cognitive sciences > micro-economics.

In such a framework, a foundation can be given to interventions whose object is test formats and qualifications without succumbing to the accusation of arbitrariness – that is to say, without these changes being open to denunciation for having as their main objective preservation of the advantages of a dominant group. One can then alter the law, which, in our societies, always represents the legitimate basis on which the procedures governing the most important tests (in particular, selection tests) rest – for example, labour law, tax law, property law, finance law – to adjust reality to the representation given of the future. But interventions of the same kind can extend little by little to most areas, like social security systems, the education system, artistic and intellectual activities and so on.

Upstream of the changes affecting test formats, we find what we have called *displacements* or shifts.[19] These shifts often follow periods when, under the impact of a strengthening of critique, important selection tests have been reordered so as to make them conform more closely to their official format – that is, make them 'just' in the meritocratic sense of the word. This is what happened in the years 1965–75, which we worked on in *The New Spirit of Capitalism*.

When the reordering of tests reaches a certain level, those whose former advantages it reduces tend to abandon the established tests to explore other profitable paths. When successful, such explorations tend to alter the state of the world, but as it were in an adjacent, tacit, not explicitly acknowledged fashion, with collateral effects – as one says of war damage – which can emerge as the unwanted results of the moves made. (Thus, to take an obvious example, the shifts of capital, required for the maximization of market opportunities and realized without any other *intention*, have the effect of producing profound changes in the texture of *the world*. And this in domains as far removed from financial logics as kinship relations, relations between the genders, forms of sociability, models of education, etc. and, more generally, with respect to the whole set of mediations that intervene in the form of objective constraints, and, as a consequence, in the orientation of subjectivities.)

These shifts tend to devalue existing tests and render them obsolete. The latter, increasingly abandoned by those who benefit, as a result of their position and past experience, from an advantage in information, nevertheless long remain sought after by those whose information is dependent on a previous state of the system of tests. This often involves newcomers (members of the popular classes in search of social mobility through schooling, foreigners, women who have newly entered the labour market, etc.) – something that is bound to create effects of *disappointment* among them in Albert Hirschman's sense,[20] when they *realize* that the investments they have made to present themselves at the tests and prove their value in them will not be reciprocated.

Downstream now of the change in test formats and modes of qualification, other processes intervene that have the effect of acting on the construction of reality. What is put to the test tends to adjust to the new test formats established to sort out what is relevant from what is not, what is recognized as possessing a value from what is adjudged uninteresting and worthless.

It would take too long to go into the details here of the multiple interventions that remodel reality by basing themselves on a change in test formats. These continuous processes are currently the subject of increasingly close attention, as indicated by recent works devoted to them. These works – for example, those of Michel Callon[21] – take as their subject processes that are increasingly labelled the *perfor-mativity of the social*.[22] This optic has been particularly developed in economics, with a view to scaling down the distinction between *economy* (the economic life of societies) and *economics* (economic science), by demonstrating the dependency of the former on the latter. But it is beginning to penetrate sociology, without (in my view) as yet having had its full impact, which should lead to a profound redefinition of a discipline still often haunted by the positivist distinction between the subject of knowledge (social science) and the object of this knowledge (society).

Especially relevant for sociology are the performative effects produced by *benchmarking* – studied notably by Alain Desrosières – the development of which in the last twenty years has marked a profound inflection of the uses of statistics by public or private operators. To be brief, by benchmarking is to be understood the construction and publication of rankings that make it possible to establish a hierarchy among organizations (firms, educational institutions, public administration, etc.) in accordance with a norm that is usually defined as efficiency. These rankings are constructed on the basis of statistical indicators whose determination is often the fruit of committees that bring actors from different spheres together – for example, senior civil servants, local actors, consultants seconded by management committees and so on.[23] The hierarchical position obtained in these rankings determines access to advantages that are very various in kind (allocations in the case of public administration, tax advantages, ease of access to markets, etc.). The very existence of these rankings produces an effect of reflexive feedback, in accordance with a logic that approximates to the self-fulfilling prophecy. The shrewdest organizational actors, those best endowed with the means required rapidly to alter their contours by taking advantage of their environment (e.g. in the case of firms, by outsourcing part of their productive apparatus), strive to maximize the recognized indicators in order to improve their rankings. The contours of reality are gradually transformed.[24]

Once modes of qualification and test formats have been recognized and established, consolidated by definitions, regulations and procedures – often stored, in Western democracies, in the form of what is called law – it becomes possible for actors in a position of power locally to base themselves on these systems to alter reality in its most ordinary and quotidian dimensions.[25]

We can find many examples of this kind in the changes that affected the world of labour in France during the 1980s. We might take the example of the substitution in these years of the term *operator* for that of *worker*, which came with a change in posts and especially in definitions formalizing the properties of those who were to be hired to fill them or, on the contrary, excluded (with a stress on communications skills), and therefore of the test formats these workers were subjected to. The new tests could then be invoked, in a multitude of local and invariably unique everyday situations, to profoundly alter the lot of people regarded as presenting particular (sometimes 'hard') cases to be resolved. But the accumulation of these particular cases has, we may be sure, had the effect of profoundly altering the reality of the world of work and hence social reality in its entirety.

A particularly pronounced feature of this *mode of governance* must be emphasized: the *instrumental*, strictly *managerial* character of the interventions and their justifications. The measures adopted have their principle of necessity in respect for a framework, most often accounting or jurisdictional in kind, without requiring any large-scale deployment of ideological discourses or, above all, the establishment of *truth tests* (in the sense defined above) validating the coherence of an order at a symbolic level. Truth tests, whose role is so important in the case of simple forms of domination geared to preserving some orthodoxy, become more or less obsolete. In the case of domination through change, everything is done without an apparat and *without ascription of worth*. The technical character of the measures renders their transmission to a broad public difficult, even pointless. Nothing, or virtually nothing, ensures the coherence of the whole, unless it is precisely the accounting and/or general jurisdictional framework that particular measures must be adjusted to.[26] This is what Laurent Thévenot calls 'government by norms'.[27]

Even so, these long periods when governance through change is conducted by means of a series of measures that are rather sectoral, technical and discreet (even opaque) is punctuated by *moments of crisis* which, in the regime of managerial domination, play a crucial role. Crisis is in fact the quintessential moment when the world finds itself incorporated into reality, which manifests itself as if it was endowed with an autonomous existence that no human will, especially not that of a ruling class (i.e. a dominant class), has laboriously fashioned through a seemingly incoherent series of small interventions, not one of which really seemed intended to have general consequences. Crisis, be it predominantly *economic* (in moments of hyper-inflation), *financial* (the bursting of financial bubbles) or *social* (in moments marked by strikes, riots, a significant increase in 'insecurity', etc.), is therefore the moment when the existence of an autonomous reality, in some sense *actual* – that is to say, a reality which can be characterized as *economic, financial, sociological,* by reference to the disciplines of the same name attached to the so-called 'social sciences'– is incontestably visible, in the way that (according to a positivist conception) nature presents itself to the so-called 'exact sciences'. These crises have a seemingly paradoxical effect. On the one hand, they call into question the relationship between symbolic forms and states of affairs on which the social order is based and introduce a radical uncertainty about the qualification of objects and the relationship between them – that is, about their *value*. Thus, for example, in crises of hyper-inflation the very possibility of a 'prediction' tends to 'disappear', because the 'relationship between individuals and goods' is profoundly disrupted as a result of 'the incoherence of systems of equivalence'.[28] But these moments of disorganization – which would be met in a regime of simple domination by a reaffirmation of orthodoxy, reparative rituals and the designation, exclusion or murder of scapegoats – are also those that provide the opportunity for a regime of domination through change to reassert its control.

Such crisis moments play at least four different roles, which can be organized in sequence. In the first place, they exonerate the dominant class, particularly in political regimes based on the authority of experts, by enabling it to escape a deconstructionist critique. Is not what manifests itself in the crisis reality *as such*, and hence the reverse of a *constructed* reality, a naked reality inhabited by its own forces, indifferent to the wills of those who are there to guide the rest by their 'knowledge', 'experience' and 'sense of responsibility'? Secondly, they thereby render patent and visible on the public stage, incontestably as it were, the existence of the *necessity* invoked by leaders to give their interventions firm backing. By the same token, and thirdly, these crisis moments are also an opportunity to hand leaders back the blank cheque they demand in order to act. Who is better placed than them to protect, so far as is possible, human beings from reality – the very one which, in its reified form, seems to escape and attack them? Fourthly, and finally, they vindicate leaders when the latter, by intervening – by 'taking things in hand' – reassert their ability to face up to disorder, but only by showing that they are *realistic* – that is to say, moulding their will to the objective will of the forces confronting them. In effect, it is by modestly acknowledging the power of these forces (i.e. also their own *relative* powerlessness) that they can claim to make them serve the common good (in their representation of it, this is rather like the paradoxical way the skipper steers his boat against the wind by 'riding' it), in such a way as to control and

135

exhaust the crisis by managing it. Certainly, the cures might invariably seem worse than the illness. But even so they are something like 'cures' and this is all that matters, above all for the 'pedagogical' effects they have in demonstrating to 'ordinary' actors the imperious character of the 'laws of economics' or 'society' and the competence of experts.[29]

Consequently, this is to say that in a regime of managerial domination, based on the prioritization and exploitation of change, moments of *panic, disorganization, moral disarray* and *everyone-for-themselves*, that is also of frenzied individualism – what Durkheim, in his naive conception of a social world democratically controlled by the wisdom of a republican elite, called moments of *anomie* – play an important role. They go together with seemingly calm periods, conducive to the multiplication of occasional interventions in reality or technical interventions in test formats which, accumulating (in a way that is never completely controlled), fashion reality such as it will reveal itself anew, with the character of an implacable necessity, during the next crisis.[30]

The Treatment of Hermeneutic Contradiction in a Managerial Mode of Domination

Let us summarize the preceding remarks by posing to the regime of managerial domination the questions contained in the terms of reference proposed at the beginning of this talk. In a regime of domination of this type, the systems that ensure domination are not geared to slowing down change or incorporating it in such a form that it can be denied as such. On the contrary, they are based on the argument of constant change, while arrogating to themselves the privilege of interpreting it, thereby providing themselves with the possibility of propelling it in a direction favourable to the preservation of existing asymmetries and forms of exploitation. This process is made possible because institutions are grounded in a form of authority – that of experts – which aims to situate itself at the point of non-distinction between reality and the world. The will of which institutions' spokespersons make themselves the expression then presents itself as being nothing other than the will of the world itself, in the necessarily modelled representation given of it by experts. But since these models are simultaneously instruments for action, they are capable of producing profound alterations in the texture of the world where it is most easily accessible – that is, where it finds itself in contact with reality

136

– alterations that enter into retroactive circuits with representations of what is, and this all the better in as much as these representations invariably possess a provisional character.

Those who fashion these representations or seize on them also have the power to make them real, because they possess resources, notably legal or regulatory resources, not to mention specifically policing resources, to alter the contours of reality. However, the constant alteration of the formats that frame and fashion reality no longer needs to be attributed to a will that is something other than the will of impersonal forces. The *leaders* [*responsables*] (to use the term given to the dominant today), because they are in charge of a totality whose designs are not those of anyone in particular, are no longer responsible for anything, even though they are in charge of everything. To designate this totality, which no longer has anything to do with a reality protected from the assaults of the world by the dominant, or with a world that the dominated seize hold of in order to attempt to challenge the reality in which they are oppressed, we might coin the neologism *wol&real* [*mon&réal*].

The seizure of the wol&real by the dominant instances does not leave much room for critique, at least for a political critique, since critique has been stripped by the dominant powers of the exteriority represented by the world, on which it was able to base itself to try to challenge reality. In effect, critique finds itself easily absorbed into the systems of domination, where it is reinterpreted in the forms that have been given it in the scientific and technical instances which serve as guarantor to institutions.[31] It then enters into controversies between expertise and counter-expertise, in which counter-expertise is necessarily dominated and invariably the loser, since it can only seek to attain expertise – that is, make itself admissible or simply audible – by conforming to the test forms laid down by the latter and adopting its formalism and, more generally, its ways of encoding reality.[32] The same applies to the constraints exercised by the current jurisdictions (especially, in the case of social struggles, labour law). Legal recognition of the existence of critical instances whose ways of acting are deemed responsible and legitimate (in contrast to critical instances that are excluded and dismissed as savagery, on the grounds that they operate outside legal frameworks) locks those that are authorized to express themselves into the tight mesh of existing law, whose recognition no longer allows for the expression of new injustices or the use of innovative forms of protest.

This way of controlling critique, by incorporating it, is reinforced by the fact that domination through change itself identifies with the critique of which it deprives those who would like to oppose it. But it identifies with an internal critique, constructed in the image of scientific disputes between those who are the exclusive possessors of the requisite authority, licensed by their competence, or rather their titles, to give a relevant opinion. What characterizes these 'controversies between experts' is precisely that their participants agree on the essentials and only oppose one another on marginal issues. No doubt this is what is meant when these debates are admiringly described as 'specialist'.

A mode of domination of this kind doubtless lends itself better than any other to the work of masking hermeneutic contradiction. Institutions resign themselves to being modest and forget their pretentions. As has already been suggested, truth tests, when they are maintained, are viewed with the rather nostalgic self-importance accorded to obsolete forms of worth. Institutions offload the power to say what is, essentially to science and technology, which play the role imparted to foundations. They are merely its interpreters. The principle of sovereignty they claim to represent is nothing other than the wol&real itself, which tends to render the distinction between the legislative and the executive obsolete. The laws or, most often, decrees promulgated by the government are presented as simple formalizations in legal language of the social or economic laws that the government claims to conform to, and hence as the manifestation of their impersonal will. As for the spokespersons, who justify themselves predominantly by their effectiveness, their preferred way of making the power they are invested manifest consists less in invoking their will, even in the democratic sense where it would simply be the expression of a general will of which they are the mere depositories, than in enumerating the constraints they must deal with and which compel them to act as they do, without any possible alternative. This is how, in their case, the *speaking the truth* we referred to above manifests itself. But it is true that they then expose themselves to the suspicion of not acting at all.

Confronted with a regime of this type, critique, when not simply disarmed, finds itself profoundly altered. The way in which it exploits hermeneutic contradiction will take a new direction. Thus, for example, in a politico-semantic regime where the institutions that say the whatness of what is are contained in architectures based on forms of representation of the political body (or the 'people'), contradiction will frequently manifest itself in the form of suspicion of representatives (this is what might be called the *Rousseauean* form of hermeneutic contradiction). By contrast, in a politico-semantic regime founded, as is increasingly the case in Western capitalist democracies, on *expertise* (whether invoking the so-called exact sciences, economic science or other social sciences), contradiction will manifest itself in the form of an antagonism between *realism* and *constructivism*. The difficulty will then revolve around whether the expert shows things 'as they are', with a transparency that excludes any mediation and confers an implacable necessity on the 'facts', or filters them through a construction 'of his own invention' of an 'arbitrary' character, such that they could just as well be presented differently. We can thus appreciate how this opposition, which was predominantly epistemological originally, has today become one of the main resources committed in political conflicts – as we have seen, for example, in recent conflicts over bio-political issues such as homosexuality or the status of the foetus – but also in a number of conflicts over ecological or economic issues.

This unease is reinforced by an intuition of the new, specifically political role attributed to the ventures in describing reality which experts rely on in a mode of domination that resorts to benchmarking. It is clear in the case of official statistics studied by Alain Desrosières. In their classical embodiment, which prevailed until roughly the 1980s, statisticians, shut up in their institutes, were supposed – at least ideally – to keep the maximum distance from the reality they were charged with describing, in accordance with a positivist conception of science based on a radical separation between subject and object of knowledge. They made it a point of honour to represent this reality, by translating it into the language of mathematics, as 'objectively' as possible, such as it was supposed to be in itself, independently of the observer, without even taking any account of the obvious fact that publication of their work was liable to alter it. It is precisely on an inversion of this position that the use of statistics by benchmarking is based. The rankings, constructed on the basis of codified statistical indicators and aiming to translate all qualitative differences into quantitative differences capable, by this token, of yielding comparisons, constitute forms of description whose explicit, admitted objective is to prompt actors to change their behaviour in such a way as to increase their hierarchical position in the rankings, in accordance with a logic which is that of maximizing the indicator. Description, in as much as it has become indivisible from an appraisal of what is described by instances possessing scarce resources whose distribution they control, then explicitly supposes the existence of circuits of feedback between subject and object of knowledge, and employs them strategically to enhance the effectiveness of measures designed to alter the contours of reality.

139

These techniques, derived from management, were first used in the administration of large private firms, with a view to increasing the efficiency of actors, enhancing their productivity and maximizing profit, without encountering much resistance, before being appropriated by state or supra-national bodies. Such a shift has had the effect of increasing unease about the ability of institutions to say the whatness of what is from an overarching point of view. As Lorraine Daston has shown, in Europe recognition of this capacity has been linked, at least since the eighteenth century, to the interchange between three denotations – one juridical, another political and the third scientific – of the term *objectivity*.[33] The notion of objectivity thus combined the idea of the *impartiality* of magistrates, that of the *detachment* associated with the overarching position occupied by government bodies, and finally that of a *separation* between subject and object of knowledge, such as to enable the observer to make, in a laboratory context, judgements that were stable in time and reproducible by others in the same experimental context. The use by institutions whose legitimacy derives from their attachment to the state of descriptive techniques aiming to alter the object described – that is to say, in the event, the behaviour of citizens – tends to call into question the impartiality and detachment attributed to state institutions, if only because they lay claim to them, reducing them to the rank of instruments of *manipulation*,[34] with no other objective than that of legitimating the viewpoint of some people so as to enable them to maximize their particular interests.

However, there remains in Western capitalist democracies, characterized by a mode of domination of the kind whose contours have just been sketched, a tension that is difficult to reduce. It stems from the fact that these regimes cannot completely liquidate the political forms inherited from the past – be they of liberal inspiration or (as is the case in France) also marked by the Jacobin interpretation of Rousseauism – that sustain the nation-state. The mode of domination we have described was forged in the laboratory of management, which accounts for its close links with the development of capitalism. It was initially through its application in the framework of governing the firm that it was gradually refined – if only in as much as it was the object of intense criticism there which, as it were, put it to the test – before being implanted in the state, which was henceforth regarded, like the firm, as an organization aiming to manage a set of resources in such a way as to extract a profit from them under the pressure of competition with other organizations of the same kind. This shift, which was favoured by the development of a new spirit of capitalism to respond to the protest movements of the 1960s and 1970s, and to restore the productivity of capital and especially shareholders' profits, followed a period in which, after the breakdown of 1930–45, the centralized, welfarist and military state had by contrast, at least in certain respects, become the model for the large firm integrated into more or less 'social' aims (what we called the 'second spirit of capitalism').[35]

But this reversal – from the state as model for the firm to the firm as model for the state – raises the issue of the articulation between these two possible instruments of domination, which have to confront different constraints. The firm, whose raison d'être in the framework of capitalism is to generate profits under the pressure of competition, claims, correctly according to its own logic, the freedom to control as it sees fit the main parameters on which profit determination depends, in a certain accounting framework, and in particular its input and output not only in commodities but also (or especially) workers. Consequently, wage-workers are not, and cannot be, 'citizens of the firm', which must be able to hire and fire them in line with its interests. Similarly, the firm is a form of organization which, not being justified by anything other than profit-creation, can emancipate itself from territorial constraints – as we see in the case of outsourcing of production sites – and from the requirement of continuing to exist. A firm is not created for all time. When profits fall or collapse, it must close to make room for other, more productive organizations.

Conversely, the state, while it disregards profit, is primarily subject to constraints of territoriality and duration. It is supposed to ensure the security of a population distributed over a territory, which has meant that, under the pressure of social struggles, it has been led to multiply forms of caring for this population of citizens but also, indivisibly, of increasing the level of state control and constraint to which it is subject.[36] But just as salaried workers are not citizens, citizens cannot easily be reduced to the condition of salaried workers of the nation-state. It is in fact only in particular historical situations that the nation-state can control the entry and exit of citizens, in accordance with the interests of the dominant classes, in the way that firms control the entry and exit of personnel: that is to say, exclude a surplus population by encouraging its emigration – as was the case in Europe from 1880–1914, with emigration to America, especially the United States (around thirty million people), and also to the colonies – or, conversely, import from poor countries or colonies a population that is undemanding as regards work conditions and wages – as was the case in Western Europe, notably from 1950–70. But in a global conjuncture marked by a shortage of territories open to colonization,[37] and by a significant increase in the number of people ready to emigrate on account of the growing differential between rich countries and poor, the problems posed by the control of entry and exit become tricky. And this is particularly the case when the nation-state itself is considered, in its materiality, as a firm to be managed by those in charge of it. The need to control entry in line with the 'needs of the economy' assumes an obsessive form and arms itself with physical violence against foreigners (and also those who, as is said, 'derive from immigration' but are nevertheless supposed to be 'citizens like the others'). As for the outgoing – that is to say, those whom capitalist firms intend to divest themselves of because they are reckoned insufficiently productive – re-baptized the 'excluded', they pose the enterprise-state with an even more difficult issue to resolve, for the simple reason that they stay put and, as a result, remain visible in the public arena, where they are even capable of making their protest heard or expressing their discontent at the ballot box. Just think what would become of a firm whose personnel, having been shown the front door, nevertheless had the possibility and even the right to continue to go about their business on the premises where they once had a job.

This historical situation runs through institutions, whose two possible foundations – on the one hand, expertise, especially of an economic kind, associated with the conception of the state as a firm; on the other, election, maintained to try to save what remains of the state's anchorage in a nation, that is, a totality constituted by a population of citizens inscribed in a territory – apply themselves to relativizing one another. This relativization is the form hermeneutic contradiction then tends to take. The will of the bodiless being of the institution, still glorified because it is supposed to emanate from the elective power entrusted to the sovereign people, is in fact carried out by corporeal beings, who find it difficult to invest themselves with the same glory, in as much as their authority has its principle in a practice – that of expertise – which is supposed to be submitted to the internalized modality of critique represented by the 'controversy of experts'. Moreover, it is in order to try to fend off such a situation that experts in social science, particularly sociologists or political scientists – well-intentioned and always inventive – undertake to imagine new, quasi-institutional systems capable of locking popular power and expert power into the same body – for example, 'hybrid forums'[38] or 'people's juries'.[39]

The semantic function performed by the institution, particularly when it fixes the terms of the law, is thus constantly concealed by the pragmatic modulations of governmental practices. But the proliferation of laws that are not applied (most often not only because they are practically inapplicable, but simply because they do not aim at being applied) then goes hand-in-hand with a proliferation of decrees or technical directives which, invariably defined in ad hoc fashion for specific, fragmented objectives, make it possible to defend policing measures whose arbitrary character paves the way for denunciation, since it is easy to show either that they are based on a network of contradictory laws, depending on the circumstances of application, or even that they have no other justification than the effectiveness, defined in strictly numerical terms, they lay claim to. Institutional violence and, especially, state violence thus find themselves on the verge of being unmasked.

The Possibility of a Dominant Class?

One of the characteristics of a managerial mode of domination is that it is based on off-shore networks and complex systems, which are much less dependent on local inscriptions than the instruments of simple domination, and whose activity can consequently be carried out just as well, or even better, from a distance. This disposition of the systems of domination can easily create the illusion of a power that has become literally systemic, in the sense that it no longer belongs to anyone and is entirely distributed among assemblages of human beings and machines control of which partially eludes each of the actors taken separately – including those of them who occupy official positions in the concretions which, rightly or wrongly, continue to be represented by the term institutions.

However, this conception of a power that has become completely, or almost completely, impersonal and mechanical tends to empty the idea of domination of much of its substance. That idea, while at least since Marx stressing structures rather than individuals (as indicated by the famous warning that features in the preface to *Capital*),[40] has nevertheless always been associated with the identification of a dominant group or class. For the idea of domination to make sense, it must be possible to show that there exists a factor of convergence between actors dispersed in space, performing different activities, occupying very different positions as regards the institutional authorities, equipped with unequal power when assessed in terms of property and capital, but who nevertheless contribute through their action to the pursuit of domination.

To make the idea of dominant class meaningful, it is therefore necessary to invoke the existence of specific links between the actors who, in different ways and to various degrees, ensure the maintenance of the established order (and benefit from it, albeit unequally) – and this without necessarily assuming the existence of explicit cooperation between them, still less a complicity realized in secret, in the manner of a conspiracy. This requirement is certainly more difficult to satisfy in contemporary democratic-capitalist societies than in societies subject to classic forms of oppression, in so far as the importance attributed to expertise and, more generally, the functioning of a managerial mode of domination, operating technically on systems, tend to distribute power between very different groups of actors, with a low level of explicit coordination. Moreover, that is why critique, when it seeks to demonstrate the systematic character of the measures adopted, is often accused of succumbing to 'conspiracy theory'. Is it not malice or sheer madness to put in the same basket – that of the dominant class – alongside the 'super-rich', 'stars', the 'powerful' and 'oligarchs', statesmen and businessmen whose province is 'global', more ordinary (and sometimes more modest) characters such as, for example, scientists, economists and social science researchers who feed centres of calculation and, in the 'reports' they publish, present descriptions of reality and its tendential changes; journalists who fill the media with news items to which these reports have drawn their attention; or again, jurists, but also management specialists, who reflect on how to alter tests as a result; and elected representatives who pass the laws (that is their duty); not to mention mere local actors, who are still more banal and innocent – the bosses of medium-sized firms, administrative heads, teachers and so on, who ensure (someone has to do it!), in situations that are always local and always unique, the adjustment of reality to the new tests.

In the first instance, ownership of the means of production and profit have served as the main criterion for bringing out the contours of the dominant class. However, in the critical sociology of the 1960s and 1970s, elaborated at the end of an era – that of the capitalism of managing directors and cadres and, in France, that of large public enterprises – when the relationship to property, while retaining great importance, nevertheless seemed less decisive, the search for more sophisticated ways of characterizing *the* dominant class or classes took priority. Thus, in the work of Pierre Bourdieu – to which reference was made in the second talk – stress was laid both on the diversity of the dominant positions ('the division of labour of domination') and on a convergence between fractions ensured by affinities

144

between *habitus* and a shared culture transmitted by schooling, in the manner of what that author often calls 'an orchestration without a conductor'. Now, these two explanatory principles – property and *habitus* – today seem inadequate to account for the links capable of ensuring the cohesion of an ensemble that is disparate and yet sufficiently coordinated to compose something like a dominant class. On the one hand, the kind of actors mentioned above cannot directly be the owners of the means of production or the main beneficiaries of profit (even if at least a fraction of them acquires a sizeable share of it through the intermediary of financial instruments, such as stock options, or fiscal instruments). On the other hand, those who today make up the globalized elites (in which it is definitely necessary also to include intellectuals often identified by the term 'global thinkers') have, in the course of their childhood and adolescence, been formed in different familial and educational cultures, so that it is less obvious than in the past to attribute the affinities that ensure their objective convergence to a shared *habitus*. These new elites, who operate at the four ends of the universe, do indeed communicate in a shared language, but the latter is no longer mainly based on schemas derived from classical culture – literary or scientific – such as were transmitted, for example, in educational establishments run by Jesuits. Instead, it is based on a new international culture that is rooted in economics and, above all, in the disciplines of management, transmitted in speech and in writing, but above all incorporated into computer, jurisdictional and accounting formats.

Even so, can we identify a *form of solidarity* capable of creating a kind of *collusion* between actors whose activity, always fragmented and technically orientated, nevertheless has general effects on the world (through the intermediary of operations on financial markets); actors whose interventions instead are applied to reality – who often present themselves as 'local actors', motivated by what they call their 'pragmatism'; and, finally, actors whose interventions are directed towards test formats and modes of qualification – actors who, prioritizing their reflexivity, define themselves as 'experts', 'intellectuals' or 'jurists'?

In accordance with the framework outlined above, I shall stress the position occupied, on the one hand, with respect to *action* and the *possibilities of action* and, on the other, with respect to the *conventions*, *procedures* and *rules* that define test formats and modes of qualification and valorization. I shall propose the idea that the dominant class brings together *leaders* – that is to say, those who, firstly, can perform a wide range of actions conducive to altering not only

145

their own life, but also the life of a more or less large number of other people and who, secondly, have acquired a particular experience of the relationship between acting on reality and acting on test formats.

The fact of possessing great capacity for action not only on the world, but also on the construction of reality and the determination of test formats, has the effect of leading them to adopt a very particular position with respect to *rules*. What members of a dominant class implicitly share, in the form of a common knowledge that they cannot avow to others – which they can scarcely avow to themselves – is, on the one hand, that it is indispensable that there should be rules – law, procedures, norms, standards, regulations and so forth; and, on the other, that *one can do nothing really profitable* (translated into their language: 'really useful'), that one simply cannot *act*, in an *uncertain* world, if one follows these rules. For these leaders, the fact that their actions are geared to the satisfaction of very general objectives which are often rather vague and mutable is the reason why their behaviour cannot be strictly defined by rules. The observance of rules therefore presents itself as a handicap for them, in as much as the context they act in is itself uncertain and constantly changing. Conversely, they are inclined to think that rules are necessary and sufficient to constrain and order the actions of underlings and, in particular, those who are dependent on them, whose limited operations contribute to the achievement of the (great) designs whereby they seek to maintain the content of reality and/or alter it.[41] While endlessly reminding people that the rules 'are the same for everyone', they thus feel justified in thinking that these rule do not in fact have anything absolute about them and are at best, contrary to what mere underlings are supposed to believe, simply *conventions* whose main virtue is that they coordinate the requisite actions without violence. Moreover, it is likely that learning a 'relativist' relationship to the rules is facilitated today by the experience of members of the dominant class, whose formation and professional activity have, on account of their international character, had the effect of leading them to pursue their objectives by exploiting variegated systems of often contradictory rules.[42]

We might perhaps summarize this leaders' knowledge by reusing the formula previously developed in the context of psychoanalysis by Octave Mannoni: '*I know very well, but even so. . .*'.[43] 'I know very well' that rules are necessary, 'but even so' I also know that the one who follows the rules, who does it 'stupidly', who follows them 'to the letter', the one who takes them *literally*, who refuses to interpret them, to adapt them to the situation and even, if necessary, to ignore them, 'well, he gets nowhere!'; 'he can no longer act'. But we should avoid assimilating this knowledge to a form of nihilism, still less to a critique of rules. Rules are regarded as absolutely *necessary*. But at the same time they have to be bent, bypassed, changed in order to be able to be effective (to have a 'grip on reality'); and that too is regarded as absolutely *necessary*.

What leaders also know is that this kind of wisdom cannot be made public, or shared with those who *are not leaders* (and thus taken to be irresponsible), because if it was everyone would feel entitled to bend the rules – and 'then where would we be? Anarchy!' Those who have been used to obeying the rules would confuse this wisdom with utter nihilism or, abandoning themselves to their craziest tendencies, give free rein to their desires, even their drives. And they would then set about *deconstructing* the rules, portraying them as *arbitrary*, as open to not being what they are, without possessing the judgement that consists in knowing that they are there – indispensable, eternal, sacrosanct, inviolable and yet destined to be always got round, interpreted, forgotten and altered, but never disavowed! That they are never as sacrosanct as when it is readily conceded that they are indeed man-made and hence are reality itself. To get round the rules or break them, without feeling that you have betrayed them, you have to believe, at least implicitly, that you embody, in your very person, the *spirit* of the rule. To belong to the dominant class is first of all to be convinced that you can break the *letter* of the rule without betraying its *spirit*. But this kind of belief only occurs to those who think they are able to embody the rule, for the very good reason that they make it.

We can describe this split relationship to the rules in the language of inauthenticity and bad faith; and, for at least a century and a half, the critique of bourgeois hypocrisy has not forgone it. However, it must be observed that the change in modes of governance has rendered this kind of moral indignation more or less obsolete. The fragmented, technical character of interventions in reality today encourages what might, to remove it from the orbit of moral judgement, be called a kind of *practical bad faith*. The opacity of the relationship everyone has to their own action is presented as the internal echo of the opacity surrounding interventions in that – external – of reality. Also, when, unfortunately, the effects of this vague relationship to the rules result in a disaster that is difficult to conceal and a *scandal* erupts, those caught out and required to justify themselves *do not feign* surprise and contrition; they are genuinely surprised and contrite. It is in utter good faith that they declare themselves both responsible and innocent ('responsible but not guilty', according to a now famous formula used by a leader accused in the so-called 'contaminated blood' affair).[44] This knowledge certainly assumes a heightened form in the context of contemporary capitalism, drawn by its own logic always to seek new differentials and, in particular, information differentials to exploit, in such a way as to circumvent even procedures aiming to regulate competition, which is however the first principle of the economic liberalism that capitalism claims to represent. Nothing is more illuminating in this regard than research on the dilemmas confronted by 'ethicists' in an investment bank, who are supposed to perform the impossible task of increasing the level of transparency, but without harming the profit rate – and this in a world where profits in large part derive from asymmetries of information.[45]

The extension of this manipulation of the rules, which has brought it from the wheeling-and-dealing periphery to the heart of institutions that pose as the most legitimate, has been facilitated by the establishment of the new relations between capitalism and the state we referred to a moment ago. In a form of state managed like a firm and penetrated by management logic, how could a leader believe in the inviolability of rules when the institutions that are supposed to guarantee them never stop bypassing or altering them to maximize political and economic asymmetries?

More generally, the situation of these leaders can be characterized today by the possibility open to them of acting simultaneously in two kinds of different arena: on the one hand, in private *organizations* or public *administration*, where they occupy official leadership positions; on the other, in financial, industrial or intellectual *networks* on which the operation of the new forms of capitalism is largely based today – networks that are largely autonomous of organizations. This dual affiliation is a source of tension. The statutory leadership of established organizations requires a certain stability and goes hand-in-hand with attachments and impediments that restrict leaders' flexibility. Conversely, the promotion of a self (it too managed as if it was a firm, 'the self as enterprise') through shifts in the networks depends upon mobility and nimbleness. The success of the actors in a dominant position is largely a function of their ability to reconcile these opposite kinds of constraint. The latter intervene in their turn in the relationship to the rules. Whereas in their official status as directors leaders are supposed to observe the laws and regulations imposed on them 'like everyone else', in their activity as network creators they are led to gamble with a multiplicity of different, and invariably irreconcilable, rules, used strategically to extend fields of intervention and maximize potential advantages.

The common knowledge of *realism* forms one of the bases of the collusion between members of the dominant class, such as it manifests itself in particular when one of them, caught in the act, is confronted with critique. Certainly, he bent the rules and, in so doing, went (it has to be said) 'a bit too far'. He went at it 'a bit hard'. But before casting a stone at him, and doing it publicly in alliance with those who are attacking him, especially when the latter are mere underlings incapable of understanding the burden shouldered by leaders, should we not examine if we have not ourselves, on other occasions, also played a little fast and loose with the rules – out of necessity, of course! But how can this be brought home to those who know no other necessity than that of the rules imposed on them, as it were from without, and in whom the ability to act on the world is simply not recognized?

— 6 —

EMANCIPATION IN THE PRAGMATIC SENSE

To conclude, I shall ask what the *pragmatic sociology of critique*, as it has been called, might be able to contribute to a social critique of domination, and therewith to the search for roads leading to *emancipation*. It cannot involve anything other than a reinforcement of *the role of critique*. By this is to be understood two things: on the one hand, an increase in the *strength* of those who are its bearers and, on the other, the consolidation of its *power* – that is to say, its capacity to engage with reality in order to alter its contours. From the standpoint of sociology, the first objective is interdependent with analyses of the way in which the collectives that enter into asymmetric relations, comprising degrees (variable depending on the historical situation and context) of exploitation, are constructed. Sketched in the previous talk in connection with the dominant, an analysis of this type should be pursued as regards the dominated. While obviously not ignoring the fact that not all relations of domination (which can involve genders, ethnic groups, etc.) can be reduced to the space of social classes, it is nevertheless by contributing to the resumption of a sociology of social classes – currently being redeployed after an eclipse lasting thirty years – that the framework presented in this work might prove useful. The second objective – an enhancement of the powers of critique – to which we shall turn shortly, might perhaps benefit from the way in which an attempt has been made to fuse in the same analytical framework, via hermeneutic contradiction, the issue of institutions and the issue of critique.

150

Social Classes and Action

A study of social classes from the perspective of domination could be based both on analysis of the relationship to the rules (sketched in the previous talk) and on consideration of capacities for action. In this respect, we could distinguish, firstly, actors who possess a wide range of capacities for action not only on their own life, but also on the life of a more or less significant number of other people; secondly, actors who possess relative control over actions that concern their own life, but who have few means for influencing that of others; and thirdly, and finally, actors who have control over neither their own life nor that of others.

From the perspective of their subjection to rules, the dominant and the dominated are in a symmetrical and converse position: the former make them but are fairly free to extricate themselves from them; the latter receive them imposed from without, but have to conform to them. To clarify this difference, we might adopt the contrast posited by Durkheim between 'technical rules' and 'moral rules'.[1] The first (says Durkheim) posit constraints that 'result mechanically from the act of violation'; the relationship between rule and sanction is 'analytical'. In the case of the second, 'there is complete heterogeneity between the act and its consequence', such that 'the consequences are attached to the act by a synthetic link'. Whereas leaders can use rules as if they were *technical rules* – that is, instrumentally – the same rules are imposed on the subordinate in the manner of a *moral rule* – that is, as if they were in some sense valid in themselves. The sanction then accompanies the violation of the rule, interpreted as a transgression whatever its effects, and not the failures to which the fact of not having followed it (or, on the contrary, having followed it) might have led.

Does this mean that leaders have no morality? Certainly not, but they have a 'higher' morality. Claiming to embody the totality (and thereby 'comprehend the unworthy people', in the dual sense – developed in *On Justification* – of being able to understand them and include them), the 'great ones' believe that they can be assessed only in the light of the ultimate success or failure of their enterprises. They therefore lay claim to a time-scale which can far exceed that of human existence ('history will judge'). As we know, the characterization 'ultimate' can always lead to controversies. The point at which the balance-sheet is closed can be brought forward or pushed into a distant future, in accordance with the interests of the relevant parties, since putting an *end* to a process assumes a labour of demarcation of the kind carried out by institutions (it is clear, e.g. in the case of clashes between historians over issues of 'periodization'). For leaders, mastery of time is an issue of major importance.

A leader's main objective is therefore to position himself in a temporal horizon defined in such a way that reality ultimately vindicates her, even if, measured by current tests, her actions seem doomed to failure. This is what is called 'surviving' or, in the language of elites, 'bouncing back' (after a period 'in the wilderness'). In this sense, the (dominant) leader is comparable to Elias Canetti's 'survivor'.[2] Above all, he wants to be there when the others, his loyal friends as well as his competitors and enemies, have succumbed – something that assures him that he is indeed the greatest: 'the one who manages to survive is a *hero*. He is stronger. He possesses more life. The higher powers are favourable to him.'[3] The leader who lasts, who survives, knows it is so only by seeing the dead pile up around him. For him, survival is the index – the sole index – of his victory. Even in the case of an apparent failure (but one can always hope to transform a failure into victory by deferring the moment of the final assessment), he will be able to pride himself on the fact that he knew how to confront *decisions* without worrying unduly about justifying them. Decisions are the leader's prerogative and his pride and joy. But they are merely the secondary effect of the capacity for action he is equipped with, and which itself depends on control of a wide range of resources. Contrary to what Elias Canetti seems to suggest at the end of his book, the quest for survival is no less associated with domination and violence when it is transferred from the physical body to the *name*. And this especially, no doubt, in the era of 'cognitive capitalism',[4] which shifts much of the work of valorizing capital onto the processing of immaterial and symbolic goods. In fact, it is increasingly often on the leader's *name* that not only the recognition secured by holding positions of power in organizations, but also the results of processes of valorization achieved through a rapid shift in networks, converge.

It is therefore, in the first instance, from having faced risks at the moment of decision and circumventing the rules that the leader (dominant) derives a personal pride, which forms the basis of his contempt for the dominated. Are they not, in this regard, those who 'have taken no risks' and remained shielded from danger because they have simply obeyed – in other words, those who, by acting in accordance with the rules, have done nothing but precisely what the leader expected of them? We can therefore say, in this respect, that the class of leaders – the dominant class – is the class of those who are ready for anything in order to survive, and who have the maximum chances of ending up doing so because they possess the most extensive range of resources for action. The most important of these, and the most useful to their survival, are none other than the dominated themselves, over whom the dominant ensure their own power by limiting the resources for action at their disposal. But also the class of those who think that this survival is *necessary*, because it realizes reality and, in so doing, brings temporary survival (at best, something to eat, a habitation, etc.) to the mass of those who, subject to the test of reality – that is, subjugated to their power – are destined to disappear, at least from collective memory.

Conversely, the dominated (whose most extreme example is the slave) is, at least tendentially, *without a name*. Even if, during his lifetime and in limited arenas among those close to him, a sequence of phonemes serves to designate him, this sequence is insufficient to compose a name. It can only have a practical existence (as in the case of the sobriquet). But, even when stabilized by the law, this simple designation is destined to be erased with the physical disappearance of the one who was its bearer. The temporal horizon of the dominated is limited to the time of their physical existence – itself always statistically shorter than that of the dominant[5] – and, when their condition improves, to the hopes they can place in their offspring. It is precisely because they are not destined to be survivors, even if they survive the struggles of their lives, that the dominated have but one recourse for enduring: to look to *affiliation* – that is, *solidarity* (of class, gender, colour, ethnicity, etc.) – for the requisite strength to achieve a worth which, taken separately, they cannot even claim, let alone attain.

It should not be deduced from this outline analysis that those whom one can, in order to distinguish them from the dominant in the sense given the term here, call the dominated – because they have few resources for acting on their own life, and still fewer on that of others, because they are subjected to tests without being able to alter the format – or (if you wish) the *non-leaders* [*irresponsables*], adhere to the rules imposed on them and accept them as valid currency. But stripped of the possibility of formatting them and taking advantage of them – that is to say, kept at a distance from economic power and political action – practically speaking, they have only two means for making the burden of the rules bearable. On the one hand, there is relativist scepticism (stored in the form of sayings like 'don't carry out the order before it's been countermanded'). It is often accompanied by a kind of splitting, with a division between situations of public representation (notably at work), where the rules are ostensibly respected, and hidden situations of close-knit intimacy, where, in joy, they are broken (practices of 'poaching' once highlighted by Michel de Certeau).[6] On the other hand (and this is what might characterize intermediate social positions), there is a mixture of scepticism and invariably disappointed faith. Like the shaman described by Claude Lévi-Strauss,[7] those who belong to intermediate categories, living close to highly placed leaders (assistants, secretaries, accountants, teachers, trainers, etc. – and it is to be noted that we are often dealing with female professions), have experienced at first hand the relationship, scandalous in their eyes, which the dominant have with the order of rules. But they nonetheless continue to think that somewhere honest leaders must exist – that is to say, leaders conforming to the ideals they themselves would like to be able to adhere to, despite everything. They continue to believe in the possibility of a society where rules, qualifications and formats, applied literally – *to the letter* – would stand solid behind a reality that is all of one piece. But it is not difficult to recognize in this meritocratic and, more generally, moralistic ideal a society which can be deemed truly 'authentic' only to the extent that it is clearly fundamentalist.[8]

Hermeneutic Contradiction and Emancipation

The critical project of a reduction in the privileges the dominant classes draw from their relationship with the rules, and that of a commitment to the emancipation of the dominated classes, hitherto compelled to obey, assumes a radical change in the political relationship to hermeneutic contradiction, so that it can be made explicit in forms equally distributed between all members of the collective.

A second reflexive look at hermeneutic contradiction would lead neither to a rejection of critique in the name of a promotion – currently in vogue, even on the left – of (putative) sources of authority (the 'Law of the Father', the impartial state, law, absolutized Science, etc.), which can only lead to an increase in the risk of reinforcing the symbolic violence exercised by institutions; nor, conversely, to renouncing the very idea of institutions – which would boil down to depriving ourselves of the positive functions they assume. One thinks, in particular, of the task of guaranteeing people a minimal semantic security, such as to enable their re-identification whatever the situation they find themselves cast into – something that helps to remove them, to a very variable extent, from the brutality of contextual forms of domination, whose nadir is complete dehumanization. This reflexive orientation would make it possible to generalize familiarity with this contradiction, which everyone would learn to look in the face, not so much to transcend it as to get used to living alongside it – that is, together – in fragility.[9]

It is difficult to assess all the effects of such a change, but it might be thought that it would open up to people the possibility of having some purchase on the collectives of which they are component parts. And this without renouncing conflicts in the name of an illusory consensus (which is invariably simply a cover for domination), but also without stopping at the moment, however necessary it is, of conflict, in as much as agreement could not be reached on anything other than the *provisional* and *revisable* character of modes of qualification, test formats and definitions of reality. Such a move, whose utopian character can indeed be stressed when judged in the light of the current political situation, would rest on a radical transformation of the relationship between instances of confirmation and critical instances. Pre-eminence would be given to the latter, which, by virtue of the very fact that they are not and cannot be institutionalized, always suffer from a deficit in strength compared with the former. In a political figure of this kind, social reality would therefore be led to recognize itself for what it is – that is to say, in its constitutive fragility and incompletion – and to get a grip on uncertainty and the disparate, to put them in the pantheon of its 'values', rather than always claiming to reduce them in the name of order and coherence. The differential between the world and reality would not thereby be abolished. But the possibility of something, wrested by critique from the opacity of the world, being inscribed in the fabric of reality, thus helping to transform it, would be less difficult to attain.

A move of this kind, proceeding in the direction of a subjection of the powers of domination, would first of all conduce to more clearly identifying and challenging processes of exploitation and, in particular, those rooted in a very unequal distribution of *property*. And this by relativizing a mode of attachment of things to people based on law, of which only those who are deprived of it believe in the literal, stable and unequivocal character,[10] established once and for all, whereas those who benefit from it know full well that it is unstable, partial and sometime quasi-random. We see it, for example, in the case of financial operations based on debt, of which a percentage difficult to assess is characterized as 'sub-prime' (in the sense not only that the creditors are deemed insolvent, but also that there is uncertainty about the portfolios these securities are in), without this in any way preventing extraction of a profit. The same could be said of the determination of the value of goods and, in particular, firms, which largely depend on the accounting conventions employed, in particular, to make a division between assets and liabilities.

This relaxation of property links, and of the values attached to goods, would be extended to people, so as to defer judgements about the qualities of actors or their level of 'excellence' for as long as possible and make them as reversible as possible . In particular, this would make it possible to say the opposite of the educational or bureaucratic appraisals that play such a big role in maintaining social hierarchies. Not to mention the effects this change could have in the direction of diminishing 'individualism' – a trend that is assumed to be implacable by sociologists and politicians who rush to deplore it, without always realizing that it is largely the result of the development of neoliberal practices of assessment which constantly place actors in competition with one another. It is reasonable to believe that a relaxation of property links and an attenuation of titles of hierarchical affiliation would have the effect of strengthening egalitarian tendencies and hence solidarities.

It remains the case that any move in this direction assumes as a precondition a better distribution of capacities for action – that is to say, to be clear, political capacities, whose use makes it possible to transform reality by opening it onto the world. Currently, it is the closure of reality on itself that discourages critique. In the situation of domination we find ourselves in, critique, although marginally impeded by *truth tests* and formally free, at least verbally ('democracy of opinion'), can only with great difficulty tear itself away from *reality tests* (or, which comes down to the same thing, from their rejection, which is as radical as it is futile), in such a way as to draw resources from *existential tests* – that is to say, the very flux of life. Hence the paradox, which is certainly one of the causes of the current malaise, and especially the malaise of the left (very obvious in the artistic world, as evinced by the forms taken by critique in contemporary theatre),[11] of a critique which is simultaneously very present, highly desirous of existing and making itself manifest, and yet very conscious of the difficulty of having the slightest purchase on reality. As if critique were exhausting itself in a permanent race with a reality that is sufficiently robust (notably because it is endlessly patched up by appointed experts, including numerous sociologists) to interdict it, integrate it and silence it even before it has arrived at a clear understanding of where it is going.

But to stress the complementary character between the role of critique and the place of institutions does not come down to positing some kind of clash of the titans condemned to the inevitability of the eternal return. Considered from the point of view of hermeneutic contradiction, the work of critique escapes circularity to focus on an axis (whose orientation is not necessarily temporal, as progressivist social philosophies would have it) directed towards *liberation* or *emancipation*. The reference to hermeneutic contradiction makes it possible to shift the denotation of these terms in such a way as to distance them from the issue of greater or lesser individual autonomy or emancipation from personal dependencies, which they have frequently been associated with since the Enlightenment. Re-orientated towards hermeneutic contradiction, emancipation refers to a path leading towards a change in the relationship between the collective and institutions. This path cannot have as its end the dissolution of every institution – as is sometimes suggested by those libertarian currents which, if not the most radical, are the most focused on self-ownership by the self qua unique being[12] – since (as we have tried to show) institutions are indispensable to collective life. But it can lead to emptying institutions of the different forms of over-determination they invoke in order to justify their existence and mask the violence they contain. This divestment would consist in unmasking what everyone possibly has prescience of without always admitting it – that not only are institutions without *foundation*, so that the power they exercise is based on an 'empty place' (as Claude Lefort puts it),[13] but also that to recognize this absence of guarantor projected from exteriority into interiority does not particularly imperil them, or (if you like) does not make them more fragile than they already are. By recognizing that their fate is bound up with that of critique, institutions would even be consolidated in a sense. It is in fact only through the intermediary of (reformist) critique, which challenges the validity of reality tests, that institutions can hope to engage with something real, and through that of (radical) forms of existential critique that they can hope to retain contact with the world. Left to themselves – that is, to truth tests and them alone – they are condemned to collapse.

To recognize the presence of hermeneutic contradiction at the heart of social life would mean not only accepting the factual character of institutions – that is to say, the fact that they are *made* – but, going a step further, that this operation never makes it possible to realize an instance that conforms to its concept. No institution can measure up to itself. And this is fortunate. It would then be admitted, without deploring the fact, that institutions are nothing but arrangements, always more or less lousy, between impermanent beings to slow the pace of change and try to give it a form. But this would in no way prevent them from playing the role, at once necessary and weak, expected of them. Far from having completed its task, critique would thereby be destined not to disappear but, on the contrary, to assert itself by establishing new forms of relationship between critical instances and institutional instances, while acknowledging its own fragility. It is to be hoped that the first victim of this reorganization of the relationship between practical collectives and institutions, between critical forces and forces of confirmation, would be nothing other than the nation-state, at least in the form it currently takes, and that those who have responsibility for making it persist in its being would have increasing difficulty continuing.

To proceed in this direction, there doubtless exists no other road than the eternal road of revolt. Such revolts are beginning to emerge and they are, for the most part, revolts *against tests*, especially selection tests, including those that are best intentioned and most impeccable in terms of a meritocratic ideal – which leads them to being taxed, not only on the right but also on the social-democratic left, with 'nihilism': revolts against schools, firms, work and even, sometimes, against the publicity systems of democracy. Currently, they invariably take the form of impulse, involving the body in violence – and this doubtless when the resources that can be committed to the action do not go much beyond those provided by one's own body – or withdrawal – especially when possession of an educationally certified competence makes it possible to survive on the edge of recognized rounds of tests, but in insecurity.

The state is still the instrument which, through public policy, makes possible a separate lifestyle, however insecure and difficult. But the state is also beginning to be ever more consciously challenged within fluid ensembles, whose mode of existence is characterized by *insecurity*, currently corresponding more to what might be called *affinitarian collectives* than social classes in the classical sense of the term. It is contested in the first instance as principal guarantor of selection tests (the adherence of numerous insecure graduates to the struggle on behalf of the *sans-papiers* is highly significant in this regard).

The lack of interest in the state as such, since it is treated as one exploitable resource among others for leading a kind of existence marked by separation – a lack of interest that can superficially be interpreted as a rejection of politics, which is certainly far from being the case – develops in favour of themes aimed at different forms, however vague, of constructing a common world, borrowing the language of communities or communes or that of networks. But, whatever forms these still largely vague and fluid aspirations will take, they attest to

158

the search for a social world where the relationship between forces of confirmation and critical forces could be established in accordance with small loops providing action with purchase – which assumes, if not the complete abandonment of the state form, then at least its profound transformation.

It might be objected that such lack of interest in the state, when it is not purely and simply contempt, risks having as its first effect liberating capitalism from the meagre constraints still imposed on it by the old states, above all in their social-democratic forms (increasingly rare and increasingly in bad shape). That is true, but I shall make two remarks in this connection. The first is that capitalism has always been bound up with the state. It cannot survive in the absence of *institutional* resources to fix property rights, qualifications and standards, or resources depending on an *administrative power* to ensure policing and, in particular, guarantee contracts. Thus we have seen that the neo-liberal turn of the last twenty years has not brought about a withering away of the state but its transformation, on the model of the firm, to adjust itself to the new forms of capitalism. The second remark is that the loss of confidence in the state would at least have the virtue of exposing capitalism and making more visible internal contradictions that the state still helps, albeit with increasing difficulty, to attenuate. Finally, by restoring initiative to actors, and particularly to those of them who currently find themselves dominated, a move like that just outlined would make it possible to mobilize significant energies against capitalism. It would thus encourage its replacement by less violent forms of utilization of the earth's resources and ways of organizing the relations between human beings that would no longer be of the order of exploitation. It could perhaps then restore to the word *communism* – become virtually unpronounceable – an emancipatory orientation that decades of state capitalism and totalitarian violence have caused it to lose.

It was suggested at the beginning of this short précis of critique that sociology – and, in particular, critical sociology – inhabited by tensions that are difficult to overcome, had something *impossible* about them and that they were worth the effort of being practised for this very reason. We are now perhaps in a position to understand more clearly why they have this character. It is because what they are concerned with – social reality – *does not hold*, at least never in a way that is, as it were, mechanical. Here we might paraphrase what Jacques Derrida says of justice: 'there is no justice without this experience, however impossible it may be, of aporia. Justice is an experience of the impossible'; a 'demand for justice' cannot correspond to

159

anything other than 'a call for justice'.[14] And we might likewise say that what manifests itself in life in common is the *appeal* of life in common, which is at once acknowledgement and denial of the impossibility of human beings connecting with one another in a way that is simultaneously coherent, stable and just. This is to say that if sociology (especially critical sociology) or anthropology never not stop telling 'tall stories', as claim the numerous (and reactionary) reactions they provoke, it is precisely in that they live in intimate proximity to their subject-matter. Their role is precisely to help society – that is, people, the people who are called 'ordinary' – deliberately maintain themselves in the state of constant imbalance in the absence of which, as the direst prophecies announce, domination would in fact seize hold of everything.

NOTES

PREFACE

1 Often more rapid and more allusive in the case of a lecture. Oral exposition does not make it possible to go into detail with as much precision as is possible in a book, for reasons that mainly stem from the speaker having regard to the memory capacity of listeners and their attention span and from the absence of a para-text.

2 In the introduction to his book on the Zapatistas (*La Rébellion zapatiste*, Flammarion, Paris, 2002), written on the margins of his practice as a Mediaevalist, Jérôme Baschet has suggested a seductive, if unproven, pattern, characterized by cycles of rebellion and restoration of order. A cycle of social struggles, which began in the first third of the twentieth century, ended around 1972–4 (a much more significant break, according to Baschet, than that, often invoked, of 1989–91). The movements of 1968 represented one of its high points, preceding a 'change in trend' marked by 'a balance of power much more favourable to capital' and therewith to a decline in critical thinking and action. From 1994, and especially 2000, a new shift began, of which the Zapatistas were one of the first manifestations, which supposedly amounted to a resurgence of both 'critical thinking and critical practice' (pp. 15–18). We find a rather similar idea, but this time applied to the issue of social classes, their forms and degrees of mobilization, in the sociologist Louis Chauvel (see, in particular, *Les Classes moyennes à la derive*, Seuil, Paris, 2006). A period of significant conflict, running from the 1890s to the 1970s and marked by important social gains, is said to have been followed by a period of low conflict, leading to a reduction in these gains and paving the way for new forms of conflict.

1 THE STRUCTURE OF CRITICAL THEORIES

1 See Luc Boltanski and Laurent Thévenot, *On Justification: Economies of Worth*, trans. Catherine Porter, Princeton University Press, Princeton, 2006.

2 See Bruno Karsenti, 'L'expérience structurale', *Gradhiva*, no. 2, 2005, pp. 89–107.

3 On the ways in which nascent sociology altered the meaning attributed to the word 'society', which at the end of the seventeenth century broke away from its old sense (the good society) to designate a collective that can be discussed without directly referring to the individuals who compose it, and then on the implicit equivalence established between these collectives and the populations assembled on the territory of a nation-state, see Robert Nisbet, *The Sociological Tradition*, Heinemann Educational, London, 1967 and Peter Wagner, *A Sociology of Modernity: Liberty and Discipline*, Routledge, London, 1994.

4 On the genesis of this founding position and, in particular, the way it is lodged by Max Horkheimer at the heart of Critical Theory, see Rolf Wiggershaus, *The Frankfurt School: Its History, Theories and Politial Significance*, trans. Michael Robertson, Polity, Cambridge, 1992, chapter 1.

5 In a way, it is to this globalizing perspective that the Foucaultian method of analysing micro-powers and the detail of their lineaments is opposed. However, the latter would remain dispersed and irrelevant without the total-izing capacities supplied by the concept of episteme.

6 The critical and systematic character of theories of domination, and their fre-quent claim to know more than actors themselves about the sources of their discontent, has in numerous cases even led their opponents to assimilate them to a kind of madness. In particular, the analogy has been suggested in connec-tion with a pathology whose description is virtually contemporaneous with the development of critical theories and, more generally, the social sciences: nothing other than paranoia. The comparison is explicitly made by the two psychiatrists to whom we owe the first descriptions of this nosological cate-gory in France: Drs Serieux and Capgras. Thus, they compare the 'paranoiac' with a 'sociologist'. Just as the paranoiac sees plots all around her, the critical sociologist sees domination everywhere, even in instances where the actors – those whom she accuses of exercising it or whom she complains suffer it – observe nothing abnormal. 'In this respect, there exists no fundamental difference,' they write, 'between a litigant determined to obtain reparation for a real or supposed denial of justice and some seeker after the philosopher's stone . . . or some sociological dreamer whose ardour is employed in propa-gating his theories and urging their implementation. . . . Where others see only chance or coincidence, he, thanks to his penetrating clairvoyance, knows how to disentangle the truth and the hidden relations of things': Serieux and Capgras, 'Délire de revendication', in Paul Bercherie, ed., *Présentation des classiques de la paranoia*, Navarin-Seuil, Paris, 1982, pp. 102–5.

7 By contrast, we can characterize the objects that are called 'natural' by an absence of reflexivity and, in particular, by their indifference to the repre-sentations given of them and the descriptions offered of their ways of being, by ordinary people or by specialists empowering themselves with science. These representations and descriptions can have an effect on their behaviour – especially in the case of animals – but only in a roundabout fashion, because they alter the action of human beings towards them – something that can prompt them, as a result, to alter their conduct. See on this point Ian Hacking, *The Social Construction of What?*, Harvard University Press, Cambridge (Mass.), 1999.

8 Far be it from us to reject this distinction, which today is often regarded with condescension as if there was something 'simplistic' about it, because it must be admitted that it marks a moment (people would once have referred to an 'epistemological break') behind which social science cannot regress without risking getting lost – and this even if (as we shall try to show later) the distinction has an element of impossibility about it. As to the issues, which have been the subject of interminable discussions, about the Nietzschean or, instead, neo-Kantian origin of the distinction in Max Weber, we shall leave it to specialists in the history of our discipline (a well-documented summary of these debates can be found in an article by Laurent Fleury, 'Max Weber sur les traces de Nietzsche?', *Revue française de sociologie*, vol. 46, no. 4, 2005, pp. 807–39). The opinion, unfortunately insufficiently informed, of the author of the present essay is that the distinction between facts and values probably has its origins in Nietzschean perspectivism, but amended by neo-Kantian rationalism, in such a way as to enable the claim of sociology to take its place among the sciences. The solution adopted – rather tortuous, it must be said – is (as is well known) built on the distinction between 'value judgements' and the 'relation to values'. Although 'ends' and 'values' cannot be the object of a foundation based on the sciences, once a certain type of benchmark value has been fixed, demonstration, in the framework of the perspective adopted, can be conducted 'objectively' with the methods of rationalism in order to release 'facts'.

9 Max Horkheimer, 'Traditional and Critical Theory', in *Critical Theory*, Seabury Press, New York, 1972.

10 Raymond Geuss, *The Idea of a Critical Theory: Habermas and the Frankfurt School*, Cambridge University Press, Cambridge, 1981.

11 Luc Boltanski, *Rendre la réalité inacceptable. A propos de 'La production de l'idéologie dominante'*, Démopolis, Paris, 2008.

12 I shall note here that the 'goods in themselves' (as Nicolas Dodier puts it in *Leçons politiques de l'épidémie de Sida*, Editions de l'EHESS, Paris, 2003, p. 19) on which the critical enterprise is based do not need to be very clearly identified. It is even less necessary to offer a precise outline of what the contours of society would be if these goods were satisfied. This is what distinguishes critical theories from *utopias*. The latter, based exclusively on moral exigencies, can free themselves from the reality principle. By contrast, critical theories, because they must be based, on the one hand, on the discourse of truth adopted by the social sciences and, on the other, on normative orientations – a perilous position that precisely explains their interest – can believe that reality does not provide sufficient purchase to sketch with precision what society would be once released from the alienations that hamper it, or even to identify clearly the goods that underlie the critique. In this sense, they can in part extricate themselves from justification, at least in its ethical forms. On this point, we can follow Bernard Yack's work on the origins of the notion of alienation. Those whom he calls 'left Kantians' seeking to understand and explain the failure of the French Revolution undertake to identify what, underneath political conditions, roots beings in a condition that does not allow them to accede to full humanity. They end up believing that the state of reality is so far removed from what conditions favourable to the realization of humanity should be that, if it is legitimate on the basis of this observation to engage in critique and commit to 'total revolution', it is not possible

to anticipate what values will emerge once the revolution is accomplished. See Bernard Yack, *The Longing for Total Revolution: Philosophic Sources of Social Discontent from Rousseau to Marx and Nietzsche*, Princeton University Press, Princeton, 1986.

13 The chapter devoted by Michael Walzer to Herbert Marcuse ends as follows: '. . . Marcuse freely chose the society he meant to criticize from within. But there was too much in American life that made him shudder. He chose to stay but always kept his distance, and his work suggests again that distance is the enemy of critical penetration. In the battles of the intellect, as in every other battle, one can win, finally, only on the ground' (*The Company of Critics: Social Criticism and Political Commitment in the Twentieth Century*, Basic Books, New York, 1988, p. 190).

14 On the different forms of totalization employed by sociology, see Nicolas Dodier and Isabelle Baszanger, 'Totalisation et alterité dans l'enquête ethno-graphique', *Revue française de sociologie*, vol. 38, 1997, pp. 37–66.

15 In this section I have forgone putting names to the schemas, taking the liberty of the more or less structuralist optic adopted here. In fact, to specify the way in which compromises between simple exteriority and complex exteriority are established by those who have written the great works that feature in the corpus of sociological classics would have required me either to be outrageously schematic, and necessarily inexact and unjust, or to go into an infinity of analyses and details that would have transformed this short passage into a thick tome. Readers can therefore read these few pages rather in the way that children amuse themselves in deciphering riddles and adults in identifying real people behind the characters in *romans à clef*. To help readers in this game, here, however, are a few of the names I had in mind when writing: Habermas, Honneth, Durkheim, Dewey, Pareto, Weber and, obviously, a whole host of authors identifying to various degrees with Marxism.

2 CRITICAL SOCIOLOGY AND PRAGMATIC SOCIOLOGY OF CRITIQUE

1 See Pierre Bourdieu, Jean-Claude Passeron and Jean-Claude Chamboredon, *Le Métier de sociologue*, Mouton, Paris, 1968.

2 See William Buxton, *Talcott Parsons and the Capitalist Nation-State*, University of Toronto Press, Toronto, 1985.

3 Today there are a large number of works that present and, sometimes, cri-tique the sociology of Pierre Bourdieu. Obviously, it would take too long to cite them all. As regards the literature in French, readers are referred in particular to Alain Accardo and Philippe Corcuff, *La Sociologie de Bourdieu*, Le Mascaret, Bordeaux, 1989; Bernard Lahire, ed., *Le Travail sociologique de Pierre Bourdieu. Dettes et critiques*, La Découverte, Paris, 1999; Louis Pinto, *Pierre Bourdieu et la théorie du monde social*, Seuil, Paris, 2002; Philippe Corcuff, *Bourdieu autrement. Fragilités d'un sociologue de combat*, Textuel, Paris, 2003; Pierre Encrevé and Rose-Marie Lagrave, eds, *Travailler avec Bourdieu*, Flammarion, Paris, 2003; Jacques Bouveresse and Daniel Roche, eds, *La Liberté par la connaissance. Pierre Bourdieu (1930–2002)*, Odile Jacob, Paris, 2004; Patrice Champagne and Olivier Christin, *Pierre Bourdieu. Mouvement d'une pensée*, Bordas, Paris, 2004. An interesting

critical viewpoint can be found in Jeffrey Alexander, *Fin de siècle Social Theory: Relativism, Reduction and the Problem of Reason*, Verso, London and New York, 1995.

4 Nevertheless, it should be noted that the work done by or around Bourdieu in the 1970s made an especially intensive use of this kind of cognitive tool – particularly socio-professional categories – while initiating research into the social conditions of their formation and their uses. This split perspective no doubt owes much to Bourdieu's dual disciplinary anchorage in sociology and social anthropology. See, in particular, Pierre Bourdieu and Luc Boltanski, 'Le titre et le poste: rapports entre système de production et système de reproduction', *Actes de la recherche en sciences sociales*, vol. 1, no. 2, March 1975, pp. 12–23; Luc Boltanski, 'Taxinomies populaires, taxinomies savants: les objets de consummation et leur classement', *Revue française de sociologie*, vol. 11, no. 3, 1970, pp. 99–118; and Alain Desrosières, 'Eléments pour l'histoire des nomenclatures socio-professionnelles', in Joelle Affichard, ed., *Pour une histoire de la statistique*, vol. 2, INSEE-Economica, Paris, pp. 35–56.

5 See Luc Boltanski and Laurent Thévenot, 'Finding One's Way in Social Space: A Study Based on Games', *Social Science Information*, vol. 22, nos 4–5, 1983, pp. 631–80. This work, based on experimental procedures appealing to the classificatory capacities of what are called 'ordinary' people, revealed the effects of reflexivity exercised by the National Institute of Statistics and Economic Studies' socio-professional categories and no doubt also by the intense and diffuse presence – in political discourse, but also in literature, films and so on – of a representation of the social world in which division into social classes was regarded as self-evident, even pre-eminent. For comparative purposes it would be interesting today, twenty years later, to conduct a similar study, which would make it possible to assess if the erasure of social classes has merely superficially affected the official field of representation, notably in the media; or, on the contrary, if it is profoundly rooted in people's cognitive capacities. See also on this point Alain Desrosières, *La Politique des grands nombres*, La Découverte, Paris, 1993 and Alain Desrosières and Laurent Thévenot, *Les Catégories socio-professionnelles*, La Découverte, Paris, 1988.

6 Reduction of the uncertainty confronting action in the course of situations is facilitated in Bourdieu by the temporal position adopted towards the object of study. In effect, this position is invariably retrospective. Envisaged retrospectively, each moment of the course of action can be invested with a kind of necessity that attaches to it from the relationship, posited by the analyst, between the moment considered and what preceded it and what followed it. To consider a sequence of events or actions in their succession in fact leads – without necessarily intending to – to reinvesting in the description a causal logic of the order of determinism. On the other hand, the position which consists in detaching each moment of action, so as to consider it as it were in itself – a position which is that of pragmatics – makes the uncertainty confronting actors more salient. (I am grateful to Matthew Carrey for this observation.)

7 On the history and foundations of the sociological theory of action, see Hans Jonas, *La Créativité de l'agir* (1992), trans. Pierre Rusch with a Preface by Alain Touraine, Cerf, Paris, 1999.

8 The first studies comparing critical sociology and pragmatic sociology of critique were done by Thomas Benatouil ('Sociologie critique et sociologie pragmatique', *Annales ESC*, 1999) and Philippe Corcuff (*Les nouvelles sociologies*, Armand Colin, Paris, 1999).

9 Jacques Rancière, *The Philosopher and his Poor*, ed. Andrew Parker, Duke University Press, Durham, 2004.

10 In some respects this critique coincided with the one Sartre was making of French Marxists – a critique, moreover, to which Pierre Bourdieu himself subscribed. See the first part of *Critique of Dialectical Reason*, 'Questions of Method' (*Search for a Method*, trans. Hazel Barnes, Vintage Books, New York, 1968).

11 Luc Boltanski and Elisabeth Claverie, 'Du monde social en tant que scène d'un procès', in Boltanski *et al.*, eds, *Affaires, scandales et grandes causes*, Stock, Paris, 2007, pp. 395–452.

12 This remark was made to me by Cyril Lemieux. See his *Le Devoir et la grace*, Economica, Paris, 2009.

13 Philippe Chateauraynaud, *La Faute professionnelle. Une sociologie des conflits de responsabilité*, Métailié, Paris, 1991; Nicolas Dodier, *Les Hommes et les machines*, Métailié, Paris, 1995; Philippe Corcuff, 'Sécurité et expertise psychologique dans les chemins de fer', in Luc Boltanski and Laurent Thévenot, eds, *Justesse et justice dans le travail*, Presses Universitaires de France, Paris, 1989, pp. 307–18.

14 Nicolas Dodier, *L'expertise médicale*, Métailié, Paris, 1993.

15 Michel Pollak, *Les Homosexuels et le sida. Sociologie d'une épidémie*, Métailié, Paris, 1988.

16 Cyril Lemieux, *Mauvaise presse. Une sociologie compréhensive du travail médiatique et des critiques*, Métailié, Paris, 2000.

17 Damien de Blic, 'Le scandale financier du siècle, ça ne vous intéresse pas? Difficile mobilisation autour de Crédit Lyonnais', *Politix*, no. 52, 2000, pp. 157–81.

18 Nathalie Heinrich, *L'art en conflit*, La Découverte, Paris, 2002.

19 François Eymard-Duvernay and Emmanuelle Marchal, *Façons de recruter. Le jugement des compétences sur le marché du travail*, Métailié, Paris, 1997.

20 Jean-Louis Derouet, *Ecole et justice*, Métailié, Paris, 1992.

21 Claudette Lafaye, 'Situations tendues et sens ordinarie de la justice au sein d'une administration municipale', *Revue française de sociologie*, vol. 31, no. 2, 1990, pp. 199–223.

22 Pierre Boisard and Marie-Thérèse Letablier, 'Un compromis d'innovation entre tradition et standardisation dans l'industrie laitière', in Boltanski and Thévenot, eds, *Justesse et justice dans le travail*, pp. 135–208.

23 Claudette Lafaye and Laurent Thévenot, 'Une justification écologique? Conflits dans l'aménagement de la nature', *Revue française de sociologie*, vol. 34, no. 4, 1993, pp. 493–524.

24 Elisabeth Claverie, *Les Guerres de la Vierge. Une anthropologie des apparitions*, Gallimard, Paris, 2003.

25 Cf., in particular, Luc Boltanski, 'La dénonciation publique', in *L'amour et la justice comme compétences. Trois essais de sociologie de l'action*, Métailié, Paris, 1990, pp. 255–366; Elisabeth Claverie, 'Procès, affaire, cause. Voltaire et l'innovation critique', *Politix*, no. 26, 1994, pp. 76–86; and Elisabeth

Claverie, 'La naissance d'une forme politique: l'affaire du chevalier de La Barre', in Philippe Roussin, ed., *Critique et affaires de blasphème à l'époque des Lumières*, Honoré Champion, Paris, 1998. See also Luc Boltanski, 'Une étude en noir', forthcoming.

26 See Damien de Blic and Cyril Lemieux, 'Le scandale comme épreuve. Eléments de sociologie pragmatique', *Politix*, no. 71, 2005, pp. 9–38.

27 Six polities were identified in *On Justification*: the inspired polity, the domestic polity, the renowned polity, the civic polity, the commercial polity and the industrial polity. Other polities, in the process of being formed, were the subject of exploratory work – in particular, an ecological polity (see Lafaye and Thévenot, 'Une justification écologique? Conflits dans l'aménagement de la nature') and a projective polity (see Luc Boltanski and Eve Chiapello, *The New Spirit of Capitalism*, trans. Gregory Elliott, Verso, London and New York, 2006).

28 The notion of test features in the work of Bruno Latour (e.g. *The Pasteurization of France*, trans. Alan Sheridan and John Law, Harvard University Press, Cambridge (Mass.), 1988). Here it is partially diverted, so as to be capable of being applied to the issues of judgement and legitimacy.

29 In the *inspired* polity, worth belongs to the saint who achieves a state of grace or the artist who receives inspiration. It reveals itself in the clean body prepared by ascesis, whose inspired expressions (saintliness, creativity, artistic sense, authenticity, etc.) constitute the privileged form of expression.

In the *domestic polity*, people's worth depends on their hierarchical position in a chain of personal dependencies. In a formula of subordination established on a domestic model, the political bond between beings is conceived as a generalization of the generational bond, conjugating tradition and proximity. The 'great one' is the elder, the ancestor, the father, to whom respect and loyalty are due and who affords protection and support.

In the *renowned polity*, worth depends exclusively on the opinion of others – that is to say, on the number of people who extend their credit and esteem. The 'great one' in the *civic polity* is the representative of a collective whose general will he or she expresses. In the *commercial polity* the 'great one' is he or she who becomes rich by offering highly desirable commodities on a competitive market. She knows how to 'seize opportunities'. Finally, in the *industrial polity* worth is based on effectiveness and determines a scale of professional capacities.

Each of these regimes of justification is based on a different principle of evaluation which, envisaging beings in a determinate respect (i.e. also by excluding other types of qualification), makes it possible to establish an order between them. This principle is called the *principle of equivalence* because it presupposes reference to a form of general equivalence (to a standard) without which comparison between beings would be impossible. We can then say: in such and such a respect (e.g. effectiveness in an industrial polity), the people put to the test turned out to possess more or less value. *Worth* is our name for the value attributed to people in certain respects when it results from a legitimate procedure.

30 See Pierre Bourdieu and Jean-Claude Passeron, *Reproduction in Education, Society and Culture* (1970), trans. Richard Nice, Sage Publications, London, 1977.

31 See Boltanski and Chiapello, *The New Spirit of Capitalism*.

32 Nicolas Dodier, 'L'espace et le mouvement du sens critique', *Annales HSS*, no. 1, January/February 2005, pp. 7–31.

33 On the relations between the notion of experiment in John Dewey and some aspects of the pragmatic sociology of critique, see Joan Stavo-Debauge and Danny Trom, 'Le pragmatisme et son public à l'épreuve du terrain', in Bruno Karsenti and Louis Queré, eds, *Le Croyance et l'enquête. Aux sources du pragmatisme, Raisons pratiques*, Editions de l'EHESS, Paris, 2004, pp. 195–226. See also, on the notion of experiment, Joëlle Zask's preface to John Dewey, *Le Public et ses probèmes*, Farrago, Léo Scheer, Paris, 2003.

34 Michael Walzer, *The Company of Critics: Social Criticism and Political Commitment in the Twentieth Century*, Basic Books, New York, 1988.

35 See Michèle Lamont and Laurent Thévenot, eds, *Rethinking Comparative Cultural Sociology: Repertoires of Evaluation in France and the United States*, Cambridge University Press, Cambridge, 2000.

36 Historical works on the great witch craze crisis that occurred in Europe (Lorraine, Germany, Switzerland and so on) at the end of the sixteenth century and the first half of the seventeenth century offer a classic, and particularly dramatic, example of reinterpretation of popular practices by power elites. In this case, it was the ecclesiastical authorities. Following denunciations in which local conflicts were at stake, they were led to reclassify acts pertaining to traditional healing techniques in terms of crimes against religion. See Robin Briggs, *Witches and Neighbours*, Fontana, London, 1996.

37 This theme was developed in the 1950s by Michael Young in his socio science fiction *The Rise of Meritocracy* (new, revised edition, Transaction Publishers, London, 1994).

38 Jean-Paul Sartre, *Critique of Dialectical Reason*, trans. Alan Sheridan and ed. Jonathan Rée, New Left Books, London, 1976, p. 310.

39 See Luc Boltanski, 'La dénonciation publique des injustices'.

40 This is something the social psychology of the 1940s and 50s, today pretty much forgotten, made one of its favourite themes. See, for example, Eleanor Maccoby, Theodor Newcomb and Eugene Hartley, eds, *Readings in Social Psychology*, Holt, Rinehart and Winston, New York, 1952.

41 See René Girard, *Deceit, Desire and the Novel: Self and Other in Literary Structure*, trans. Yvonne Freccero, Johns Hopkins University Press, Baltimore, 1965.

42 I am referring here to the forthcoming work of Natalia Suarez on everyday life in a situation of civil war in Colombia.

43 See Luc Boltanski, *The Making of a Class: Cadres in French Society*, trans. Arthur Goldhammer, Cambridge University Press, Cambridge, 1987 and Alain Desrosières and Laurent Thévenot, *Les Catégories socio-professionnelles*.

44 See Boltanski and Chiapello, *The New Spirit of Capitalism*, pp. 296–323.

45 See Alain Desrosières, 'L'Etat et la formation des classes sociales. Quelques particularités françaises', in Desrosières, *Gouverner par les nombres*, vol. 2, Mines-Paris Tech, Paris, 2008, pp. 293–304.

46 Boltanski, *The Making of a Class*.

47 See Pierre Bourdieu and Luc Boltanski, 'Le titre et le poste: rapports entre système de production et système de reproduction'.

48 See Christian Laval, *L'homme économique. Essai sur les racines du néolibéralisme*, Gallimard, Paris, 2007 and Pierre Dardot and Christian Laval, *La*

nouvelle raison du monde. Essai sur la société néolibérale, La Découverte, Paris, 2009.

49 Nicholas Abercrombie and Bryan Turner, 'The Dominant Ideology Thesis', *The British Journal of Sociology*, vol. 29, no. 2, June 1978, pp. 149–70.

50 See Raymond Aron, *Main Currents of Sociological Thought*, vol. 2, trans. Richard Howard and Helen Weaver, Weidenfeld and Nicolson, London, 1968.

51 Sartre, *Critique of Dialectical Reason*, vol. 1, book. 1, 'From Individual Praxis to the Practico-Inert'.

52 Giorgio Agamben, *State of Exception*, trans. Kevin Attell, Chicago University Press, Chicago, 2005.

53 See Michael Mann, *State, War and Capitalism: Studies in Political Sociology*, Basil Blackwell, Oxford, 1988.

54 See Nancy Fraser, *Abnormal Justice*, forthcoming.

55 As are the beings about whom Bruno Latour poses the question of their entry into politics. See Latour, *Politics of Nature: How to Bring the Sciences into Democracy*, trans. Catherine Porter, Harvard University Press, Cambridge (Mass.) and London, 2004.

56 Herbert Marcuse, *Eros and Civilization: A Philosophical Inquiry into Freud*, Beacon Press, Boston, 1955.

57 Axel Honneth, *Reification: A New Look at an Old Idea*, ed. and introd. Martin Jay, Oxford University Press, Oxford, 2008.

58 Cf. Zygmunt Bauman, *Modernity and Ambivalence*, Polity, Cambridge, 1993 and Malcolm Bull, *Seeing Things Hidden: Apocalypse, Vision and Totality*, Verso, London and New York, 1999.

59 A work inspired by a similar intention, but conducted with methods that differ in part, has been carried out by Cyril Lemieux. See, in particular, 'De la théorie de l'habitus à la sociologie des épreuves: relire *L'expérience con-centrationnaire*', in Liora Israël and Danièle Voldman, eds, *Michael Pollak. De l'identité blessée à une sociologie des possibles*, Complexe, Paris, 2008, pp. 179–206.

3 THE POWER OF INSTITUTIONS

1 John R. Searle, *The Construction of Social Reality*, Free Press, New York, 1995.

2 Noting the polysemic character of the term 'institution', especially among historians, Jacques Revel distinguishes at least three usages. 'The first defines the institution as "a juridico-political reality": it is what is illustrated by the "history of institutions".' The second comprises 'any organization function-ing in a regular fashion in society, in accordance with explicit and implicit rules, and which is presumed to respond to a particular collective demand', such as 'the family, the school, the hospital, the trade union'. Finally, by insti-tution the third refers to 'any form of social organization that links values, norms, models of relation and conduct, roles'. (This final definition is taken from Georges Balandier's preface to the French edition of Mary Douglas's *How Institutions Think* (*Comment pensent les institutions*, La Découverte, Paris, 1989).) See Jacques Revel, 'L'institution et le social', in *Un Parcours critique. Douze exercices d'histoire sociale*, Galaade, Paris, 2006, pp. 85–110.

3 John Searle, 'What is an Institution?', *Journal of Institutional Economics*, no. 1, 2005, pp. 1–22.
4 Erving Goffman, *Asylums: An Essay on the Social Situation of Mental Patients and Other Inmates*, Penguin, Harmondsworth, 1968.
5 See, for example, Sandra Laugier, 'Care et perception', in *Le Souci des autres. Ethique et politique du care, Raisons pratiques*, Editions de l'EHESS, Paris, 2005, pp. 317–48.
6 See Jean-Claude Gens, 'Le partage du sens à l'origine de l'humanité', in Pierre Guenancia and Jean-Pierre Sylvestre, eds, *Le Sens commun. Théories et pratiques*, Editions Universitaires de Dijon, Dijon, 2004, pp. 75–89.
7 The most remarkable example is perhaps Erik H. Erikson's book, *Childhood and Society*, 2nd edn, Norton, New York, 1963.
8 For a critical discussion of economic rationality from the standpoint of sociology, see Richard Swedberg, *Economics and Sociology*, Princeton University Press, Princeton, 1990 and the same author's *Principles of Economic Sociology*, Princeton University Press, Princeton, 2003.
9 See Philippe Batifoulier, ed., *Théorie des conventions*, Economica, Paris, 2001 and also the founding issue of *Revue économique* (*L'économie des conventions*, vol. 40, no. 2, March 1989). At the heart of conventionalism, in its standard form, is the idea that behaviour can be arbitrary but rational if the basic objective is the coordination of actions. The classic example is that of cars driving on the left or right. But that said, it remains to make a distinction between forms of behaviour which it seems to us inconsequential to judge 'arbitrary' (as in the case of driving cars) and forms of behaviour which (for reasons that we shall seek clarify later) appear to lose all pertinence if we do not give them a basis that can confer an intrinsic necessity and authenticity on them. To discredit them, they will then be characterized as 'conventional' precisely in order to bring out their 'arbitrary' character. This is particularly clear in cases, to which we shall refer later, where the establishment of conventions demands *slicing up* a continuum and establishing *thresholds* or *boundaries*, whose tracing has to be justified.
10 See, for example, Daniel Cefaï, *Phénoménologie et sciences sociales. Alfred Schutz. Naissance d'une anthropologie philosophique*, Droz, Geneva, 1998 and Jocelyn Benoist and Bruno Karsenti, eds, *Phénoménologie et sociologie*, Presses Universitaires de France, Paris, 2001.
11 Jürgen Habermas, *Moral Consciousness and Communicative Action*, Polity, Cambridge, 1990.
12 See René Daval, *Moore et la philosophie analytique*, Presses Universitaires de France, Paris, 1997, pp. 28–31 and also the special issue of *Revue de métaphysique et de morale* devoted to G.E. Moore (no. 3, July/September 2006), especially the contributions by Christophe Alsaleh ('Quand est-il valide de dire je sais?') and Elise Domenach ('Scepticisme, sens commun et langage ordinaire chez Moore').
13 Cf. Luc Boltanski, *L'amour et la justice comme compétences. Trois essais de sociologie de l'action*, Métailié, Paris, 1990, pp. 110–24.
14 See Laurent Thévenot, *L'action au pluriel. Sociologie des régimes d'engagement*, La Découverte, Paris, 2006.
15 It will be noted that the link between radical uncertainty and state of nature and that between the 'floating' of meanings and violence, at least potential, is established by Hobbes in particular in the chapter of *Leviathan* on speech.

The same themes are developed when the issue of contracts is broached (Thomas Hobbes, *Leviathan*, Penguin edition, Harmondsworth, 1981, pp. 100–10, 189–201). Nevertheless, it is more to the theme of envy that the Hobbesian problematic has drifted when it has been taken up by social science, and then towards that of the unlimited character of human appetites as a source of violence – an argument used to justify the necessity of the state. We find this theme in Durkheim, where it plays an important role in the genesis of the notion of institution (see, e.g. *Socialism and Saint-Simon* (1928), trans. Charlotte Sattler, London, 1959 and also *The Social Division of Labour in Society* (1893), trans. W.D. Halls, Macmillan, Basingstoke, 1984, especially the second preface of 1902). Let us finally add that the stress in Durkheim on the need to put a brake on the anarchy of desire resonates (as has often been remarked) with Freudian conceptions (see, e.g. Robert A. Nisbet, *The Sociological Tradition*, Heinemann Educational, London, 1970). Departing from these classical positions, it is instead the semantic role of institutions that is stressed in the present work.

16 On the extension in the domain of social science of the theme of the social construction of reality, see Ian Hacking, *The Social Construction of What?*, Harvard University Press, Cambridge (Mass.) and London, 1999. Readers will find a remarkable presentation of constructionism and the issues it raises in the presentation ('Quel naturalisme pour les sciences sociales?') by Michel de Fornel and Cyril Lemieux to the special issue of the journal *Enquête* (no. 6, 2007, pp. 9–28), *Naturalisme versus constructivisme*, edited by them.

17 Blaise Benoit thus suggests (analysing the uses of *Realität* and *Wirklichkeit* in Nietzsche) that one finds in him a tension between reality conceived as a sort of fiction constructed to discover some stability in the world and reality envisaged as ungraspable, chaotic becoming, to which experience neverthe-less affords access ('La réalité selon Nietzsche', *Revue philosophique*, vol. 131, no. 4, 2006, pp. 403–20).

18 Albeit posited differently and, in particular, from within psychoanalysis, the difference between reality and world underlies Cornelius Castoriadis's gran-diose attempt to construct the framework for an analysis of 'the institution of the world by society' (*The Imaginary Institution of Society* [1975], trans. Kathleen Blamey, Polity, Cambridge, 1987).

19 Frank Knight, *Risk, Uncertainty and Profit* (1921), University of Chicago Press, Chicago, 1985.

20 Michel Foucault, *Sécurité, territoire, population. Cours au Collège de France (1977–78)*, Hautes Etudes, Gallimard/Seuil, Paris, 2004.

21 See Frédéric Keck, *Claude Lévi-Strauss, une introduction*, La Découverte, Paris, 2005, pp. 136–43.

22 Frédéric Nef, *L'objet quelconque. Recherches sur l'ontologie de l'objet*, Vrin, Paris, 2000.

23 Bruno Karsenti, *Politique de l'esprit. Auguste Comte et la naissance des sci-ences sociales*, Hermann, Paris, 2006.

24 Readers are referred on this point to Durkheim's course on pragma-tism (*Pragmatisme et sociologie*, Vrin, Paris, 1955, published by Armand Cuvilier), and to Bruno Karsenti's illuminating analysis of Durkheim's oppo-sition to pragmatism (which does not prevent some areas of convergence), in *La Société en personnes. Etudes durkheimiennes*, Economica, Paris, 2006, pp. 183–212.

25 Pierre Bourdieu, *Outline of a Theory of Practice*, trans. Richard Nice, Cambridge University Press, Cambridge, 1977.

26 On the regime of planned action, see Laurent Thévenot, 'L'action en plan', *Sociologie du travail*, vol. 37, no. 3, 1995, pp. 411–34.

27 This notion is borrowed from Thomas Schelling, *The Strategy of Conflict*, Oxford University Press, New York, 1960.

28 In the analyses of practical sense developed by Pierre Bourdieu, this theme appears in the form of a critique of what he describes as the stranglehold of 'legalism' on the social sciences – for example, when he contrasts 'practical kinship' with the kinship rules modelled in Claude Lévi-Strauss's *The Elementary Structures of Kinship* (see *The Logic of Practice*, trans. Richard Nice, Polity, Cambridge, 1990).

29 See Laurent Thévenot, 'L'action qui convient', in *Les Formes de l'action*, *Raisons pratiques*, no. 1, Editions de l'EHESS, Paris, 1990.

30 Jack Goody, *The Domestication of the Savage Mind*, Cambridge University Press, Cambridge, 1977.

31 See Irène Chauviré, *Voir le visible. La seconde philosophie de Wittgenstein*, Presses Universitaires de France, Paris, 2003, pp. 71–2; and, for an experimental application of Wittgenstein's positions in the domain of cognitive anthropology, Eleanor Rosch, 'Classification of Real-World Objects: Origins and Representation in Cognition', in P.N. Johnson-Laird and P.C. Watson, eds, *Thinking: Readings in Cognitive Science*, Cambridge University Press, Cambridge, 1977, pp. 212–23. Finally, readers will find in Bernard Conein's work *Les Sens sociaux. Trois essais de sociologie cognitive* (Economica, Paris, 2005) the most recent and, to my knowledge, fullest discussion of the problems raised by the different way of making use of categories.

32 Boltanski, *L'amour et la justice comme compétences*, pp. 137–244.

33 One of the characteristics of a regime of unconditional love is that the people in interaction cooperate to maintain the lowest possible level of reflexivity. Thus, for example, a reflexive statement of the kind 'you see, I'm giving it to you without counting', when accompanying a gift presented as free, would immediately cause the actors to leave this regime and re-enter the logic of exchange under equivalence.

34 See, in particular, the work edited by John Lucy, *Reflexive Language: Reported Speech and Metapragmatics*, Cambridge University Press, Cambridge, 1993.

35 On this distinction, see Nef, *L'objet quelconque*, p. 97.

36 In *Fixer le sens. La sémantique spontanée des gloses de spécification du sens* (Presses de la Sorbonne nouvelle, Paris, 2001, p. 41), Catherine Julia underlines the proximity between what she calls 'reflexive glosses' and 'modalized statements containing a subjective adjective carrying an evaluation within an axiology of the beautiful, the true and the good'. She gives as examples: 'a great poet' (evaluative judgement) and 'a true woman'. 'Great and true state a judgement about the referent's membership of the class denoted by the noun. This membership is evaluated in terms of conformity to an ideal associated with this noun.'

37 For the origins of cognitive anthropology, see Ernst Cassirer, *The Philosophy of Symbolic Forms* (1923), vol. I, trans. Ralph Mannheim, Yale University Press, New Haven and London, 1953 and, in particular on Wilhelm von Humboldt, pp. 155–63.

38 See Laurent Thévenot, 'Jugements ordinaries et jugements de droit', *Annales ESC*, no. 6, November/December 1992, pp. 1279–99.

39 Irène Rosier, *La Parole comme acte. Sur la grammaire et la sémantique au XIIIe siècle*, Vrin, Paris, 1994, pp. 14–15.

40 The link between establishing reference and determining value is inherent in the sense given by legal disciplines to operations of qualification. As Olivier Cayla writes, 'Before saying of an object that it must not be, in order to condemn it, or on the contrary saying that it can or must be, in order to permit its existence, tolerate it or demand its advent, it is necessary to start by saying what it is. Of a fact which, in the raw "natural" state, presents itself, for example, as the transfer of a good from the hands of one person into those of another, it is necessary to start by saying if it must be called "sale", "gift" or "theft", before applying to its case the corresponding regime commanded by law'. But the author then shows how this process is at the same time one of valorization or devalorization (of 'disqualification' in his terms), so that it is 'now barely conceivable to argue that law makes it possible to establish, in a descriptive register, what is, but rather to impose prescriptively what must be'. Cayla thus ends up in the same article making the power of qualifying the sovereign's principal prerogative (Olivier Cayla, 'La qualification, ou la vérité du droit', *Droits. Revue française de théorie juridique*, vol. 18, 1993, pp. 1–18).

41 See Julia, *Fixer le sens*, p. 41.

42 The contrast between these two ways of mobilizing categories is clear when we contrast the use of terms referring to groups or classes in the course of verbal exchanges between ordinary people and the use by professionals of socio-professional categories (see Luc Boltanski and Laurent Thévenot, 'Finding One's Way in Social Space: A Study Based on Games', *Social Science Information*, vol. 22, nos 4–5, 1983, pp. 631–80.

43 See, in particular, Josette Rey-Debove, *Le Métalangage. Etude linguistique du discours sur le langage*, Armand Colin, Paris, 1997. As another classic example we might offer: 'all cat' and not 'a four-legged cat'. When metalinguistic possibilities are activated, evaluation – that is to say, 'the conformity of a referent to some ideal' – takes the form (as Catherine Julia also notes in *Fixer le sens*) of a 'representation of the act of enunciation', as is the case when people speak of a 'poet in the major sense of the word' or a 'woman in the true sense of the word'. Similarly, using a word in inverted commas in a text is a metalinguistic procedure (often employed by sociologists to indicate their detachment from their object), since it consists in simultaneously using the word and making a derogatory judgement on it, by making it clear that the author does not want the reader to think that he shares the connotations associated with the term.

44 See also Josette Rey-Debove, *Lexique de la sémiotique*, Presses Universitaires de France, Paris, 1979, p. 95. The paradox is that this reflexivity is internal, without transition to a different 'level'. We can therefore emphasize either this reflexive uncoupling or the fact that one remains, including in moments of enunciation when metalanguage is preponderant, within the limits of the language in question. 'Every language,' writes Jacqueline Authier-Revuz, 'is for itself its own language object and its own metalanguage'. While she agrees 'that there is no metalanguage', according to Jacques Lacan's famous formula (*Le Séminaire, Livre III, Les psychoses*, Editions du Seuil, Paris,

1981, p. 258), in the sense of the logicians, it is nevertheless the case that 'there is something metalinguistic', since 'language . . . is reproduced within itself'. See Authier-Revuz, 'Le fait autonymique: Langage, langue, discours'. Quelques repères', in Jacqueline Authier-Revuz, Marianne Doury and Sandrine Reboul-Touré, *Parler des mots. Le fait autonymique en discours*, Presses de la Sorbonne nouvelle, Paris, 2003, pp. 67–96.

45 Jacqueline Authier-Revuz (*Ces mots qui ne vont pas de soi. Boucles réflexives et non-coïncidences du dire*, Larousse, Paris, 1995, vol. 1, p. 19) gives the following example: 'She does dressmaking for the people of the quarter, if you can call that dressmaking, because, as dressmaking, it's rather. . .' As another example we could take this sentence, heard on the occasion of a 'civil baptism': 'You call that a baptism!'

46 If 'metalinguistic competence', which makes it possible to 'produce acceptable sentences on language' (Josette Rey-Debove, *Le Métalangage*, p. 21) is part of the normal linguistic competence that makes it possible to 'construct acceptable sentences on the world', it would seem (as John Lucy, *Reflexive Language*, pp. 20–24 notes) that the former – which is an operator of reflexivity – is employed even more unconsciously than the second.

47 Rhetoric takes in hand the formal tautology to reduce or increase the gap between that of which one speaks and the definition given of it ('a penny is a penny', 'a woman is a woman'): Rey-Debove, *Lexique de la sémiotique*, p. 146.

48 Josette Rey-Debove, *La Linguistique du signe. Une approche sémiotique du langage*, Armand Colin, Paris, 1998, p. 31.

49 On the role of epideictic discourse in the confirmation of what everyone is supposed to know already, see Loïc Nicolas, 'La function héroïque: parole épidictique et enjeux de qualification', *Rhetorica: A Journal of the History of Rhetoric*, no. 27/2, 2009.

50 See, for example, Lucie Ménager and Olivier Tercieux, 'Fondements épistémiques du concept d'équilibre en théorie des jeux', *Revue d'économie industrielle*, nos 114–15, 2006, pp. 67–84.

51 This kind of performance thus has things in common with the promise (see Mohamed Nachi, *Ethique de la promesse. L'agir responsable*, Presses Universitaires de France, Paris, 2003).

52 Olivier Cayla, 'Les deux figures du juge', *Le Débat*, no. 74, March/April 1993, pp. 164–74.

53 'By virtue of the preceding – the illegibility of intentions in the text of statements – there never exists any means of *verifying* that the interpretation finally *decided on* by the interlocutor coincides with the intention actually harboured by the speaker. In such uncertainty, agreement is never attestable and misunderstanding is always lodged at the heart of any interlocution. Always affected by doubt, discussion is never capable of spontaneously issuing in a reduction of interpretative diversity to unity . . . for (hermeneutic) seriousness can do nothing about the *play* that always remains, as between two disconnected rooms, between the general meaning of the statement and the particular force of the enunciation – that is to say, can do nothing about the phenomenological gap between the letter and the spirit of every proposition': Cayla, 'Les deux figures du juge'.

54 'The usual way of looking at things sees objects as it were from the midst of them, the view *sub specie aeternitatis* from outside. In such a way that they

174

have the whole world as background. Is this it perhaps – in this view the object is seen *together with* space and time instead of *in* space and time?': Ludwig Wittgenstein, *Notebooks, 1914–1916*, eds G.H. von Wright and G.E.M. Anscombe and trans. G.E.M. Anscombe, Blackwell, Oxford, 1961, p. 83e.

55 These definitions are semantic in the sense that, although associated with domains of usage, they do not take account of variations in context. In more developed collections, like dictionaries, the lexicographical text has a circular character that invites the reader to move from definition to definition. We can thus say that definition is tautological from a semantic point of view, in its relationship with other statements of the same type ('a single man is an unmarried man'), but not in its relation to reference. See Centre d'étude du lexique, *La Définition*, Larousse, Paris, 1990.

56 These phrases are cited from a comment by Frege in Claire Ortiz Hill, *Rethinking Identity and Metaphysics*, Yale University Press, New Haven, 1997, p. 146. But as we know, this kind of problem was at the heart of the debates that developed around the work of Bertrand Russell and also of the Vienna Circle. For a synthetic history of it, see Jocelyn Benoist, *Représentations sans objets aux origines de la phenomenologie et de la philosophie analytique*, Presses Universitaires de France, Paris, 2001.

57 After the seminal works of John J. Gumperz and Dell Hymes (see, in particular, *Directions in Sociolinguistics: The Ethnography of Communication*, Blackwell, New York, 1986).

58 Giorgio Agamben, 'Les langues et les peuples', in *Moyens sans fin. Notes sur la politique*, Rivages, Paris, 2002, pp. 73–81.

59 Michel de Certeau, Dominique Julia and Jacques Revel, *Une Politique de la langue*, reprinted, Gallimard Folio, Paris, 2002.

60 In contemporary French literature, exploration of the most extreme limits of the language has been carried out by Pierre Guyotat in *Prostitution* (1975; new edition, Gallimard, Paris, 2007) and especially *Progénitures* (Gallimard, Paris, 2000). The author explains himself by claiming that 'what is of the order of mystery cannot be expressed in a common language'. According to the author, 'mystery' here refers to the place where 'ordure and metaphysics, let us say God . . . touch' (Pierre Guyotat, *Explications. Entretiens avec Marianne Alphant*, Léo Scheer, Paris, 2000, p. 35).

61 See, for example, François Eymard-Duvernay, 'Conventions de qualité et formes de coordination', in 'L'économie des conventions', *Revue économique*, vol. 40, no. 2, 1989, pp. 329–59.

62 Hernando de Soto, *Le Mystère du capital*, Flammarion, Paris, 2007.

63 See Simon Cerutti, 'A qui appartiennent les biens qui n'appartiennent à personne? Citoyenneté et droit d'aubaine à l'époque moderne', *Annales HSS*, no. 2, March/April 2007, pp. 355–83.

64 Alessandro Stanziani thus shows how the market in agrofood products is constantly supervised by operations of qualification that define the properties products must possess to achieve protected designation status. These operations of qualification are particularly necessary to confront the changes introduced by technological innovations. What is really butter has thus been defined so as to confront competition from the new product that is margarine sold under the designation of butter. See Alessandro Stanziani, *Histoire de la qualité alimentaire*, Seuil, Paris, 2005, pp. 173–90.

65 See George Akerlof, *An Economic Theorist's Book of Tales*, Cambridge University Press, Cambridge, 1984.

66 See François Eymard-Duvernay, 'Coordination par l'entreprise et qualité des biens', in A. Orléan, ed., *Analyse économique des conventions*, Presses Universitaires de France, Paris, 1994, pp. 307–34.

67 Laurent Thévenot, 'Essai sur les objets usuels: propriétés, fonctions, usages', in *Les objets dans l'action, Raison pratique*, no. 4, Editions de l'EHESS, Paris, 1993, pp. 85–111.

68 Eve Chiapello and Alain Desrosières, 'La quantification de l'économie et la recherche en sciences sociales: paradoxes, contradictions et omissions. Le cas exemplaire de la "Positive accounting theory"', in François Eymard-Duvernay, ed., *L'économie des conventions. Méthodes et résultats, Tome I. Débats*, La Découverte, Paris, 2006, pp. 297–310. And, in a historical perspective, see Eve Chiapello, 'Accounting and the Birth of the Notion of Capitalism', *Critical Perspectives on Accounting*, vol. 18, 2007, pp. 283–96.

69 Boltanski, *La Condition foetale*, pp. 171–207.

70 John Searle also regards the process of institutionalization itself as a process of creation of power. Without altering 'the physical power of individuals', it creates the conditions for acknowledging power and for consent. Searle's analysis is here very close to that of Bourdieu (for a commentary, see Jean de Munck, 'L'institution selon John Searle', in *Institutions et conventions. Raisons pratiques*, Editions de l'EHESS, Paris, 1989, pp. 173–225).

71 See Owen Lattimore's seminal work, *Inner Asian Frontiers of China*, Oxford University Press, New York, 1989 (reprint) and, for more recent work, Robert R. Alvarez, 'The Mexican-US Border: The Making of an Anthropology of Borderlands', *Annual Review of Anthropology*, no. 24, 1995, pp. 447–70 and A. Murphy, 'Historical Justification for Territorial Claims', *Annals of the Association of American Geographers*, vol. 80, no. 4, 1990, pp. 531–48.

72 Cf. William J. Goode, *The Celebration of Heroes: Prestige as a Control System*, University of California Press, Berkeley, 1978, pp. 67–70.

73 On the cognitive processes of re-identification of human beings in connection with the theory of recognition in Axel Honneth, see Bernard Conein, 'Reconnaissance et identification: qualification et sensibilité sociale', a text presented at the conference 'De l'inclusion: reconnaissance et identification sociale en France et en Allemagne', 23–25 May 2007, Maison Heinrich Heine.

74 In the abundant anthropological literature on slavery, I have particularly benefited from the works of Jean Bazin ('Guerre et servitude à Segou', in Claude Meillassoux, ed., *L'esclavage en Afrique précoloniale*, Maspero, Paris, 1975, pp. 135–81), Claude Meillassoux (*The Anthropology of Slavery: The Womb of Iron and Gold*, trans. Alide Dasnois, Athlone Press, London, 1991), and Alain Testart ('L'esclavage comme institution', *L'Homme*, no. 145, 1998, pp. 31–69).

75 The term is used here in the dual sense given it by Paolo Napoli of 'governmental practice' and 'function of judicial power', in his study of the way 'modern policing' was established at the end of the Ancien Régime and under the French Revolution, by combining 'regulatory measures' ranging from 'prevention' to repression. See Napoli, *Naissance de la police moderne*, La Découverte, Paris, 2003.

76 The kind of unease that becomes manifest in the transition to the formal moment is, at the same time, a *vertigo* (in Roger Caillois's sense in *Les Jeux et les hommes*, Gallimard, Paris, 1992) and an *intense pleasure*. The vertigo and pleasure of a reflexivity that make it possible to be aware of the mystery of the institution and its fragility: is it the institution or is it *simply* us? It is us and, at the same time, not us – something incomprehensible of which we are merely the servants. But this something does not exist, or rather it exists only because we make it exist. And yet the opposite is also true: it is we who do not exist, who are nothing, nothing but the creatures of this being that confers on us our humble grandeur, which transmits to us part of its authority and so on.

77 Thus, in France there exist 'ministerial decrees on terminology' that fix the definitions of terms, no doubt with a view to preventing conflicts of interpretation in the course of disputes. For example, in 1988 a decree was published in the *Journal officiel* on sports terminology. It is divided into domains, with the same term being open to different interpretation in different sports (e.g. in rugby and football the word *chandelle* [up-and-under] does not refer to the same way of imparting motion to the ball). The decree, whose objective is normative, distinguishes terms whose 'use is mandatory' and 'recommended terms'. It also provides a list of 'inappropriate terms and terms to be avoided' (see Centre d'étude du lexique, *La Définition*, pp. 262–7).

78 See, for example, Martine Segalen, *Rites et rituels contemporains*, Nathan, Paris, 1998.

79 See, in particular, Victor Witter Turner, *The Ritual Process: Structure and Anti-Structure*, Routledge and Kegan Paul, London, 1969.

80 It remains the case that this requirement of de-differentiation, which is aimed at in ritual, is never realized in the case of theatre, which is often precisely denounced – particularly by Rousseau, in his *Lettre sur les spectacles*, for whom the morally respectable spectacle is a feast the people gives itself – for the distance it introduces between spectators and actors, understood as inauthenticity (see Jonas Barish, *The Antitheatrical Prejudice*, University of California Press, Berkeley, 1981). It is the often unavailing search for practices that might bridge this gap which largely inspires contemporary theatre and, in particular, numerous attempts identifying with the theatre of cruelty of Antonin Artaud, who was himself inspired by the example of ritual.

81 Victor Turner (*The Ritual Process*, pp. 97–106) thus describes African rituals of enthronement in the chiefdom, where the applicant is left for a whole night, on the eve of the ceremony, clothed in rags and associated with a female slave treated as if she was his wife. He must remain cowering with an air of shame and endure insults without turning a hair, and this in order to make manifest (says Turner) the tension between the feebleness of the flesh-and-blood man, who like the others is merely dust, and the grandeur of the responsibility which, in being conferred on him, is going to transform him.

4 THE NECESSITY OF CRITIQUE

1 On the fiction of the 'original moment' and the circularity between 'constituent power' and 'constituted power', cf. Olivier Cayla, 'L'obscure théorie du pouvoir constituant originaire ou l'illusion d'une identité souveraine

inaltérable', in *L'architecture du droit. Mélanges en l'honneur du Professeur Michel Troper*, Economica, Paris, 2006, pp. 249–65.

2 The argument of circularity (the language used to establish conventions is itself already based on established conventions) is one of the origins of David Lewis's theory of conventions (see Daniel Urrutiaguer, Philippe Batifoulier and Jacques Merchier, 'Peut-on se coordonner sur une base arbitraire? Lewis et la rationalité des conventions', in Philippe Batifoulier, ed., *Théorie des conventions*, Economica, Paris, 2001, pp. 63–95).

3 Catherine Alès, *L'ire et le désir*, Karthala, Paris, 2006, pp. 38, 134–5, 166–9, 286–8. See also 'Speeches and Assemblies among the Yanomami: Ways for Creating Society', communication to the symposium on 'The Interplay of Polity and the Social in Native Amazonia', 52nd International Congress of Americanists, University of Seville, July 2006.

4 It is precisely the tension between ritual organization and gaps, whose origin is often contingent with respect to the main activity being performed, which is at the centre of the work of Albert Piette on what he calls 'the minor mode of reality' (see his *Ethnographie de l'action*, Métailié, Paris, 1996). Actions of a pragmatic order, dictated by circumstances, arrive to parasite a course of action that is metapragmatic in character. That is why (as Catherine Rémy has shown) these gaps are all the more visible, and all the more 'shockingly' so, the more the action underway is ritualized. See Catherine Rémy, 'Activité sociale et latéralisation. Pour une étude micro-ethnographique de la tension déterminisme – marge de manoeuvre', *Recherches sociologiques*, vol. 34, no. 3, 2003, pp. 95–114.

5 Here, if I may be permitted, a personal anecdote. As a child I went with my parents and sister to attend Sunday mass in unheated churches (it was after the war). A lot of people used to cough. Believing that coughing was one of the gestures required by performance of the ritual, I forced myself to cough as well, just as I made the sign of the cross when I saw the others do it. Losing its contingent character, coughing was thus integrated into the liturgical ritual.

6 Julien Bonhomme, *Le Miroir et le crâne. Parcours initiatique du Bwete Misoko (Gabon)*, CNRS Editions and Editions de la Maison des Sciences de l'Homme, Paris, 2006, p. 19. Taking initiatory journeys as his subject, Julien Bonhomme aims to develop a pragmatic analysis of rituals that reveals components different from those stressed by the hitherto predominant semantic and semiotic analyses inspired by structuralism. The study of 'abstract relations between symbols' is replaced by that of 'dynamic relations between agents'. But this shift tends to conceive symbolism itself from a different angle by bringing out its plasticity.

7 See Elisabeth Claverie's anthropological study of ritual journeys to sites where the Virgin Mary has appeared: *Les Guerres de la Vierge. Une anthropologie des apparitions*, Gallimard, Paris, 2003.

8 Erving Goffman, *Asylums: Essays on the Social Situation of Mental Patients and Other Inmates*, Penguin, Harmondsworth, 1968.

9 Walter Benjamin, 'Critique of Violence', in *One-Way Street and Other Writings*, trans. Edmund Jephcott and Kingsley Shorter, New Left Books, London, 1979, p. 142.

10 Commenting on this text by Benjamin, Jacques Derrida writes: '. . . it [violence] is, in *droit*, what suspends *droit*. It interrupts the established *droit* to found another. This moment of suspense, this *épokhè*, this founding or

178

revolutionary moment of law is, in law, an instance of non-law. But it is also the whole history of law. *This moment always takes place and never takes place in a presence.* It is the moment in which the foundation of law remains suspended in the void or over the abyss, suspended by a pure performative act that would not have to answer to or before anyone' ('Force of Law: The "Mystical Foundation of Authority"', trans. Mary Quaintance, in Drucilla Cornell, Michel Rosenfeld and David Gray Carlson, eds, *Deconstruction and the Possibility of Justice*, Routledge, New York and London, 1992, p. 36).

11 For an example of 'deconstruction' of ritual reinterpreted in terms of domination, see Catherine Bell, *Ritual Theory, Ritual Practice*, Oxford University Press, Oxford, 1992.

12 On the history of forms of protest, see Charles Tilly, *The Contentious French*, Belknap Press, Cambridge (Mass.) and London, 1986; and, by the same author, *From Mobilization to Revolution*, Addison-Wesley, New York, 1978.

13 See François Tricaud, *L'accusation. Recherche sur les figures de l'agression éthnique*, Dalloz, Paris, 1977.

14 See Luc Boltanski, 'La dénonciation publique', in *L'amour et la justice comme compétences. Trois essais de sociologie de l'action*, Métailié, Paris, 1990, pp. 255–366.

15 I am grateful to Bruno Karsenti, to whom I owe this observation. This feature is revealed most obviously in *commemoration*, one of the activities in which institutions perform their functions with the greatest meticulousness and devotion. But it always underlies institutional acts (see Gérard Namer, *La Commémoration en France de 1945 à nos jours*, L'Harmattan, Paris, 1987).

16 On this point, see Cornelius Castoriadis, *The Imaginary Institution of Society*, trans. Kathleen Blamey, Polity, Cambridge, 1987.

17 Boltanski, 'La dénonication publique'.

18 Robert Descimon, *Les Ligueurs de l'exil. Le refuge catholique français après 1594*, Champ Vallon, Seyssel, 2005.

19 Christian Jouhaud, *Mazarinades. La fronde des mots*, Aubier, Paris, 1985.

20 Elisabeth Claverie, 'Procès, affaire, cause. Voltaire et l'innovation critique', *Politix*, no. 26, 1994, pp. 76–86.

21 Marc Angenot, *La Parole pamphlétaire. Typologie des discours modernes*, Payot, Paris, 1983.

22 Readers will find some particularly relevant examples of the role played by emotions in situations of this type in François Berthomé's thesis on ceremonial devices for 'dispute resolution' (see his 'Remarques sur trois dispositifs cérémoniels de "règlement de disputes"', forthcoming). See also Thomas Scheff, *Catharsis in Healing, Ritual and Drama*, University of California Press, Berkeley, 1980.

23 François Héran, 'L'institution démotivée. De Fustel de Coulanges à Durkheim et au-delà', *Revue française de sociologie*, vol. 28, 1987, pp. 67–97.

24 See, for example, Sarah Hanley, *Le 'Lit de justice' des rois de France. L'idéologie constitutionnelle dans la légende, le rituel et le discours*, Aubier, Paris, 1991. For more diverse scenarios, see, in particular, Alain Dierkens and Jacques Marx, eds, *La Sacralisation du pouvoir. Images et mises en scène*, Editions de l'Université libre, Brussels, 2003; and, for contemporary examples, Jean-William Dereymez, Olivier Ihl and Gérard Sabatier, eds, *Un*

Cérémonial politique. Les voyages officiels des chefs d'Etats, L'Harmattan, Paris, 1998.

25 Marcel Hénaff, '"La condition brisée des langues": diversité humaine, altérité et traduction', *Esprit*, no. 323, March/April 2006, pp. 68–83.

26 It is precisely because these words and gestures refer to one another, and therefore have a self-referential character, that the attempt to explain them in accordance with the logic of an external causality is meaningless (see Jacques Bouveresse's postface to Ludwig Wittgenstein, *Remarques sur le rameau d'or de Frazer*, L'âge d'homme, Paris, 1990).

27 The formula can be inscribed in dialogical structures. One then responds to a formula with another formula. But it remains the case that a characteristic of the formula, as a form, is that it cannot form the object of a commentary or gloss composed in the same form. If we want to comment on a formula, we have to change forms and use argumentative discourse. In this respect the formula might be compared to poetry, commentary or gloss on which cannot be undertaken while remaining in poem form, rather like the way in which glosses on music must necessarily quit musical language to use natural languages, while being based on musical examples (whether played, e.g. on the piano in the case of a lecture; or represented by extracts from scores in the case of a written text). By contrast, we can comment on a sociological or philosophical text in the language of sociology or philosophy without changing forms, no doubt because these texts are so constructed as to be open to the possibility of critique. The formula, although it is a typical form of the metapragmatic register of confirmation, is not reflexive vis-à-vis itself, in the sense of the argumentative reflexivity employed by critique.

28 'Our language can be seen as an ancient city: a maze of little streets and squares, of old and new houses, and of houses with additions from different periods; and this surrounded by a multitude of new boroughs with straight regular streets and uniform houses': Ludwig Wittgenstein, *Philosophical Investigations*, trans. G.E.M. Anscombe, Blackwell, Oxford, 1968, p. 8e.

29 As Tomaso Vitale remarks, campaigns thus transform 'private problems' and 'experiences undergone by individuals' into 'public problems' that concern 'the collectivity as a whole' (Vitale, 'Le tensioni tra partecipazione e rappresentanza e i dilemmi dell'azione collettiva nelle mobilitazioni locali', in Vitale, ed., *In nome di chi? Partecipazione e rappresentanza nelle mobilitazioni locali*, Franco Angeli, Milan, 2007, pp. 9–40).

30 See Luc Boltanski and Laurent Thévenot, *On Justification: Economies of Worth*, trans. Catherine Porter, Princeton University Press, Princeton, 2006.

31 In the sense in which cognitive anthropology refers to 'covert categories' (see B. Berlin, D.E. Breedlove and P.H. Raven, 'Covert Categories and Folk Toxinomies', *American Anthropologist*, vol. 72, no. 2, 1968, pp. 290–9).

32 Similar remarks can be made on the basis of an analysis of the way that the foetus is referred to in the course of a medical examination. The body of the foetus identified by ultrasound can constitute the same object of reference while being assigned different meanings, depending on whether the pregnant woman has decided to keep it or have it removed from her body. See Luc Boltanski, *La Condition foetale. Une sociologie de l'engendrement et de l'avortement*, Gallimard, Paris, 2004, pp. 171–8.

33 Luc Boltanski, *La Souffrance à distance. Morale humanitaire, medias et politique* (1993), new expanded edition, Gallimard, Paris, 2007.

34 I rely here on the ongoing work of Delphine Moreau. This work focuses on the close friends and relatives of young people who have been diagnosed as schizophrenic and, in particular, on the way these friends began to suspect that the one whose 'eccentricities' surprised them was, in fact, mentally ill. See Delphine Moreau, *Faire interner un proche? Le travail sur l'autonomie en contexte de troubles psychiatres*, CNAF, Paris, Dossiers d'études no. 94, July 2007 (available on the website).

35 See Dominique Linhardt, 'Guerrilla diffusa. Clandestinité, soupçon et provocation dans le conflit entre organisations révolutionnaires subversive et l'Etat ouest-allemand (années 1970)', *Politix*, no. 74, 2006, pp. 75–102.

36 It must, however, be noted that this kind of critique can seek to take shape by rooting itself in a 'reality' which is idealized but distant and, as a result, easily mystified in the sense that it has been reconstructed in imaginary fashion from fragments detached from written or oral 'testimony', to the extent that those who evoke it or claim to represent it have not had any direct experience of it. And it is precisely because this 'reality' has not been directly tested (no reality test incorporates it) that critiques invoking it have a character that is at once artificial, rigid and irrefutable, whatever the objects they claim to apply to.

5 POLITICAL REGIMES OF DOMINATION

1 As Michel Serres puts it, commenting on Carpaccio's painting of Saint George fighting the dragon (*Esthétiques sur Carpaccio*, Hermann, Paris, 1975, p. 34).

2 The term arrangement, in the sense it is used in here, has been elaborated in *La Condition foetale*. The form of reasoning adopted is the same, since in that book what is involved is a generic contradiction that is at once embodied and masked in different arrangements.

3 As is well known, the term is used by Durkheim in *The Rules of Sociological Method* (1895), ed. Steven Lukes and trans. W.D. Halls, Macmillan, London, 1982. But it is also found from the pen of Axel Honneth, when he refers to the 'pathologies of capitalism' (see *Disrespect: The Normative Foundations of Critical Theory*, Polity, Cambridge, 2007).

4 This theme is developed in Arnaud Esquerre, *La Manipulation mentale. Sociologie des sectes en France*, Fayard, Paris, 2009.

5 On the design of a social world containing a plurality of worlds, see Luc Boltanski and Laurent Thévenot, *On Justification: Economies of Worth*, trans. Catherine Porter, Princeton University Press, Princeton, 2006.

6 Cf. Luc Boltanski, 'L'espace positionnel', *Revue française de sociologie*, vol. XIV, no. 1, 1973, pp. 3–20.

7 Philippe Descola, *Par-delà nature et culture*, Gallimard, Paris, 2005.

8 The possibility of metamorphosis depends, if we follow Philippe Descola, on the possibility open to beings to change externally while remaining identical internally or, on the contrary (which is invariably the case in our society), of remaining identical in their external appearance while altering internally. According to Hans Blumenberg (*Work on Myth*, trans. Robert M. Wallace, MIT Press, Cambridge (Mass.) and London, 1985), the biblical tradition and, in its wake, Christianity, fought incessantly against the possibility, central

in Greek mythology, of metamorphosis and also against its resurgence in heresies. Nevertheless, we may consider that metamorphosis was a kind of self-evident fact difficult to exclude, since it resurfaced in the twelfth century in the Christian West, in particular in the form of the werewolf and, in theology, in unsuccessful attempts to interpret the trans-substantiation of species in terms of metamorphosis (see Caroline Walter Bynum, *Metamorphosis and Identity*, New York, Zone Books, 2005).

9 Bruno Latour, *We Have Never Been Modern*, trans. Catherine Porter, Harvester Wheatsheaf, Hemel Hempstead, 1993.

10 'The ignominy of such an authority . . . lies in the fact that in this authority the separation of law-making and law-preserving violence is suspended. If the first is required to prove its worth in victory, the second is subject to the restriction that it may not set itself new ends. Police violence is emancipated from both conditions. It is law-making, for its characteristic function is not the promulgation of laws but the assertion of legal claims for any decree, and law-preserving, because it is at the disposal of these ends': Walter Benjamin, 'Critique of Violence', in *One-Way Street and Other Writings*, trans. Edmund Jephcott and Kingsley Shorter, New Left Books, London, 1979, p. 141.

11 See Giorgio Agamben, *Le Règne et la gloire*, Seuil, Paris, 2008 and Bruno Karsenti's commentary on it, 'Y-a-t-il un mystère du gouvernement? Généalogie du politique *versus* théologie politique', *Critique*, no. 744, 2009.

12 Oliver E. Williamson, *The Economic Institutions of Capitalism*, Free Press, New York, 1985.

13 Readers will find a description of some of these managerial forms of state power in Albert Ogien, *L'esprit gestionnaire*, Editions de l'EHESS, Paris, 1995.

14 Albert O. Hirschman, *The Rhetoric of Reaction: Perversity, Futility, Jeopardy*, Belknap Press, Cambridge (Mass.) and London, 1991.

15 William Ryan, *Blaming the Victim*, Vintage Books, New York, 1988.

16 Emilie Hache, 'La responsabilité, une technique de gouvernementalité néoliberale', *Raisons politiques*, no. 28, 2007, pp. 49–66.

17 Pierre Bourdieu and Luc Boltanski, 'La production de l'idéologie dominante', *Actes de la recherche en sciences sociales*, vol. 2, no. 2, 1976. This text has been reprinted in book form by Demopolis and Raisons d'agir, Paris, 2008.

18 One of the first books in France devoted to analysing this new way of understanding politics was Bruno Jobert's *Le Tournant néo-libéral en Europe. Idées et recettes dans les pratiques gouvernementales*, L'Harmattan, Paris, 1994.

19 See Luc Boltanski and Eve Chiapello, *The New Spirit of Capitalism*, trans. Gregory Elliott, Verso, London and New York, 2006, pp. 34–5 for a definition of the notion.

20 Albert O. Hirschman, *The Passions and the Interests: Political Arguments for Capitalism before Its Triumph*, Princeton University Press, Princeton, 1977.

21 Michel Callon, ed., *The Laws of the Markets*, Blackwell, Oxford, 1998. See also D. MacKenzie, D. Muniesa and F. Siu, *Do Economists Make Markets?*, Princeton University Press, Princeton, 2007.

22 These works benefit from the breaches in positivism and behaviourism made by various currents whose influence made itself felt above all (at least in

Europe) in the years 1975–90, such as ethnomethodology, science studies, the historical sociology of statistics and the cameral sciences and so on. In the case of economics, they also benefited from a renewed interest in the work of Karl Polanyi, belatedly and partially translated into French in the 1980s (*The Great Transformation* was published by Gallimard in 1983).

23 On the way in which this process occurred in Britain from 1980–2000, see Patrick Le Galès and Alan Scott, 'Une révolution bureaucratique britannique? Autonomie sans contrôle ou "free markets, more rules"', *Revue française de sociologie*, vol. 49, no. 2, 2008, pp. 301–30.

24 On the role of rankings and benchmarking instruments in systems of management and government, see in particular the works of Alain Desrosières, especially 'Historiciser l'action publique. L'Etat, le marché et les statistiques', in P. Laborier and D. Trom, *Historicités de l'action publique*, Presses Universitaires de France, Paris, 2003, pp. 207–21. Readers will find an excellent description of these processes, on the basis of a case study of the effects of rankings on the transformation of law schools in the United States, in Wendy Espeland and Michael Sauder, 'Rankings and Reactivity: How Public Measures Recreate Social Worlds', *American Journal of Sociology*, vol. 113, no. 1, July 2007, pp. 1–40. Another highly relevant example is the guidance of research at a European level (the 'Lisbon process') studied by Isabelle Bruno (*A vos marques, prêts . . . cherchez. La stratégie européenne de Lisbonne. Vers un marché de la recherche*, Editions du Croquant, Paris, 2008).

25 See Pierre Lascoumes and Patrick Le Galès, eds, *Gouverner par les instruments*, Presses de Sciences Po, Paris, 2005.

26 On the importance of accountancy in the instruments of government, see the works of Eve Chiapello, especially 'Les normes comptables comme institution du capitalisme. Une analyse du passage aux norms IFRS en Europe à partir de 2005', *Sociologie du travail*, vol. 47, July/September 2005, pp. 362–82 and (with Karim Medjad) 'Une privatisation inédite de la norme: le cas de la politique comptable européenne', *Sociologie du travail*, vol. 49, 2007, pp. 46–64.

27 Laurent Thévenot, 'Un gouvernement par les normes. Pratiques et politiques des formats d'information', in Bernard Conein and Laurent Thévenot, eds, *Cognition et information en société, Raisons pratiques*, no. 8, Editions de l'EHESS, Paris, pp. 205–42.

28 See Gabriel Kessler and Sylvia Sigal, 'Survivre: réflexion sur l'action en situation de chaos. Comportements et représentations face à la dislocation des regulations sociales: l'hyperinflation en Argentine', *Cultures and Conflicts*, nos 24–5, 1997, pp. 37–77.

29 On the pedagogical role accorded to crises, see Federico Neiburg, 'Inflation: Economists and Economic Cultures in Brazil and Argentina', *Comparative Studies in Society and History*, vol. 48, no. 3, 2006, pp. 604–33.

30 But this is also to register, although this is not the object of the present text, the naivety of conceptions of political action which base revolutionary hope entirely on moments, portrayed as *historical* – i.e. as exceptional – of disaggregation of the dominant social order. Certainly, such moments can be favourable to the manifestation of critique and the expression of a challenge. However, invariably coinciding with the moments of crisis that a regime of domination in the strict sense feeds off, they always risk being reincorporated

into the logic of an order which perpetuates itself through change. At least if they do not intervene in the wake of a prolonged labour of critique based, in the first instance, on challenging existing reality tests and hence on an everyday experience of revolt, capable of restoring to people, individually and collectively, some purchase on action and an ability to formulate expectations based on a resumption of their existential tests.

31 On the way that the domination of experts and, in particular, economists has ended up emptying politics of any critical content – i.e. of any content – see Mariana Heredia's remarkable thesis on the forms taken by this process in Argentina over the last 30 years (Mariana Heredia, *Les Métamorphoses de la représentation. Les économistes et la politique en Argentine (1975–2001)*, sociology thesis, Ecole des Hautes Etudes en Sciences Sociales, Paris, 2007).

32 Thomas Angeletti has studied the functioning of the Conseil d'analyse économique, created in 1997 with the brief of enlightening the French government on its economic options, and made up of economists supposed to belong to different 'trends' between whom a 'debate' was to be initiated. In his work he shows that this erudite body, which claimed to be pluralist, in fact only produced uniform notes and advice conforming to the neo-classical mainstream, while the positions of so-called 'heterodox' economists did not make themselves heard. In effect, the latter found themselves placed in the position of either adopting the dominant models and formalisms to gain recognition – which necessarily had the result of homogenizing and censoring at least some of what they had to say; or censoring themselves by avoiding adopting clear positions on certain problems; or simply keeping quiet. See Thomas Angeletti, 'Economistes, Etats, démocratie: du peuple souverain à l'expert institué', forthcoming in *Tracés*.

33 Lorraine Daston, 'Objectivity and the Escape from Perspective', *Social Studies of Science*, vol. 22, 1982, pp. 597–618.

34 On the history and social uses of the notion of 'manipulation', see Arnaud Esquerre, *La Manipulation mentale*.

35 Boltanski and Chiapello, *The New Spirit of Capitalism*.

36 See Michael Mann, 'The Autonomous Power of the State: Its Origins, Mechanisms and Results', *Archives européennes de sociologie*, vol. 25, 1984, pp. 185–213.

37 See Zygmunt Bauman, *Wasted Lives: Modernity and its Outcasts*, Polity, Cambridge, 2004.

38 See Michel Callon, Pierre Lascoumes and Yannick Barthe, *Agir dans un monde incertain. Essai sur la démocratie technique*, Seuil, Paris, 2001.

39 See Loïc Blondiaux and Yves Sintomer, 'L'impératif délibératif', *Politix*, vol. 15, no. 57, 2002, pp. 17–35 and Yves Sintomer, *Le Pouvoir au peuple. Jurys citoyens, triage au sort et démocratie participative*, La Découverte, Paris, 2007.

40 'To prevent possible misunderstandings, let me say this. I do not by any means depict the capitalist and the landowner in rosy colours. But individuals are dealt with here only in so far as they are the personifications of economic categories, the bearers . . . of particular class-relations and interests': Karl Marx, Preface to the First Edition (1867), *Capital*, vol. I, Penguin edn, trans. Ben Fowkes, Harmondsworth, 1976, p. 92.

41 I am grateful to Eve Chiapello for drawing my attention to the distinction

between following a rule and pursuing an objective – a distinction that plays a notably important role in theories of control pertaining to management. On this distinction, see also the different modalities of action plans as analysed by Laurent Thévenot in *L'action au pluriel. Sociologie des régimes d'engagement*, La Découverte, Paris, 2006.

42 See Anne-Christine Wagner, *Les Classes sociales dans la mondialisation*, La Découverte, Paris, 2007. Karim Medjad's excellent *Droit international des affaires* (Armand Colin, Paris, 2005), one of whose lessons is demonstration of the non-existence of such a law, clearly shows how the conduct of international economic operations (which today occupy a central role in the functioning of economies) first of all presupposes the acquisition of great dexterity in operating rules, norms and usages. The latter, which are often contradictory, rely on bodies of law that are valid in different national territories. Their heteroclite multiplicity gives regulation a plasticity that is treated as a resource by operators.

43 'Je sais bien, mais quand même. . .', an article by Octave Mannoni first published in 1964 and recently reprinted in the journal *Incidence*, no. 2, October 2006, pp. 167–90.

44 Marie-Angèle Hermitte, *Le Sang et le droit. Essai sur la transfusion sanguine*, Seuil, Paris, 1998.

45 See Judith Assouly, 'La mise en place des normes déontologiques et la question de la vérité de la finance' (working document) and 'Que vaut la valeur fondamentale des actions calculées par les analystes financiers?', forthcoming in *Sociologie du travail*.

6 EMANCIPATION IN THE PRAGMATIC SENSE

1 Emile Durkheim, *Sociologie et philosophie*, Presses Universitaires de France, Paris, 1967, pp. 46–51.

2 Elias Canetti, *Masse et puissance*, Gallimard, Paris, 1966, pp. 241–66.

3 In the first volume of his work on '*La Servitude volontaire*'. *Les morts d'accompagnement* (Editions Errance, Paris, 2004), Alain Testart studies the well-nigh universal custom of killing all the collaborators of a chief when he dies and burying them in the ground around his tomb. These right-hand men were often high-ranking slaves or poor, subjected men who, free from any other form of affiliation and any other kind of tie (notably of kinship), were loyal exclusively to their chief. Testart regards this practice as one of the origins of the state. It disappears (e.g. in China) when bureaucracies are established.

4 Yann Moulier Boutang, *Le Capitalisme cognitif. La nouvelle grande transformation*, Editions Amsterdam, Paris, 2007.

5 In Western societies let alone those of the South, we know that the life expectancy of the poorest is still statistically far below that of members of the elites.

6 Michel de Certeau, *The Practice of Everyday Life*, trans. Steven Rendall, University of California Press, Berkeley and London, 1984.

7 Claude Lévi-Strauss, 'The Sorcerer and his Magic', in *Structural Anthropology* (1958), trans. Claire Jacobson and Brooke Grundfest Schoepf, Penguin, Harmondsworth, 1977, pp. 167–85.

8 This schema – admittedly, as it stands, very simplistic – draws on numerous descriptions provided by the social anthropology of societies that are based upon an initiatory model. See, in particular, the issue of the journal *Incidence*, no. 2, October 2006, devoted to this theme and containing, in connection with the reprinting of the article by Octave Mannoni to which we have already referred ('Je sais bien, mais quand même . . .') and that of Claude Lévi-Strauss ('Le père Noël supplicié'), studies by (and about) Donald Tuzin on the Tambaran – a masculine initiation ritual among the Arapesh of New Guinea. We can take as an example the case of the Hopi society, invoked by Mannoni, as it is presented in the autobiographical memoir of Talayesva (*Soleil Hopi*, Plon, Paris, 1959). Such a model contains four kinds of actors. The first is *deceived children*: they really believe that the katcinas come to dance during certain feasts in the village and that they have the power to punish or reward them. Secondly, there are *adolescents* undergoing initiation who, realizing that the katcinas are nothing but their own fathers and uncles in masks, succumb to a kind of unease verging on nihilism, which has something to do with what in our societies we call an adolescent crisis. Thirdly, we have *adult men*, the initiators, who restore the confidence of the adolescents by *initiating* them – that is to say, by getting them to concede that, even if the bodies they saw, with fear and trembling, dancing in the village were not really, literally, *to the letter*, those of spirits, nevertheless the spirits were indeed there, but – if we might be allowed this pleonasm – *in spirit*. Fourthly and finally, there are *women* who, excluded from the initiation process, are both assumed to be deceived by the men's tricks, like the children, while being aware of their subterfuges, to which they discreetly lend a helping hand (which confirms the idea that male domination constitutes the archetype of domination, since, ultimately, it is the women whom this process keeps under the enduring domination of men with their at least apparent consent).

9 Philippe Corcuff, *La Société de verre. Pour une éthique de la fragilité*, Armand Colin, Paris, 2002.

10 On the plasticity of the notion of property, see Mikhaïl Xifaras, *La Propriété. Etude de philosophie du droit*, Presses Universitaires de France, Paris, 2004. In this work, which focuses on legal thinking in the nineteenth century, especially relevant for our purposes are the pages on difficulties in defining the notion of property created by the issue of the sale of labour power, treated as an entity distinct from the worker and of which she has the 'ownership' (pp. 43–84).

11 I am referring to the thesis of Bérénice Hamidi-Kim, *Les Cités du théâtre politique en France de 1989 à 2007*, Entretemps, Paris, 2009.

12 This is one of the main tensions that has had to be confronted by libertarian currents of thought and anarchist movements, which (to be brief) are distributed between an individualist pole, whose main reference is Max Stirner, and a communist pole represented by Mikhail Bakunin, or an altruistic and egalitarian pole represented by Peter Kropotkin (see Daniel Guérin, *No Gods, No Masters*, two vols, trans. Paul Sharkey, AK Press, Edinburgh, 1998 and Peter Marschall, *Demanding the Impossible: A History of Anarchism*, Harper Perennial, London, 2008). As is shown by Irène Pereira in her thesis ('Un nouvel esprit contestataire. Une grammaire pragmatiste dans le syndicalisme d'action directe d'inspiration libertaire'), these tensions could be

reduced by the convergence we are currently witnessing between currents inspired by pragmatism and currents attached to the libertarian tradition. Let us add that Philippe Corcuff's endeavour to fashion compromises between 'contemporary individualism' and 'social justice' proceeds in the same direction (see Philippe Corcuff, Jacques Ion and François de Singly, *Politiques de l'individualisme*, Textuel, Paris, 2005).

13 Claude Lefort, 'Permanence du théologico-politique', in *Essais sur le politique*, Seuil, Paris, 1986.

14 Jacques Derrida, 'Force of Law: The "Mystical Foundation of Authority"', trans. Mary Quaintance, in Drucilla Cornell, Michel Rosenfeld and David Gray Carlson, eds, *Deconstruction and the Possibility of Justice*, Routledge, London and New York, 1992, p. 16.

INDEX

Desrosières, Alain 133, 139
disputes/protests 24, 26–8, 31–2
  and agreement 59–60
  expansion 37–9
  and institutions 95–7, 98–9
  practical register 67
  self-limitation of 34, 35, 65
  tests/test formats 27–9, 32–5, 37–8,
    39–40
  and uncertainty 60–1
Dodier, Nicolas 29
domination
  critical sociology of 18–19, 19–23,
    43–9
  and exploitation 8–9, 14
  male 39
  theories 1–3, 4–5, 6, 8, 42–3
  see also institutions; political
    regimes; social classes
Durkheim, Emile 3, 18–19, 47, 52,
  53, 102, 117, 136, 151

emancipation 5, 14–15, 22
  hermeneutic contradiction 154–60
  social classes and action 151–4
epideictic discourse 73
ethnomethodology 24, 25
existential tests 103, 107–10, 113,
  125, 156
expertise 7, 142
  and counter-expertise 137–8
  realism and constructivism 138–9
exploitation and domination 8–9, 14
exteriority, simple and complex 6–8,
  10

Foucault, Michael 47, 57
Frankfurt School 18
French intellectual tradition 23, 24
Freud, Sigmund 46–7, 99

Garfinkel, Harold 20
gender inequality 39
generality, rise towards 37, 81, 95,
  97
Girard, René 36
Goffman, Erving 52, 63–4, 92, 127
goods and property 155–6
Goody, Jack 64–5
grammars 59, 111–12

habitus and shared culture 144–5
Hénaff, Marcel 104
Héran, François 103
hermeneutic contradictions
  emancipation 154–60
  embodiment in spokesperson 84–7
  in political regimes 116–19, 121–2,
    123, 136–43
  semantics vs pragmatics 87–93
Hirschman, Albert 128, 132
Hobbes, Thomas 14, 42, 52
Honneth, Axel 47
Humboldt, Wilhelm von 69

idealist and analogist institutions
  120–2
individualization and collectivization
  38–9
injustice model and tests 27–9, 30–3
injustices, public denunciation of 35,
  36, 37, 100
institutions 51–4
  analogical and idealist 120–2
  bodiless being of 74–8, 89–90, 93,
    101–2
  construction of reality by 91–2,
    97–8
  disputes/protests and 95–7, 98–9
  language functions of 74–7, 78–81,
    92–7
  and rituals 81–2, 91–2
  see also hermeneutic contradictions;
    political regimes
internalization of norms and
  ideologies 15, 20, 22, 38, 40–1

justifications, official and unofficial
  124–5

Knight, Frank 57
knowledge
  common 73
  objective and subjective 139–40
  of structures 20–1
  theories 9

language/semantics 8–9, 24–5, 65–6
  functions of institutions 74–7,
    78–81, 92–7
  grammars 59, 111–12